WILL EUROPE FIGHT FOR OIL?

Energy Relations in the Atlantic Area

Edited by
Robert J. Lieber

AF

Published in Cooperation with
the Committee on Atlantic Studies,
Washington, D.C.

PRAEGER

PRAEGER SPECIAL STUDIES • PRAEGER SCIENTIFIC

Library of Congress Cataloging in Publication Data
Main entry under title:

Will Europe fight for oil?

"Based on papers given at the Committee on Atlantic
Studies conference on energy and the Atlantic Alliance,
held at Courmayeur, Val D'Aosta, Italy, October 8–11,
1981"—Introd.
   Includes bibliographical references.
   Contents: Must Europe fight for oil?/Robert J.
Lieber—The energy outlook/Frederick W. Gorbet—
Khrushchev's oil and Brezhnev's natural gas pipelines/
Bruce W. Jentleson—Energy trade relations between
the Federal Republic of Germany and the USSR/Reimund
Seidelmann—[etc.]
   1. Energy industries—Political aspects—Congresses.
2. Petroleum industry and trade—Political aspects—
Congresses.   3. North Atlantic Treaty organization—
Congresses.   4. World politics—1975–1985—Congresses.
I. Lieber, Robert J., 1941.   II. Committee on
Atlantic Studies.
HD9502.A2W53   1983   327.1'11'091821   82-24598
ISBN 0-03-062032-5

Published in 1983 by Praeger Publishers
CBS Educational and Professional Publishing
a Division of CBS Inc.
521 Fifth Avenue, New York, New York 10175 U.S.A.

©1983 by the Committee on Atlantic Studies

3456789 052 987654321

Printed in the United States of America
on acid-free paper

FOREWORD

Charles Foster

The Committee on Atlantic Studies, founded in 1964, is an international group of approximately 50 scholars from Europe and North America who are dedicated to generating and improving scholarly dialogues on issues of common concern to the Atlantic nations. The annual colloquia, held alternately in Europe and North America, are attended by both committee members and invited guests.

This volume originated from the 14th annual conference of the Committee on Atlantic Stuides, held in Courmayeur, Aosta, Italy, in October 1981. Some 35 scholars from Europe and the United States attended the meeting, and, thanks to the efforts of our host, Mario Andrione, President of the Autonomous Region of Aosta, the conference was both successful and productive.

In a time when energy relations have become a vital and controversial subject in the Atlantic Community, we hope this volume will contribute to a constructive international dialogue.

Charles Foster
Executive Secretary
Committee on Atlantic Studies

iii

14210

CONTENTS

NA

INTRODUCTION

Robert J. Lieber

This book is based on papers given at the Committee on Atlantic Studies' Conference on Energy and the Atlantic Alliance, held at Courmayeur, Val d'Aosta, Italy, October 8-11, 1981. This meeting, and the book that has developed from it, reflect a shared concern with the impact of energy problems on European-American relations. As we know from the experience of two world oil shocks (in 1973-74 and in 1979), allied differences over the Middle East and Persian Gulf, and European-U.S. recriminations over the Soviet gas pipeline, the energy problem has become not only a central security concern but also a major source of tension in relations among the Western allies. To ask "Will Europe Fight for Oil?"[1] is thus to inquire whether Europeans and North Americans will quarrel among themselves as much as it is to ask whether their energy security concerns may involve conflict in their relations with the Middle East and the Soviet Union.

This volume provides a series of studies on security implications, the energy outlook, the Soviet gas and oil pipelines, the cases of France and of Mexico, and economic and domestic constraints. Equally important, it offers contributions and perspectives from four non-American authors. For an understanding of why the energy problem is sometimes perceived so differently by America's allies, the direct expression of divergent views is especially valuable. American readers may well disagree sharply with analyses presented by one or more of the European contributors to this effort. Indeed, as editor of this volume, I do so myself. Yet these differences embody in microcosm many of the tensions inherent in allied relations over energy.

The volume begins with an assessment of the security consequences of the energy problem in its distinct military, economic, and political components. In the course of a decade, the subject of energy — which had once seemed to be the province of technical and resource analysts or regional specialists — has come to occupy a central position on security agendas.

Frederick W. Gorbet (at the time of his writing, head of long-term planning for the International Energy Agency) provides an authoritative treatment of the energy outlook. His essay is especially useful in calling attention to the long-term importance of decreased dependence on imported oil. He emphasizes the slow pace at which progress toward this goal has taken place, the long lead times that adaptation requires, and the very costly impact of the two oil shocks of the 1970s.[2]

Any long-range energy scenarios involve considerable uncertainty. Indeed, projections made during the 1970s often proved remarkably off target within only a few years. Yet Gorbet's scenarios for 1990 and 2000 offer valuable reference points for any analysis of energy problems. Despite the emergence of an oil "glut" in 1981-83, the risk of future disruption of the oil supply, particularly in the late 1980s, remains substantial. As suggested by past experience, such an event can unleash serious tension among the allies.

A special contribution of this book is its three chapters on the Soviet pipeline controversy. Chapter Three, by Bruce W. Jentleson ("Khrushchev's Oil and Brezhnev's National Gas Pipelines"), is especially useful because it contrasts the 1981-82 allied confrontation over western Europe's role in building the Soviet gas pipeline with a comparable argument in the early 1960s. The earlier dispute involved European imports of Soviet oil and German exports of wide-diameter pipe. Jentleson provides striking comparisons of events occurring some two decades apart. Consider, for example, the sharp differences that emerged in the early 1960s. These pitted the United States against governments in Bonn and London that were conservative and anti-Communist yet had a compelling interest in trade with the Soviet Union. In the early 1960s, as in the early 1980s, policy on sanctions or East-West trade restraint proved a source of transatlantic friction. The United States' inability to prevail over its allies in exerting leverage upon European energy trade is all the more noteworthy in the earlier period. At the time the political and economic conditions that maximized America's relative strength were far greater than they would be some two decades later.

Reimund Seidelmann provides a West German perspective on energy trade relations between the Federal Republic and the Soviet Union. He asks whether increased dependence on energy imports from the Soviet Union will lead to economic dependence, vulnerability, and Finlandization of the Federal Republic, or to an overall decrease of vulnerability through better diversification of energy security risks, the increase of economic interdependence, and a growing Soviet stake in détente. Seidelmann finds the latter set of outcomes more probable, and asserts that fears associated with the gas pipeline deal are exaggerated. He bases this conclusion, in part, on the Soviets' pressing hard currency requirements and their dependence on Western imports. However, he emphasizes their need to maintain economic growth in order to meet demands from the COMECON countries, foreign policy commitments, military spending, and domestic and agricultural investment priorities. Whether or not one is convinced by the author's controversial and optimistic assessment (particularly in its assumptions about the effects of interdependence and the existence of symmetrical pro-détente lobbies in East and West), the essay does provide a forthright statement of views strongly held by important segments of West German opinion.

"Energy and Soviet Foreign Policy," by Nils Andrén, offers a different perspective on the Soviet gas pipeline. He provides a detailed examination of the Soviet energy balance and offers both "best" and "worst" case analyses. He weighs the merits of seeking to squeeze the Soviet Union, by refusing to cooperate in its energy development, against the broader energy security of the West and the possible consequences of instability in eastern Europe. While acknowledging considerable long-range uncertainties, Andrén argues for maintaining the pipeline deal, but emphasizes that this must be done in ways that minimize Soviet capacity for leverage against the West.

Guy de Carmoy, in "Oil and Security in the Middle East: The French-Iraqi Case," treats one facet of a subject — the Middle East and the Arab-Israeli conflict — that has often involved sharp disagreement among the allies. The analysis remains quite controversial, but it does embody a viewpoint shared by a number of French and other European observers of the Middle East. The starting point is French dependence on Middle East oil and the special relationship that France sought to establish with a key oil-producing country. After 1967 this included a pro-Arab position on Arab-Israeli questions, as well as the export of sophisticated arms and highly sensitive nuclear materials and technology. Professor Carmoy is highly critical of the Israeli attack on the Osiraq reactor, and implies in his conclusion that resolution of the Palestinian question is the

key to avoiding nuclear proliferation in the Middle East as well
as to allied energy security and regional stability.

However, the tragic record of Middle East turmoil, including
upheaval in Iran, Iraq's September 1980 invasion of Iran, and a wide
range of intra-Arab tensions (religious, political, and military) may
suggest an entirely different conclusion. It is that even a satisfactory
settlement of the Israeli-Palestinian conflict might well find the
Middle East still subject to manifold problems of instability, and
hence to persistent risks of interruption of the oil supply. In addition,
not all analysts will agree with Professor Carmoy's view of the Iraqi
nuclear program. Other detailed assessments find strong indications
of an intent to develop nuclear weapons. The evidence includes
purchase from France of a gas-graphite reactor, noneconomical for
electric power generation but capable of producing plutonium
(a source of nuclear weapons); the buying of a 70-megawatt material
testing reactor, which a country not producing its own nuclear
power reactors would not normally need; Iraq's demand that its
Osiraq research reactor be supplied with 92 percent enriched
(weapons-grade) uranium rather than 7 percent enriched "caramel"
fuel; purchase of 250 tons of natural uranium, which made sense
only if Iraq intended to produce plutonium; and purchase of plu-
tonium-separation "hot-cell" simulators from Italy, used in the
handling of sensitive nuclear materials.[3] Testimony to the U.S.
Congress, in the aftermath of the Israeli attack, also casts doubt on
the efficacy of International Atomic Energy Agency inspections in
preventing production of nuclear weapons.[4] An important question
here is one of timing: Professor Carmoy finds it improbable that
the Iraqis would have acquired nuclear weapons for a decade; others
saw a more immediate risk.

Ironically, the Middle East policies of France did not produce
significant payoffs either in an appreciable advantage in the price
of oil or in additions to supply during the 1980 oil shock.[5] At the
same time, trade advantages were modest. Apart from weapons sales,
French exporters derived little benefit from the pro-Arab policies of
the Pompidou and Giscard governments. At most, they may have had
what one of Giscard's cabinet members privately termed a 3 percent
factor — a favorable reception if the price of French products came
within 3 percent of those offered by major competitors.

With the election of François Mitterrand's Socialist government in
June 1981, French policy on the Arab-Israeli conflict became more

evenhanded. The French government made an effort to differentiate between understanding and sympathy for Israel as a country, and disagreements with the Begin government. As a result, the gap between the United States and France over Middle East policy lessened substantially, as did differences among the Europeans.

The three remaining essays in the volume address different sets of questions of importance in Atlantic energy relations. In "Mexican Oil and the Western Alliance," Edward Wonder analyzes the triangular relationship among the United States, Mexico, and western Europe. He explores the sources of Mexico's oil policy, political and economic constraints that shape it, the tensions that affect U.S.-Mexican energy relations, and differences over Central America. While competition for Mexican oil among the allies may be less of a problem than often thought to be the case, the combination of oil, industrialization, and economic difficulties will ensure the increased importance of Mexico to the economies and foreign policies of the Western alliance countries.

Walter Goldstein provides a valuable consideration of the economic damage triggered by the oil problem. In his view, the two oil shocks have been succeeded by a third one, in which Europeans have had to pay higher prices for oil because of the sharp appreciation of the dollar in 1981-82. A decade of energy crisis has dealt a major economic blow to the economies of the advanced industrial countries. As a result, the turmoil in world trade has become increasingly severe, with risks of systemwide disruption. These events have given rise to strong economic nationalism among major trading blocs and countries, and they constitute an area of serious tension in the alliance.

Finally, Ronald Inglehart considers domestic political constraints on an Atlantic energy policy. He brings to bear his work on public opinion in the United States and the major countries of western Europe, and relates attitudes toward nuclear power to his previous studies of postmaterialist attitudes and values.

In sum, these essays provide a broad perspective on the range and depth of energy problems as a source of serious strain among the allies. The difficulties extend not only to oil and the Middle East, but also to an array of different energy resources and geographic areas as well as to security, economic, and attitudinal concerns. There is much in these chapters that suggests how powerful the centrifugal forces of economic nationalism and unilateral policy choices can be. There are few long-term problems that approach energy in their importance or difficulty. The question "Will Europe Fight for Oil?" thus symbolizes the array of tensions within the Atlantic Alliance.

NOTES

1. For suggesting this title, I am indebted to Catherine Kelleher.

2. For a valuable appraisal of the ecnomic impact of the oil shocks and the risks that a future crisis would pose, see Daniel Yergin and Martin Hillenbrand, eds., *Global Insecurity: A Strategy for Energy and Economic Renewal* (Boston: Houghton Mifflin, 1982), esp. pp. 1-28, 58-137.

3. See the detailed assessment of Shai Feldman, "The Bombing of Osiraq— Revisited," *International Security* 7, no. 2 (Fall 1982): 114-42, at 115 ff.

4. After the outbreak of the Iran-Iraq war, the Iraqi nuclear facility was damaged by Iranian air attack. Iraq then kept IAEA inspectors away for several months. Iran's nuclear facilities have been closed to IAEA inspectors since December 1979. See Ronald Koven, "Baghdad Blocks Inspection of Its Nuclear Reactors," *Washington Post*, November 11, 1980, and Feldman, op. cit., p. 121.

5. For an analysis of the constraints on French energy diplomacy, see Robert J. Lieber, "Energy Policies of the Fifth Republic: Autonomy Versus Constraint," in William G. Andrews and Stanley Hoffman, eds., *The Impact of the Fifth Republic on France* (Albany, N. Y.: State University of New York Press, 1981), pp. 179-96.

MUST EUROPE FIGHT FOR OIL?
ENERGY AND ATLANTIC SECURITY

Robert J. Lieber

The emergence of energy as a major problem in Western security has seemed to develop suddenly, particularly as the result of dramatic oil crises in 1973-74 and 1979-80. Yet the movement of this issue onto the security "chessboard" is not without precedent. Historically, resource questions have counted heavily in geopolitical calculations, and have played a role up to and including that of *casus belli*. For example, the problem of petroleum had a significant impact on Japanese calculations on the eve of World War II. In that case, U.S. and Dutch measures to restrict the flow of oil were crucial in affecting the substance and timing of Japanese decisions prior to the attack on Pearl Harbor.

In the postwar era, concern over the security consequences of Western oil dependence has not been confined to the years after October 1973. For example, President Dwight Eisenhower wrote to Winston Churchill in March 1956:

> The free nations know that the prosperity and welfare of the entire Western world is inescapably dependent upon Mideast oil and free access thereto.[1]

More recently, cries of alarm about Western energy security have been widely expressed. In the words of one analyst:

1

> The world, as we know it now, will probably not be able to maintain its cohesion . . . against the onslaught of future oil shocks – with all that this might imply for the . . . internal and external security [of the West].[2]

This kind of anxiety was reflected in the January 1980 Carter Doctrine. Worries about Persian Gulf security have also figured prominently in the defense planning of the Reagan administration. But what does the energy security problem really entail? Under what circumstances is Western security affected by the energy problem? How severe is its impact upon the Western alliance? These security consequences are more complex than often assumed. To appreciate them, we need to consider the military, economic, and political realms separately.

MILITARY CONSEQUENCES AND THE SOVIET ROLE

The well-being of the oil-consuming countries rests on the stability and oil production of one of the most unstable regions on earth. Most concern has been focused on the Middle East and especially the Persian Gulf. Particular attention has been paid to deterring Soviet threats to this region. Fears have been expressed that Russian control of the Persian Gulf would give it a stranglehold over Europe's petroleum lifeline, thus neutralizing the western Europeans and dividing them from the United States. Thus, in the words of a former high American official, "It is probably easier to defeat Europe at the Straits of Hormuz than it is on the Central Front."[3]

There is ample reason for concern over European oil security. However, the likelihood of a direct Soviet challenge is almost certainly less than a series of other threats. The risks of upheaval and of potential oil disruption in the Persian Gulf are many and varied. In order of probability they are national instability, regional instability, indirect Soviet threat or action, and – least probable though potentially most serious – direct Soviet attack.[4]

From the standpoint of alliance cohesion, overt military threats may be easier to deal with, even though they would pose serious risk of oil supply interruption. This is suggested by the November 1980 dispatch of British and French naval forces to the Indian Ocean. However, internal instability within major oil-producing states is both a more probable threat to the West's energy security and a more ambiguous and difficult problem to manage effectively. The autonomous nature of this problem is what makes it particularly troublesome. That is, indigenous sources of instability and the tumultuous nature of the development process leave most OPEC countries vulnerable to serious internal tensions, regardless of outside interest in either fomenting or preventing those tensions.

Internal change or upheaval need not interfere with petroleum production and shipment, since even the most radical, weak, or ephemeral regimes will usually need substantial oil revenues. On the other hand, domestic political factors, such as Islamic fundamentalism and reaction against modernization, can cause oil production to be held to lower levels than would otherwise be the case. More important, the chaotic circumstances that accompany instability — as in the case of the Iranian revolution — may disrupt oil production regardless of intent.

Among the long list of potential crisis catalysts, the Soviet role does provide a source of concern, but one that must be appreciated as much or more for the indirect risks it poses as for the kind of threat embodied in the invasion of Afghanistan. A direct military move by the USSR toward Middle Eastern oil is not the most immediately pressing threat. While it is conceivable that Soviet oil production will fall from a peak of 12.5 million barrels per day in 1981 to roughly 10.5-11.5 million in 1985,[5] this would have the effect of forcing Russia's customers (mainly those from western Europe and, to a lesser extent, the Communist countries) onto the world oil market. The Soviets themselves are less likely to be compelled to turn there for large amounts of oil, whether to purchase or to "grab."

Even without the necessity to obtain Middle East oil, the opportunity to gain influence over the producing countries would be an attractive source of leverage for the USSR. Such a role would be likely to provide significant advantages in political and economic power vis-à-vis the oil-consuming countries, particularly the European nations and Japan.

A Soviet military involvement in northern Iran, especially in support of the pro-Soviet Tudeh party during an Iranian civil war, is one scenario for enhanced Soviet influence (although the maintenance of effective Soviet domination would be a difficult task). More broadly, Soviet actions contributing to internal upheavals —

supplying arms and training to revolutionary groups, supporting terrorism, or intervening in a local civil war — pose conceivable threats to Middle Eastern and North African oil-producing regimes. Soviet involvement, or anticipation of it, may also make it more difficult for Western countries to bolster sympathetic but vulnerable governments in these regions.

The maintenance and enhancement of an allied military presence within or near the oil-producing countries is desirable. This is less a matter of providing protection against an invasion than of deterring possible external pressures (including those supported by Soviet client states or Soviet-backed groups). However, it is a difficult and delicate task, particularly where internal upheavals are concerned. Too much overt military presence risks triggering local and regional antagonism as well as disagreement among the allies. There also must be a recognition that individual Western countries will have different roles to play in various countries of the Middle East, and that these efforts can be complementary. In this light, U.S. response to the September 1980 outbreak of the Iran-Iraq war was appropriate. In stationing American-controlled airborne radar warning systems (AWACS) in Saudi Arabia and in moving naval power near the Straits of Hormuz, the United States responded at a suitable level. However, striking a balance between too much and too little military presence is not easy.

The western Europeans and Japanese may face increased political differences with the United States over the emphasis to be placed on military means for assuring oil supplies. For example, despite their greater dependence on the Persian Gulf, the Europeans remained skeptical of the Carter Doctrine offered in January 1980. The absence of substantial support for this doctrine owed as much to the lack of consultation with allies (and even Congress) and to a dearth of confidence in the judgment of the American administration, as to disagreements about the use of force. European responses to the Reagan administration's Persian Gulf defense policies also remained cautious. Prime Minister Margaret Thatcher did express the willingness of the United Kingdom to contribute to a rapid deployment force,[6] yet British economic problems and defense budget constraints were likely to limit the impact of any such commitment.

Allied agreement on military responses to the problem of Persian Gulf security is by no means unanimous. Western European governments tend to place greater emphasis on national instability, regional conflicts, and Arab-Israeli tensions than on direct or indirect Soviet action.

Regional military capabilities of the United States and the western Europeans also constitute an area of imbalance. France and the United Kingdom have some military presence in the region: the French at Djibouti, Réunion Island, and Mayotte in the Comoro Islands; the British through arrangements with Oman, Bahrain, Qatar, and the United Arab Emirates. However, most allied forces are committed to NATO theaters of operation on the European continent and its adjacent oceans. The Europeans also face budgetary pressures merely to maintain their existing forces. European capabilities available for Middle East contingencies are thus modest in size. France and the United Kingdom, along with Australia, did contribute ships to the allied force deployed near the Straits of Hormuz after the outbreak of the Iran-Iraq war. However, these forces numbered well under half the ships provided by the United States.[7]

The energy problem poses an additional and more indirect military security problem. This lies in the consequences for allied capability of constraints on economic growth. The energy problem has been a major element in reduced economic performance since 1973. As a result, resources that Europeans, Japanese, and Americans have available to satisfy competing social, economic, and defense needs are affected. Tradeoffs become more explicit and more politically contentious.

Consider the competing claims among investment in energy production, economic growth, social welfare, and defense spending. In 1978 the NATO countries had committed themselves to boost defense budgets by 3 percent in real terms. In the immediate aftermath of the second oil crisis, there appeared to be an initial determination to proceed with the military increases. Indeed, France (though not a party to the 3 percent commitment) even decided to build a sixth strategic nuclear submarine, and did so with little domestic opposition. Anxieties over Middle East instability and Soviet behavior appeared to outweigh increased economic stringency. However, with the passage of time the endurance of these commitments was called into question. In substantial part this resulted from a widespread lag in economic performance and the politically difficult choices required among social and defense priorities. It also reflected internal disagreements over the appropriate defense policy response to the ensemble of problems faced by the Europeans.

For 1979 and 1980 as a whole, the only countries to meet or exceed the 3 percent objective were Luxembourg (9.9 percent), the United States (3.6 percent), Portugal (3.2 percent), and France (3 percent). Others fell below the target: the United Kingdom (2.8 percent), West Germany (2.3 percent), the Netherlands (2.3 percent), Norway (2.3 percent), Turkey (2.3 percent), Belgium (2.0 percent), and Italy (1.6 percent).[8]

In the spring of 1981 the West German government decided not to increase defense spending by 3 percent in real terms. This was followed by further budget reductions in October and November. Although the Federal Republic's 1982 budget provided for a nominal 3.2 percent increase, this represented an actual decrease in real terms after inflation was taken into account.

Even the Christian Democratic Coalition government that came to power in October 1982 found its defense budget choices tightly constrained. It increased military spending, in its initial budget, by only a small, token amount. These budgetary pressures suggest the kind of difficulties that governments face, as well as the potential for acrimony among alliance members. Comparable problems have occurred in the Low Countries and Scandinavia. French military choices may also be affected as the Mitterrand government is forced to choose among competing budget priorities.

American preference for a greater European military role in the Middle East and Persian Gulf will encounter not only allied resistance due to budgetary constraints; differences over policy toward the region and domestic divisions over foreign military commitments will also play a part. Yet these factors do not entirely preclude an allied military presence. The residual British participation in the Persian Gulf remains a factor, for example. In addition, on one notable occasion, the French government played a limited but effective role in Saudi Arabia, providing weapons and a handful of security advisers to coordinate the Saudi assault on terrorists who had seized the Mecca Grand Mosque in November 1979.

The alliance countries could find themselves in disagreement over strategic choices in energy security policy. One perspective involves greater emphasis on increased military capabilities in order to deter or defend against threats to Persian Gulf oil supplies. The other would place greater weight upon investments to reduce the level of

oil dependence and vulnerability, through increasing and diversifying energy production, improving energy efficiency, building strategic
stockpiles, and other measures. The choice does not require the
selection of one strategy to the total exclusion of the other, but
substantial differences in the mix or emphasis placed on each choice
could occur.[9]

ECONOMIC CONSEQUENCES

Energy crisis problems can affect the economic security of the
Western countries in three broad ways: by threatening to curtail
economic life in the event of a major supply interruption, by their
damage to economic performance through sudden disruptive price
increases, and by the competitive tensions they unleash among the
oil-consuming states.

The risks of oil supply interruption leave the consuming countries
vulnerable to external disturbances over which they may have little
or no control. They can undertake crisis planning as well as longer-
term measures to reduce their dependence and vulnerability, but
risks to energy security will remain a cause for long-term concern.
For many countries the effects of economic vulnerability spill over
into the political realm.

Damage to Western economic performance as a result of the
1973 and 1979 oil shocks has been a tangible and ongoing problem.
Lower economic growth, higher inflation, and growing unemployment are a direct result. The direct and indirect impact of oil price
increases after the second oil crisis caused the 1981 GNP of the
OECD countries as a whole to be 6.5 percent less (some $550 billion
lower) than it might otherwise have been.[10] Oil price increases
caused consumer prices to rise from an initial 8.25 percent inflation
rate in the first half of 1979 to around 12 percent a year later, and
contributed to an increase in OECD unemployment from 20 to 25
million between mid-1980 and mid-1981.[11] Economic consequences
of the energy problem also subject the societies of the oil-consuming
countries to greater strain by exacerbating domestic conflicts.

A tangible impact of this economic stress has been to make life
more difficult for incumbent governments. With their freedom to
maneuver narrowed and their policy choices both more pressing and
more difficult, governments have found themselves under increased

domestic political pressure. The defeat of the Carter administration in November 1980 and of Valery Giscard d'Estaing and his conservative allies in May and June 1981 are cases in point.[1][2]

By tightening of economic constraints, the energy problem also increases the difficulties for reformist parties and governments of the democratic left. They find their ability to maneuver increasingly restricted as they seek to initiate policies aimed at alleviating unemployment, increasing economic growth, meeting social welfare needs, and implementing redistributive policies. A series of conspicuous failures by these governments could produce new political alignments. These might include the undermining of their credibility and political support vis-à-vis conservative parties, a more concerted and radical choice of policy measures by democratic left parties and governments seeking to overcome the constraints that bind them, or a growth in support for movements of the extreme left or extreme right.

Economic security also includes effective functioning of the international economy. The consequences of past and future energy shocks place an enormously greater load on this system. To date it has withstood these shocks and avoided financial perils on the scale of the 1930s. However, very serious problems remain and the impact of another energy crisis would subject this system to still greater strains.

The economic security of the United States, Europe, and Japan is affected by the increasing competitive tensions among them. Rivalry among the allies encompasses a wide array of common problems. The pressures engendered by oil import costs and resultant balance-of-payments anxieties lie at the heart of this rivalry, as do concerns over unemployment and deindustrialization. The pressures have been explicitly set out, for example, in a State of the Nation address by the then chancellor of Germany, Helmut Schmidt:

> *Our chief concern is to reduce our Current Account Deficit.* In other words, we cannot keep on paying bills to other countries that are higher than the amounts we ourselves receive from abroad. This means first and foremost: further cuts in our oil imports, but at the same time the conservation of energy all round. And *it also means making our products even more competitive on world markets to be able to sell more.*[13]

These pressures make it difficult for Western countries to cooperate over the rules of the game in export promotion, trade sanctions, arms exports, nuclear proliferation, and trade policy and technology transfer to the Soviet Union.

Differences between the Reagan administration and the western Europeans over the Soviet natural gas pipeline derive in part from competitive pressures and from differences of perspective. For the Europeans, lessening of oil import dependence on the Middle East seems paramount. From a U.S. perspective it appears risky for these countries to rely on the Soviet Union for supplies that, by 1990, could constitute as much as 30 percent of French and German natural gas.[14]

Despite a tendency for the Europeans to downplay the risks of dependence on Soviet gas and for the Americans to stress them, the key issue is vulnerability. If the Europeans can manage to insulate themselves against the effects of a potential cutoff, the likelihood of the Soviets ever turning off the tap or — more plausibly — of implicitly or explicitly threatening to do so, would be virtually eliminated. Such measures include gas stockpiles, dual-capacity (gas-oil or gas-coal) boilers, surge capacity, use of the Dutch Groningen gas fields as a strategic reserve, improved integration of western European gas pipeline networks, and interruptable contracts (which would shift the burden of an unexpected shortage to a few large enterprises rather than let it affect large numbers of individual residences). Increases in Norwegian gas supply would also be useful, although lead times involve nearly a decade. (In the early 1970s Norwegian fears of too rapid development presented an obstacle. In the early 1980s the prospect of lower-than-expected gas demand in the next decade and questions of cost may delay expansion.)

From the perspective of the U.S. government, another concern became more important than European vulnerability. It was the prospect of massive Soviet foreign exchange earnings through the export of natural gas. By the mid-1980s, just as Soviet oil exports to the West were likely to have fallen sharply or ended (and, along with them, the source of more than half the USSR's hard-currency earnings), gas would provide an alternative source of foreign exchange. From the standpoint of the Reagan administration, this would help the Soviets to maintain high levels of military spending that they might otherwise find themselves under increased pressure to curtail.

European governments differed sharply with the United States. From their standpoint the American sanctions of December 1981 and (especially) June 1982 were too late, likely to be ineffective, unnecessary, an unacceptable interference in their internal affairs, and – in view of continued American grain sales to the USSR – inconsistent.

From a German perspective, for example, there were advantages in diversifying the sources of energy imports. (The Soviet natural gas would provide roughly the same proportion of German primary energy supply as Libyan oil.) The Germans also were concerned with the health of their domestic steel industry. The provision of large quantities of German pipe for the project would preserve thousands of jobs in that hard-pressed industry. The Federal Republic benefited from a joint German-French contract to provide pumping stations for the Soviet pipeline project. In the case of France, the possible ability to sustain up to a one-year supply interruption, due to underground gas storage and contingency arrangements with the Dutch, would alleviate the dangers posed by excessive reliance on Soviet gas.

Conflict among the allies over the Soviet pipeline issue was less constructive than focusing attention primarily on measures to lessen allied vulnerability. Thus, it would be important to minimize shipment of Soviet gas directly to millions of individual homes, as opposed to large industrial installations and power plants, and to keep the gas purchases from reaching a percentage level that would surpass the ability of the western Europeans to insure themselves against disruption.

Short of a major and long-term reduction in international oil prices, economic pressures caused by the energy problem are unlikely to disappear. Hence, U.S.-European tensions over these issues will persist, particularly as long as domestic problems make it more difficult for each of the major oil-consuming countries to cooperate. As a result, economic implications spill over into the political realm.

POLITICAL CONSEQUENCES

Europe's dependence on imported oil, with the attendant risks of supply disruptions, market disturbances, and periodic price upheavals increases, has led to its increased vulnerability. The energy dimension has thus been added to those of conventional and strategic nuclear military threat. Each poses major risks to security against which the Europeans have — at best — limited means of protecting themselves from externally originated shocks. In part, this contributes to a sense of powerlessness, as well as a perspective different from that of their North American allies. The individual countries of Europe do possess sufficient combined weight — population, economic strength, resources, economic power — to give them a potential for much greater influence in deterring or responding to these external security dangers. Yet differences of interest, history, language, geography, and internal politics are enduring, as are existing national institutions. As a result of these and other obstacles to unity, the exercise of collective European power is severely limited.

Europe's room for diplomatic maneuver has been further circumscribed by the threats and events of the 1970s. The destruction of Persian Gulf oil facilities and a major interruption of Europe's petroleum supply would cause grave economic damage, although the International Energy Agency (IEA) emergency oil-sharing system, as well as national measures of stockpiling, demand reduction, and fuel switching provide tools for alleviating some of this harm.

Control of Persian Gulf oil by a hostile Soviet Union is a specter haunting some strategists. Their political concern is that with Soviet control of Europe's petroleum supply, the western Europeans and Japanese would become "Finlandized." This remains an improbable scenario: the likelihood of a direct Soviet takeover in the Persian Gulf is less substantial and the uses of oil power more complex. Even hostile regimes in oil-producing regions will continue to sell oil, and their power over price and distribution is by no means unlimited (witness the oil gluts of 1975-78 and 1981-83). Yet their emergence could influence political, economic, and strategic relationships in the Middle East and Europe, with the nature of the resultant interchanges becoming more unfavorable to oil consumers.[1][5]

The political consequences of European energy dependence are not entirely one-sided. Most of the oil-producing countries of the less developed world find themselves dependent on Western technology, markets, and even personnel. Saudi Arabia, for example, has little prospect of establishing a strong and self-sustaining economy based on anything except oil and natural gas. It must, thus, continue indefinitely in a massive two-way trading relationship with the

Western allies. To be sure, the terms of this trade, the mix of bargaining advantages, and the nature of the domestic regimes will vary — along with the possibility of change in oil production levels — but there is a powerful propensity for the relationship to continue in any case.

The political implications of European and Japanese energy dependence also depend on allied perceptions of the United States. American leadership, power, and policies are at least as important in security equations as Middle East factors or allied views of the Soviet Union. One element has been crucial to the relationship among the allies: America's ability to guarantee the security of Japan and Europe. This has continued to hold the alliance together, despite a series of differences over political, economic, and military issues virtually throughout the postwar period. In broad terms, it implies that tensions — even serious ones — over energy issues can nonetheless be assimilated within the overall U.S.-European-Japanese relationship. However, the fabric of these ties could be seriously weakened if the energy crisis were to leave the United States significantly more vulnerable, and thus with reduced capabilities. This in turn could indirectly undercut the credibility of U.S. security guarantees, and hence increase the possibilities for disruption within the alliance.

Political cohesion among alliance countries over energy and security issues will also be shaped by the atmosphere of East-West relations. More direct Soviet threats — especially in the Persian Gulf — could produce an environment in which cooperation over energy and other political and security issues was seen to be more urgent. On the other hand, if a period of energy stringency were accompanied by an apparent easing of tension in East-West relations, this could contribute to reduced willingness to cooperate on energy and security issues, as well as leave the alliance countries more open to disruptive competition as oil consumers.

Western energy and security policies have been unevenly affected by the oscillations between oil crisis and apparent glut, as well as by the Iranian hostage episode, the Soviet invasion of Afghanistan, the Iran-Iraq war, and continued tensions in Arab-Israeli relations. As a result, the potential for tensions within the alliance remains substantial.

Although the allies do not share identical views with the United States regarding the uses of political and military power in response to threats to energy security, their positions do not preclude collaboration. In effect, a division of labor may take place as the allies respond to security problems in the Middle East and the Mediterranean. For historical, geographic, and even cultural reasons, European commitments to some of the states in these regions may be more politically effective than exclusive American commitments. Possible methods to lessen the risks of instability and regional conflict, or conceivably to provide alternatives to a Soviet presence, are offered by the French in Iraq and North Africa, the British in certain of the Persian Gulf states, and the Germans in Turkey.

If America succeeds during the 1980s in becoming substantially less reliant on Middle East oil, its credibility in the region will be enhanced. This would affect relations not only with allies, but also with oil-producing states and U.S. adversaries. Yet even if American pressure for a greater allied military role did not elicit a ready response, the United States could not afford a policy of benign neglect. A massive oil disruption in the late 1980s, even if not directly impinging on large portions of the American oil supply, would still have a significant effect on the United States. This would be felt through price increases for oil throughout the world, competition for scarce supplies, and triggering of the IEA's International Energy Program. The United States would be unable to remain a disinterested spectator while Europe and Japan experienced major energy supply disruptions.

IMPLICATIONS

The allied countries have begun to adapt to the military, economic, and political consequences of their energy dependence and vulnerability. This adaptation, however, has not been without substantial cost. Approximately half the cause of the stubborn economic troubles of the late 1970s and early 1980s lies directly or indirectly in the energy problem. Militarily, the alliance countries are spread more thinly, with commitments to defend an area of great strategic importance in which their preponderance of power is by no means certain. They are in full agreement neither on the nature of military threats to the Persian Gulf nor on the criteria for Western response. Politically, their room to maneuver has become more circumscribed. The allies are faced with significant areas of potential discord.

But despite real differences among the allies, the energy problem has not destroyed their ability to cooperate on security matters of mutual interest. The direct and indirect effects of the energy and oil crises create tensions, disturbances, and even shocks; these do not prevent the alliance countries from cooperating on fundamental matters.[16] The lack of viable alternatives for the Europeans and Japanese, their inability to go it alone, the American need to retain allied support, and a mutual recognition (however grudging) of overriding strategic realities continue to provide ties that hold these countries together.

NOTES

1. Letter, Eisenhower to Winston Churchill, March 29, 1956, p. 2 (in Eisenhower Library, Abilene, Kan.). Quoted in Steven Spiegel, *The War for Washington* (New York: Twentieth Century Fund, forthcoming), ch. 3.

2. Walter J. Levy, "Oil and the Decline of the West," *Foreign Affairs* 53, no. 5 (Summer 1980): 1015.

3. Statement by General Brent Scowcroft, American Enterprise Institute Public Policy Forum, "U.S. Foreign Policy: What Are Our Vital Interests?" Washington, D.C., December 8, 1981.

4. The conclusion that internal upheaval is likely to be a greater threat to Persian Gulf stability than direct Soviet attack is similar to that of a major study of U.S. national security by the Carnegie Endowment. ". . . [T]he principal threats to the West's oil and strategic interests in the Persian Gulf stem much more from the political instability of the area than from the likelihood of Moscow's direct use of force." It also concludes that of the military threats, those from within the region are more likely than any originating from the USSR. See Carnegie Panel on U.S. National Security and the Future of Arms Control, *Challenges for U.S. National Security. Assessing the Balance: Defense Spending and Conventional Forces, A Preliminary Report*, pt. II (Washington, D.C.: Carnegie Endowment for International Peace, 1981), pp. 4, 23.

5. The U.S. Defense Intelligence Agency anticipates a slight increase in Soviet oil production by 1985. (See *New York Times*, September 3, 1981). However, CIA projections of a decline remain more plausible.

6. In Thatcher's words, Britain was prepared to contribute "in the same way as, in conjunction with the U.S. and France, we have already stationed naval units in the Gulf in response to the situation arising from the Iran/Iraq war" (statement in the House of Commons, March 2, 1981). See American Relations: Prime Minister's Visit to the U.S." (New York: British Information Services, Policy and Reference Division, March 4, 1981: mimeograph), p. 3.

7. For a detailed analysis and critique of U.S. Persian Gulf commitments, see "The Persian Gulf: Are We Committed? At What Cost?" prepared for the use of the Joint Economic Committee with the assistance of the Congressional Research Service (Washington, D.C.: October 26, 1981: mimeograph).

8. Figures from Stanley R. Sloan, *Defense Burden Sharing: U.S. Relations with NATO Allies and Japan* (Washington, D.C.: Library of Congress, Congressional Research Service, August 25, 1981).

9. American policy in energy and energy security reflects one such mix of choices. For example, administration budget requests for 1983 included $4 billion for the Rapid Deployment Force, $2.3 billion for the Strategic Petroleum Reserve, $1.6 billion for nuclear power, but only $83 million for solar power and $22 million for conservation. (America's 1981 oil import bill was $77 billion.) Critics of this policy mix suggested it showed a lack of priority — especially in the relative amounts for the RDF and nuclear power vis-à-vis conservation and solar. See Daniel Yergin, "America in the Strait of Stringency," in Daniel Yergin and Martin Hillenbrand, eds., *Global Insecurity: A Strategy for Energy and Economic Renewal* (Boston: Houghton Mifflin, 1982) p. 112. Others have expressed concern about the adequacy of preparations for dealing with a large-scale interruption of oil supply.

10. OECD, *Economic Outlook* no. 28 (December 1980): 9. The OECD figures include the effects of tighter fiscal policies adopted in response to oil price increases. These were responsible for OECD's GNP being 2 percent lower than if policy had been neutral.

11. OECD, *Economic Outlook* 27 (July 1980): 7; no. 30 (July 1982): 21.

12. On the impact of economic dissatisfaction as the most direct influence in the 1980 U.S. presidential vote, see Gerald Pomper, *The Election of 1980: Reports and Interpretations* (Chatham, N.J.: Chatham House, 1980), pp. 85-89.

13. State of the Nation Address by Chancellor Helmut Schmidt before the Bundestag on April 9, 1981. Published in German Information Center, *Statements and Speeches* 4, no. 6 (April 10, 1981). Italics added.

14. According to figures published just after the contract was signed, French dependence on Soviet natural gas could reach 32 percent (*New York Times*, February 4, 1982). However, according to French officials interviewed by this author in March 1982, the actual percentage would be substantially lower, since France was quite unlikely to take the maximum amount of gas available under the contract. For an earlier set of figures suggesting a rate of 17-20 percent, see U.S. Department of State, Bureau of Public Affairs, *Soviet-West European Natural Gas Pipeline* (Statement by Robert Hormats, Assistant Secretary for Economic and Business Affairs), Current Policy No. 331 (Washington, D.C., October 14, 1981).

15. This is a variant of what Keohane and Nye have called "asymmetrical interdependence." It connotes a relationship in which interchange is carried on in a bargaining situation where one side is more dependent than the other and is more vulnerable to changes in the relationship. See Robert O. Keohane and Joseph S. Nye, "World Politics and the International Economic System," in C. Fred Bergsten, ed., *The Future of the International Economic Order: An Agenda for Research* (Lexington, Mass.: D. C. Heath/Lexington Books, 1973), pp. 118-22.

16. The durability of the Atlantic relationship is stressed by A. W. Deporte, *Europe Between the Superpowers: The Enduring Balance* (New Haven: Yale University Press, 1979).

2

THE ENERGY OUTLOOK

Frederick W. Gorbet

INTRODUCTION

The transition away from oil that began in the early to mid-1970s is gathering momentum, and we are now moving toward more balanced and resilient energy systems. Although progress is being made, the process is a slow one, and it will not be until well into the next century that energy systems may cease to be dominated by fossil fuels. The critical challenge for the rest of the century is to reduce dependence on oil — both to minimize the political and strategic risks of overdependence on a few major producers and to protect against the possibility of further price shocks that could lead once again to recession, higher inflation, and more unemployment. The economic and social strains that have emerged since 1973 have been greatly influenced by the need to absorb and adjust to a fifteen- to twentyfold increase in oil prices. The underlying conditions leading to those price increases, as well as their timing and their explosive character, not only have exacerbated the adjustment process but also have demonstrated clearly the political dimension of the problem.

Rapid, fundamental, and largely unanticipated changes in world oil markets have taken place since the end of 1978. Triggered by the revolution in Iran and sustained by the outbreak of war between Iran and Iraq, oil prices increased by almost 170 percent between the end of 1978 and March 1981 (from about $12.90 to $34.80 per barrel). These higher prices played a critically important role in reducing oil consumption, both directly and indirectly through their impact on economic activity. As a result, oil use in International Energy Agency (IEA) countries[1] fell from about 38.3 million barrels per day (mbd) in 1979 to an anticipated 32.9 mbd in 1981. OPEC production over the same period fell from 31.6 mbd to about 23.3 mbd. The oil market was relatively soft for some months and, toward the end of 1981, OPEC successfully realigned official selling prices around a benchmark of $34 per barrel and narrowed the very large differentials that had developed in the course of 1979 and 1980. Prices fell back slightly after the first quarter of 1981, but were still around $34 per barrel, about 160 percent higher than they were at the end of 1978.

Increasingly we hear public statements that the energy problem is over. I would agree that the world oil market may remain relatively stable over the next few years, barring political surprises. But as we look forward through the 1980s, the possibility is very real that renewed economic growth in the industrial countries, together with rapidly growing demands for oil in OPEC countries, other less developed countries (LDCs), and the centrally planned economies will once again put increasing pressure on the oil market.

And we should not forget that even in the relative calm of today's market, we continue to suffer the economic impacts of the recent price increases. In statistical and economic terms, those price increases cost the OECD countries more than $1 trillion from 1979 to 1981, lost income amounting to almost $1,300 per person. They also contributed to the continued existence of inflationary pressures and the high interest rates that are necessary to contain them. In human terms, the price increases had some responsibility for the increase in unemployment from less than 19 million people in 1979 to an expected level of 26 million people in 1982. These broader economic and human impacts are becoming manifest in increasing social tensions within countries and in more difficult relations among countries. They reflect the too often ignored, but very real, costs of the energy problem.

It is essential that those responsible for energy policy – and ultimately that includes all of us – ensure that every reasonable effort is made to protect against the economic consequences of a further oil price shock. If a calmer oil market in the next year or two frees us from short-term supply disruptions, governments and the private sector should use the time to move ahead with the strategies necessary to implement energy objectives. Energy investments require long lead times before they become productive – typically ten years or more for nuclear power plants, for example. So the decisions we make – or do not make – today will affect us in the late 1980s and early 1990s.

CURRENT MARKET OUTLOOK

It may seem strange to talk about further price shocks in today's market, but there are basically three reasons for concern.

First, we do not yet know how much of the decline in oil demand – which amounted to about 8 percent in 1980 and possibly a further 7 percent in 1981 – reflects permanent changes in energy structures rather than the impact of cyclical and other factors that may be reversed quickly. A large part is obviously due to lower economic growth. And special factors, such as climate and consumer stocking decisions, have also played a role. Some preliminary work suggests that these factors may have accounted for almost 50 percent of the total reduction in oil use in those two years. The balance is due to consumer reaction to higher prices and government policies encouraging reduced oil use. But it would not be correct to categorize all of the response to price and policies as structural. Some fuel switching has taken place and some conservation investment has occurred; the effects of these actions will persist. But some of the price response undoubtedly reflects only changes in habits (turning thermostats down, driving less), and these could easily be reversed if oil prices stay relatively constant, or decline in real terms, and incomes begin to grow again.

In current circumstances it is relevant to note that during the last economic recovery (1976-78), oil use in IEA countries grew at about 4.1 percent per year and net oil imports grew by about 2.5 mbd despite a rapid increase in domestic production. Many of the factors in the current situation differ from the previous economic slowdown;

in particular the energy policy framework in most countries, and specifically in North America, is much better developed now than it was earlier. Nevertheless, it would be only prudent to expect some increase in oil use as economic growth accelerates in the industrialized countries.

Second, an important part of the reason for market weakness was the continuation of high production levels by Saudi Arabia. OPEC has now agreed to unify prices around a benchmark of $34 per barrel, and this consensus has already resulted in lower levels of Saudi production, which should move the oil market closer to balance through 1982. Saudi Arabia has also expressed its intention to protect the $34 benchmark price.

Finally, in addition to uncertainty about future oil demand and supply, we are living with continuing uncertainty about the overall political situation in the Middle East. The one hard lesson we have learned since 1973 is that politics and oil do mix, and it would be imprudent to plan our energy futures on the belief that there will be no further surprises in the Middle East.

Overall, I see the market reaching balance in the course of 1982, with the timing depending very much on the timing of economic recovery. Barring political surprises, the oil market could remain in comfortable balance for a few more years. Over the longer run, however, assuming satisfactory economic growth is restored and sustained, the market is likely to become increasingly tight and the underlying conditions that could lead to yet another oil price shock could emerge once more. We have a breathing space at the moment, but it is important to recognize that it is nothing more than a breathing space. It is essential to use this time wisely to follow through with energy policies that can bring about lasting structural change, leading to reduced dependence on oil.

RECENT PERFORMANCE: THE BEGINNING OF ADJUSTMENT

There is no doubt that a process of structural adjustment is now under way in the industrialized countries. Since 1973, for example:

- Energy used to produce a dollar's worth of real GDP in IEA countries has fallen by almost 13 percent. Oil use is now lower than it was in 1973 and oil intensity − that is, oil use relative to GDP – has decreased by almost 20 percent. These trends reflect increasing efficiency and a growing trend to substitute other fuels for oil.

Progress has also been made on the supply side. From 1973 to 1980 indigenous production of energy in IEA countries grew by more than 12 percent, equivalent to about 5.5 mbd of oil. Of the total increase, 70 percent occurred in 1979 and 1980, reflecting long lead times but also indicating that the process is now under way. It is also worth noting that of the total increase, about 45 percent came from coal and 30 percent from nuclear power.

The development of energy and oil use over the 1973-79 period (shown in Table 2.1) indicates that oil use grew at just under half the rate of total primary energy for the IEA as a whole. This, however, masks very wide differences in results for different regions. In Europe oil use actually declined by almost 10 million tons oil equivalent (mtoe), with a substantial decrease in industrial consumption more than offsetting increased use in transportation. In the Pacific region oil use increased by only 3.8 percent, compared with an increase in total primary energy (TPE) of 13.5 percent. The relative importance of oil over this period fell from 71 percent of TPE in 1973 to 65 percent in 1979. Oil use in North America grew substantially more quickly than total energy use, reflecting the impact of price controls and also of natural gas delivery problems in the mid-1970s, which resulted in some industrial substitution of oil for natural gas.

Overall, oil use grew quite strongly in the industrial and transportation sectors but declined markedly in residential/commercial use and for electricity generation. Regional experience in these sectors varied greatly. Transportation use increased markedly in all regions. This may well have been due to lower rates of increase in consumer prices in this sector than in other sectors, because of the existence prior to 1973 of relatively substantial tax components on motor gasoline prices, fixed in specific rather than ad valorem terms.[2] Finally, all regions registered some progress in reducing oil used for electricity generation.

Developments in net oil imports are shown in Table 2.2. Although oil use declined substantially in 1980, it was still almost

TABLE 2.1
Energy and Oil Use, 1973-79
(mtoe)[a]

		Regional Breakdown		
	IEA Total	North America	Europe	Pacific
AGGREGATES				
Total primary energy				
1973	3,373	1,987	978	408
1979	3,612	2,088	1,059	463
Percent change	7.1	5.1	8.3	13.5
Total final consumption				
1973	2,463	1,436	737	290
1979	2,617	1,500	786	331
Percent change	6.3	4.5	6.6	14.1
Total oil use				
1973	1,755	898	567	290
1979	1,818	958	559	301
Percent change	3.6	6.7	−1.4	3.8
Percent of incremental demand (1973-79) supplied by nonoil fuels	73.5	40.6	109.9	80.0
SECTORAL BREAKDOWN OF OIL USE				
Residential/commercial				
1973	364	179	146	39
1979	325	142	142	41
Percent change	−10.7	−20.7	−2.7	5.1
Industrial sector[b]				
1973	425	150	180	95
1979	475	203	162	110
Percent change	11.7	35.3	−10.0	15.8
Transportation				
1973	634	444	133	57
1979	732	502	159	71
Percent change	15.5	13.1	19.6	24.6
Electricity generation				
1973	233	90	71	72
1979	216	87	68	61
Percent change	−7.3	−3.3	−4.2	−15.3

[a]1 million barrels per day is approximately equal to 49.2 mtoe per year.
[b]Including nonenergy use.
Source: IEA energy statistics.

1 mbd above the level it had reached in 1975, at the trough of the previous recession. Oil production has increased through the period, reflecting developments in the North Sea and the North Slope; as a result, net oil imports declined in 1980 to their lowest post-1973 level. The decline has been most substantial in Europe, reflecting in large part growing production from the North Sea. In North America imports increased steadily and markedly from 1973 to 1977, but have since fallen dramatically.

FUTURE PROSPECTS

I am convinced that the trends developing since 1973 on both the demand and the supply side will continue. The critical question is whether results will occur quickly enough to protect our economies against the possibility of another oil price shock in the 1980s.

At the IEA we have developed a reference case scenario for 1990 and 2000.[3] This has been constructed in the form of complete and consistent energy balances, on a regional basis and for the major energy economies; it thus provides a look at one possible future

TABLE 2.2
Oil Use, Production, and Net Oil Imports:
1973-80
(mtoe)

Year	Oil Use	Oil Production	Net Oil Import[a] IEA Total	Regional Breakdown N. America	Europe	Pacific
1973	1,754.9	659.3	1,179.4	295.3	591.3	292.8
1974	1,676.5	639.1	1,140.7	291.6	565.4	283.6
1975	1,617.7	603.6	1,074.6	313.4	498.9	262.3
1976	1,728.6	600.6	1,191.2	384.1	534.1	272.8
1977	1,784.5	632.7	1,244.7	460.1	502.9	281.7
1978	1,827.5	676.2	1,200.6	433.6	488.8	278.2
1979	1,818.2	706.6	1,205.8	425.6	486.0	294.3
1980[b]	1,665.0	714.9	1,033.1	335.2	432.1	265.7

[a]Includes international marine bunkers.
[b]Preliminary figures.

pattern of production, trade, conversion, and use. The methodology employed was to begin with sets of national projections for 1990, then adjust and extend them with a view to indicating what might be achievable in reducing oil use, taking into account technological, economic, and institutional factors and allowing for the continued development and implementation of energy policies.

The purpose of the scenario is not to present a projection of what is likely to happen, but to provide a quantitative and internally consistent framework within which issues of energy policy can be addressed and discussed. The numbers themselves are secondary to the directional trends and their implications.

Our analysis (see Table 2.3) suggests that even with a healthy economic recovery over the next few years and sustained economic growth at about 3.2 percent per year thereafter, it is possible to limit IEA net oil imports in 1990 to roughly 19-20 mbd, and reduce them to about 15 mbd by the end of the century. This would imply that total oil consumption would fall from a little less than 50 percent of total energy requirements today to about 26 percent by 2000.

This outcome is possible, but achieving it will not be easy. Further efforts to conserve energy and oil will be essential in order to hold growth of final energy consumption to about 1.2 percent per year. The overall efficiency of energy, as reflected by the TPE/ GDP ratio,[4] will increase by about 25 percent by the end of the century. Relative to GDP, oil use will fall by 37 percent in the 1980s and a further 38 percent in the 1990s, a rough measure of both increasing efficiency and substitution.

The scenario also requires substantial increases in new energy supplies. For example, we are assuming the following:

- Growth in coal production and use on the order of 150 percent by 2000

- An increase in nuclear power of 170 percent in the 1980s and a further 65 percent in the 1990s

- Stabilization, or perhaps even some increase, in IEA oil and gas production, with new finds, enhanced recovery, and some synthetic production making up for declines in other fields.

The resulting pattern of declining oil use, on both a sectoral and a regional basis, is shown in Tables 2.4 and 2.5. In the 1980s

TABLE 2.3
IEA Reference Scenario
(mtoe)

		Reference Case	
	1979	*1990*	*2000*
Total primary energy	3,612	4,236	5,100
Nonoil energy consumption	1,794	2,666	3,780
Oil consumption	1,818	1,570	1,320
Of which: net oil imports[a]	1,206	974	730
Domestic energy production	2,486	3,142	4,205
Coal	727	1,100	1,770
Oil	707	678	680
Gas	695	713	750
Nuclear	123	336	555
Hydro	232	285	350
Other	2	30	100
Net nonoil imports			
Coal	11	60	40
Gas	30	142	215
Total final consumption	2,617	2,918	3,369
Industry (inc. nonenergy use)	1,040	1,270	1,667
Transport	737	709	680
Residential/commercial	840	939	1,022
Oil use			
Industry (inc. nonenergy use)	475	375	420
Transport	732	707	670
Residential/commercial	325	265	135
Electricity generation	215	136	50
Memorandum items			
Net oil imports (mbd)[a]	24.5	19.8	14.8
Oil consumption as percent TPE	50.3	37.1	25.9
TPE/GDP ratio (1973 = 100)	91.2	77.7	68.3
Oil/GDP ratio (1973 = 100)	88.4	55.4	34.0

TABLE 2.3, continued

| | 1979 | Reference Case | |
		1990	2000
Electricity consumption (mtoe)	358	494	655
Electricity consumption as percent TFC	13.6	16.9	19.7
Share of oil in total sectoral energy use (percent)			
Industry	45.6	29.5	25.2
Residential/commercial	38.7	28.2	19.8
Electricity generation[b]	18.6	8.6	2.4

[a]Includes marine bunkers. Conversion at 49.2 mtoe/year = 1 mbd.
[b]Measured on the basis of fuel inputs.

Source: IEA Secretariat estimates.

virtually all of the absolute decline in oil use is expected to occur
in North America, reflecting the possibilities for larger efficiency
gains as well as more easily available options for substitution. By the
end of the century North America is seen to be virtually self-sufficient
in energy, with oil imports of only about 2 mbd. The degree of self-
sufficiency is also expected to increase in Europe and the Pacific
region, as a result of more extensive use of coal, nuclear power,
and natural gas. In Europe the decline in oil use will accelerate in
the 1990s, and through that decade the absolute reduction will
amount to almost half the total IEA reduction. In the Pacific region
oil use will remain at about 1979 levels through 2000, but decline
substantially in relative terms, from 66 percent of TPE in 1979
to 35 percent by 2000. Overall, oil use will be reduced to about
26 percent of TPE by the end of the century, accounting for 28
percent in Europe and only 22 percent in North America.

On a sectoral basis the general picture is one of transition to a
much more energy-efficient economy, and one in which oil is increasingly reserved for premium industrial use and transportation.
The strong performance witnessed in the residential/commercial
sector is anticipated to continue, and indeed accelerate, in response
to price incentives, government conservation measures, and increasing substitution of natural gas and electricity. Oil use in this
sector could fall to less than 20 percent of total energy use, with

TABLE 2.4
Changing Patterns of Oil Use, 1979-2000
(mtoe)

| | IEA Total | Regional Breakdown | | |
		N. America	Europe	Pacific
1979 levels				
Total oil use [a]	1,818	958	559	301
Industry [b]	474	203	161	110
Transport	732	502	159	71
Residential/commercial	325	142	142	41
Elec. generation	216	87	67	61
Net oil imports [c]	1,206	426	486	294
1979-90 change				
Total oil use	−248	−226	−23	1
Industry [b]	−99	−70	−10	−19
Transport	−25	−62	21	16
Residential/commercial	−60	−32	−34	6
Elec. generation	−80	−54	−17	−8
Net oil imports [c]	−232	−167	−64	−1
1990-2000 change				
Total oil use	−250	−132	−116	−2
Industry [b]	45	27	−16	34
Transport	−37	−50	5	8
Residential/commercial	−130	−70	−53	−7
Elec. generation	−86	−18	−40	−28
Net oil imports [c]	−244	−159	−77	−8

[a]Including conversion losses and stock changes.
[b]Including nonenergy use.
[c]Including marine bunkers.

Source: IEA Secretariat estimates.

TABLE 2.5
Regional Breakdown of Reference Scenario
(mtoe)

	North America			IEA Europe			IEA Pacific		
	1979	*1990*	*2000*	*1979*	*1990*	*2000*	*1979*	*1990*	*2000*
Total primary energy	2,088	2,311	2,750	1,061	1,285	1,500	463	640	850
Domestic production	1,757	2,097	2,725	573	738	910	153	307	570
Oil	569	500	530	114	150	110	24	28	40
Gas	529	510	535	155	170	180	11	33	35
Coal	458	707	1,150	197	233	280	72	160	340
Nuclear	74	200	270	32	101	210	17	35	75
Import requirements	397	241	55	522	583	625	328	352	305
Oil*	426	259	100	486	422	345	294	293	285
Gas	5	45	55	8	49	85	17	48	75
Coal	−33	−63	−100	27	112	195	17	11	−55
Domestic production as percent TPE	84.1	90.7	99.1	54.0	57.4	60.7	33.0	48.0	67.1
Oil consumption as percent TPE	45.9	31.6	21.8	52.7	41.7	28.0	64.8	47.1	35.2
Imported oil									
as percent of TPE	20.4	11.2	3.6	45.8	32.8	23.0	63.4	45.8	33.5
as percent of oil consumption	44.5	35.4	16.7	86.8	78.7	82.1	98.0	97.0	95.0
Million barrels/day	8.7	5.3	2.0	9.9	8.6	7.0	6.0	5.9	5.8

*Includes marine bunkers.

Source: IEA Secretariat estimates.

28

the decline concentrated in North America. Progress will also continue in phasing oil out of electricity generation, with the result that by the end of the century only about 1 mbd would be used in this sector. Coal and nuclear power are the major substitutes, together accounting for almost 80 percent of electricity generation in 2000.

The scenario has a number of encouraging aspects, but obviously presents a number of challenges as well. On the encouraging side, it suggests that the possibility to reduce potential oil market pressure in a significant way does in fact exist, and that the link between oil use and economic growth can be substantially bent, if not broken. Moreover, this picture is not constrained by resource availability or by technology: energy resources and the technology to use them on the scale suggested in the scenario currently exist. Finally, at today's oil prices, most of the required developments are economically attractive.

None of this is to say, however, that the developments will automatically proceed at the desired pace or on the required scale. There are some serious social, institutional, and political constraints that need to be looked at very hard if an attractive investment climate — which is the fundamental requirement for these developments to take place — is to be created and sustained.

KEY AREAS OF UNCERTAINTY

Against the background of this reference scenario, there are a number of specific issues that will become increasingly important on the "energy policy agenda." Particular areas that warrant further consideration include the following.

The Role of Electricity

Relatively rapid rates of growth of electricity demand are essential if coal and nuclear power are to play a major role in displacing oil over the next few decades. Recent declines in projected load growth need to be scrutinized carefully in order to disentangle cyclical and structural factors. Further, for any given load growth estimates, greater attention needs to be given to the risks of underbuilding as opposed to risks of ending up with some excess capacity.

From a public policy perspective, and in view of recent oil price increases from a utility perspective, the risks may be highly asymmetrical — with excess capacity providing opportunities to displace oil in end use or to phase out more costly oil generating plants earlier than would otherwise be possible. Finally, in some specific cases attention needs to be given to the regulatory regime governing the setting of tariffs and the impact of such regimes on the financial health of utilities and their ability to undertake investment in new and relatively capital-intensive facilities.

Energy Pricing

The increasing role of governments in energy markets, particularly as rent collectors, requires that greater attention be given to energy prices and specifically to relative price structures for competing fuels. Rising oil prices generate economic rents for other energy sources, particularly in the short term. To the degree that such rents are appropriated by producers, suppliers of equipment or services, or governments, the process of substitution of alternative fuels for oil will be slowed. As a result, the dominating influence of the oil price, which is not a free market price, on energy and economic prospects will be reinforced.

A second issue related to energy pricing concerns the extent to which, and the appropriate conditions under which, government policies should reinforce market forces with the aim of speeding up, or reducing the overall cost of, responses to market forces. A relative price structure that is economically attractive is a necessary condition to promote substitution and reduced oil dependence, but it may not be sufficient in all cases. For example, where development of alternatives is constrained by regulatory frameworks, environmental conditions, or simply the lack of information about available options, consideration needs to be given to addressing these constraints directly, since positive actions in these areas may facilitate substitution at a lower oil price than would otherwise be necessary to bring about similar results.

Security of Supply

Security of oil supply continues to be a major concern, but there are also growing concerns about the security of future natural gas supplies, particularly in Europe, where most of the growth is expected to come through Algerian and Soviet exports. Greater attention needs to be given to possibilities for reducing risks of interruption through greater connection of gas grids, enhanced emergency storage capability, and increased use of dual-fired equipment. Appropriate international arrangements for greater access to secure sources of gas on a standby basis, particularly from the Netherlands, can also reduce the risks of greater reliance on potentially insecure imports.

Nuclear Power

Nuclear power is surrounded by the greatest uncertainties. Nuclear power capacity almost tripled from 1973 to 1979, but since 1979 little has happened. In 1980 only four units came on-line, and although 16 new units were ordered in Europe and Japan, there was an equal number of cancellations in the United States. The anticipated growth in nuclear power foreseen for the 1980s could well materialize, given the reactors that are now under construction and on order, although the possibility of future cancellations and continuing increases in lead times must be recognized. For the 1990s there is much greater uncertainty, and the possibility exists that, without substantial changes in the overall climate affecting nuclear power development, a contribution on the scale we have assumed will not materialize. The consequences of such a shortfall could be far-reaching. For example, if only half the foreseen increase in nuclear power occurs by 2000, an additional 4.5 mbd of oil equivalent would have to be "supplied" in 2000 — through greater use of other fuels, through greater energy efficiency, or perhaps through lower economic growth. This example clearly illustrates the integrated nature of the scenario and the need to consider all the options in a comprehensive and consistent framework.

CONCLUSIONS

Although the most recent price increase has been very costly, it has brought about relative calm in the international oil market. Nevertheless, we must recognize that the energy problem has not gone away. Lead times in energy are so long that we are effectively shaping the energy outcome in the late 1980s and early 1990s by the decisions we make, or fail to make, today.

The issue before us is clear. Do we have the foresight, by taking appropriate decisions now, to avoid a further tightening of oil markets in the late 1980s, with the lower economic growth, higher inflation, greater unemployment, and increasing political tensions that would inevitably follow? Or are we doomed to a future in which hard decisions are made only after the situation has deteriorated to the point where the level of pain becomes socially and politically intolerable?

The longer-term outlook presented in this chapter can serve as a directional framework for decisions that must be made by consumers, industry, and governments if our dependence on oil is to be reduced to acceptable levels and better and more sustainable balance in our energy economies achieved. Its attainment will not be easy, but the consequences of not attaining it will be severe.

NOTES

1. Member countries of the IEA are Australia, Austria, Belgium, Canada, Denmark, Germany, Greece, Ireland, Italy, Japan, Luxembourg, the Netherlands, New Zealand, Norway, Portugal, Spain, Sweden, Switzerland, Turkey, the United Kingdom, and the United States.

2. See A. Tait and D. R. Morgan, "Gasoline Taxation in Selected OECD Countries, 1970-79," International Monetary Fund, *Staff Papers* (January 1980).

3. R. Lamb, *Shaping the Energy Transition*, IEA Monograph no. 2 (Paris: OECD, November 1981).

4. The TPE/GDP ratio is a very rough measure of overall energy efficiency. It suffers from many drawbacks, however, including an inability to take account of structural changes in GDP over long periods of time and the inclusion of conversion losses in TPE, which can be particularly important if, for example, the share of electricity in total energy use grows markedly over time, as it does in the reference scenarios. To overcome the latter difficulty, total final consumption (TFC) provides a better measure of energy use. The TFC/GDP ratio falls by about 32 percent (1979-2000) in the reference scenario, compared with a decrease of almost 10 percent from 1973 to 1979.

3

KHRUSHCHEV'S OIL AND BREZHNEV'S NATURAL GAS PIPELINES

Bruce W. Jentleson

European participation as natural gas importer, wide-diameter pipe and gas turbine-compressor exporter, and financier of the west Siberian natural gas pipeline project raises a corollary to the question of whether Europe will fight for oil. Will the increased reliance on Soviet supplies of natural gas sap Europe of the will to continue to "fight" alongside the United States in East-West bloc politics? The Reagan administration appears to think so. Assistant Secretary of Defense Richard N. Perle told a congressional committee, "We believe that the increasing dependence of our European allies on Soviet energy, and especially natural gas, will weaken the alliance politically and militarily." Perle went on in his testimony to delineate the negative strategic consequences of the west Siberian pipeline for the Western alliance:

> It will generate substantial hard currency earnings for the Soviet Union that will finance . . . the modernization of the Soviet military and industrial establishment.

The author wishes to thank Arch Dotson, Peter Katzenstein, Walter LaFeber, Ariel Levite, Theodore Lowi, and Richard Rosecrance for their comments and assistance on earlier versions of this chapter.

Where jobs and profits emanate from Moscow, it would be naive to think that politics will stay far behind.

In a crisis the Soviets might interrupt the flow of gas to achieve political purposes.

There is the day-to-day influence that must flow, like the gas itself . . . . Practical men will find alternatives to angering their [energy] suppliers more easily than they will find new ones. Whether one calls it sensitivity or solicitousness or simply "reality," is there any doubt that our allies listen more carefully to kings and rulers who supply them with energy than to those who do not?[1]

This is not the first time that the issue of transbloc energy trade has threatened to split the Western alliance. In the early 1960s the analogous issues were large volumes of oil imports from the Soviet Union and wide-diameter pipe exports for the construction of its so-called Friendship Pipeline. With intelligence agency and private oil industry estimates of Soviet petroleum exports all pointing upward, American officials were concerned that oil exports were becoming "the latest and in some ways the most effective weapon the Soviets have found in their well-stocked arsenal against the Free World."[2] Oil exports both brought in substantial hard currency earnings and, even more important from the American perspective, were considered a valuable means for expanding Soviet political influence. The Friendship Pipeline would vastly increase the Soviets' oil export capacity. It also was seen as having military significance because of the logistical support it would provide for conventional forces. Because wide-diameter pipe, like gas turbines and compressors today, was in short supply within the Soviet Union, the denial of Western exports held out the prospect of delaying, if not undermining, the pipeline project.

Both the 1960s oil pipeline case and the 1980s natural gas pipeline case raise questions concerning the conditions under which American leverage over European transbloc energy trade policies is likely to be maximized. This chapter seeks to provide insights into the current natural gas pipeline case through a comparison with the earlier oil pipeline case. Patterns of behavior will be identified, some general explanatory propositions formulated, and empirically grounded policy prescriptions offered as an alternative to the ideologically infused and emotionally charged arguments that have tended to dominate discussions of East-West trade.

COCOM AND THE EARLY COLD WAR:
WEAK REGIME BUT HIGH AMERICAN LEVERAGE

For the United States the regulation of East-West trade was a logical extension of the basic politico-strategic doctrine of containment. By denying the Soviets the benefits of trade with the West, it was expected that their military capabilities and overall economic development could be significantly retarded. Multilateral Western trade controls also would reduce the possibility that the Soviets could manipulate any bilateral trade relations in order to gain political influence. Toward that end the Consultative Group-Coordinating Committee (COCOM) was created in late 1949 as the institutional basis for a multilateral Western embargo. The membership list essentially duplicated that of NATO, with the exception of Iceland and the addition of Japan.

It was only under sustained pressure from the Truman administration, however, that other nations consented to the creation of COCOM.[3] The western Europeans, notably the British, were reluctant to subjugate their national trade policies to a multilateral institution with a politico-strategic mission. Overall trade traditionally had represented a larger percentage of GNP in Europe than in the United States. Trade between western and eastern Europe (including the Soviet Union) had reached relatively high levels during the interwar period. For example, total British trade with eastern Europe in 1937 was $420 million, compared with only $250 million for the United States. The terms of trade were attractive because manufactured goods were exported in exchange for such primary products as food, timber, and oil. In addition, the debacle of the League of Nations sanctions against Italy had left most European leaders with little confidence in the efficacy of economic coercion for achieving political objectives.[4]

The limited enthusiasm of the Europeans was reflected in COCOM's weak institutional structure and narrow scope of authority. It was not given a basis in treaty; instead, it was created by less formal, and for years highly secretive, executive agreements. Its rule-making authority was circumscribed by the granting of veto power to individual members. Resources allocated for enforcement were extremely limited. In essence, it was true to its name: it was a forum for consultation more than a governing body, and decision making was by committee rather than through a strong executive.

These weaknesses in COCOM's structure were patched over during the early 1950s by the unusually high degree of leverage that the United States possessed over its allies. This American capacity to influence the policy choices of other nations without the overt use of force[5] had two principal sources. First, Europe's almost total dependence on the United States for its defense created a relationship of foreign policy dominance. Without the American nuclear umbrella and American funding, manning, and equipping of NATO's conventional forces, Europe would have been left virtually defenseless. The rearmament that was under way was limited in scope and was possible only because of the $4.5 billion in direct military assistance that Europe received from the United States between 1950 and 1953. Moreover, the threat of Stalinist aggression and totalitarianism made security concerns even more paramount than would have been the case under more stable conditions. As the guarantor of European security, the United States was well positioned to exert leverage over trade controls and other security-related issues.

The second principal source of leverage was the economic dependence of a continent still ravaged by wartime destruction. The large volumes of American capital and technical assistance that flowed through the Marshall Plan were vital to Europe's economic reconstruction. However, in 1950, amid reports that trade with the Soviet Union was continuing in Europe, the U.S. Congress passed the Mutual Defense Assistance Control Act (also known as the Battle Act after its chief sponsor, Rep. Laurie Battle, Democrat of Alabama). Under the provisions of the Battle Act, any nation that violated the COCOM export controls was liable to a cutoff of economic assistance. Given that Marshall Plan economic aid totaled $15 billion between 1949 and 1953, it was extremely doubtful that any transbloc trade could provide comparable benefits. This economic leverage through capital flows was further reinforced by the targeted subsidization of private foreign direct investment through the Investment Guaranty Program (IGP).[6] While there was no statutory link between the IGP and trade controls, it was the same Congress that controlled the purse strings.

Thus, as Table 3.1 shows, the volume of exports to the Soviet Union in the early 1950s was far below the interwar and immediate postwar periods. American exports showed the most precipitous decline, falling from $149 million in 1947 to $1 million in 1950.

TABLE 3.1
Exports to the Soviet Union, 1938, 1947-54 (millions of U.S. dollars)

	Total COCOM	United States	Great Britain	France	West Germany
Interwar period					
1938	226.2	73	55	7.6	48
Postwar, Pre-COCOM					
1947	234.7	149	49	0.1	0.2
1948	115.7	28	21	0.2	0
1949	123.3	6	32	0.6	0
Cold war, COCOM					
1950	86.9	1	32	2.7	0
1951	71.0	2.8	10	4.9	0
1952	85.0	1.1	11	6.5	0.2
1953	130.4	0.6	9	16.0	1.7
1954	206.3	0.4	27	30.9	12.6

Sources: Gunnar Adler-Karlsson, *Western Economic Warfare* (Stockholm: Almqvist and Wiksell, 1968), p. 316-A; United Nations, *Yearbook of International Trade Statistics* (New York: United Nations, various years).

Britain, the most reluctant member of the trade controls regime, cut its exports from a high of $55 million to $9 million. The same pattern held for COCOM exports taken in the aggregate, which did not again reach interwar levels until 1956.

Among the most strictly controlled sectors of trade was energy. In the 1930s Italy, France, Germany, England, Belgium, and Denmark all imported substantial quantities of Soviet oil. The German economist Heinrich Hassmann asserts that it was "Russia's pursuance of its oil export policy" that disrupted the Achnacarry orderly marketing system in Europe and set off the violent price wars of the 1930s.[7] But in the postwar period western European imports of Soviet oil fell to negligible levels. In 1950 the largest non-Communist importer of Soviet oil (with the exception of Finland) was Italy, with only 5,700 metric tons.[8] Oil was an economically strategic commodity and, especially among American strategists, there was concern that Soviet political influence would flow along with Soviet oil.

According to the State Department's 1950 *Battle Act Report*, "All basic specialized equipment for the exploration, production and refining of petroleum and natural gas" was on the COCOM embargo list.[9] While oil was neither arms nor ammunition, World War II had demonstrated the direct military significance of a secure oil supply and of mastery of the refinery technologies for producing high-performance petroleum products. In November 1945 the American Joint Chiefs of Staff called the Allies' ability to meet the demand for oil of their economies and armed forces "without question one of the greatest industrial accomplishments in the history of warfare."[10] Because strategic bombers required high-octane fuels, the technological sophistication of a nation's oil industry had become even more militarily relevant in the nuclear age. In addition, the oil industry was a central part of the industrial base on which a nation's economic mobilization capacity, as well as its overall economic growth, depended.

In theory, export controls can have the greatest economic impact when the nation at which the sanctions are aimed has limited indigenous capacity to produce for itself, cannot do without the embargoed goods, and is unable to find substitute trade partners.[11] Because of the economic and military importance of a strong oil industry, the "do-without" option carried high costs for the Soviets. Strict COCOM rules and extensive American leverage reduced the availability of substitute trade partners.

As a result the Soviets were left with no other option than to produce for themselves. Yet, as a 1950 CIA report concluded, without Western exports the Soviet oil industry "cannot be expected to make any spectacular improvements in the near future."[12] Prewar levels of crude oil production were not reached again until 1950. Then, despite the ambitious goals of Stalin's Fifth Five-Year Plan (1951-55), the crude oil production growth rate fell from the 1948-50 average of 13.3 percent to 11.6 percent in 1951-53. Even with the coming on line of a number of refineries built at least in part with American wartime lend-lease assistance (technology as well as capital), the Soviets could not produce petroleum products in the needed quantity or of the needed quality. In fact, at the time of Stalin's death the Soviet Union relied on Romania to meet its need for high-quality petroleum products. The Soviet oil industry was so beset with problems that in a report prepared for the National Security Council in early 1952, Secretary of the Interior Oscar Chapman (who still also carried the title petroleum administrator for defense) declared in ringing terms:

> The story of world exploration and discovery of crude oil reserves is largely the story of American ingenuity, technological advancement and the financial incentives of private enterprise under our form of government.[13]

KHRUSHCHEV'S OIL PIPELINE
AND THE SOVIET OIL OFFENSIVE

In the late 1950s, however, the scenario changed dramatically. One of the more notable achievements of the government of Nikita Khrushehev (1953-64) was the dynamic development of the Soviet oil industry. By 1958 total oil production was 100 percent greater than at Stalin's death only five years earlier. When production reached 147.8 million metric tons in 1960 (3 million barrels per day), the Soviet Union displaced Venezuela as the world's second leading producer of oil behind the United States. Khrushchev's Seven-Year Plan (1959-65) forecast even more rapid growth of production to 240 million metric tons by 1965, a figure disputed by American government and oil industry analysts only to the extent that they anticipated that the goal would be exceeded.[14]

For the most part the Soviets achieved these gains through indigenous production, an option that earlier in the 1950s American strategists had presumed held little prospect for reducing their vulnerability to Western export controls. Undoubtedly, some Western technology reached the Soviet Union through illegal transshipment, as was the general rule in most sectors. But studies by an industry-government delegation that visited the Soviet Union and by the National Petroleum Council concluded that indigenous technologies such as the turbodrill and favorable shifts in the resources allocated to the energy sector were the principal determinants of the reversal of fortunes.[15]

The rapid growth in oil production was sufficient not only to fuel Khrushchev's domestic economic development projects but also to leave a substantial surplus available for export. This surplus provided a valuable foreign policy instrument. Within the USSR's sphere of influence in eastern Europe, the Polish and Hungarian uprisings of 1956 had served notice that more rapid economic growth was a necessary condition for political stability. Soviet oil had to be available in sufficient quantities to fuel this economic development, or President Dwight Eisenhower and his Secretary of State, John Foster Dulles might get the opening they sought for their "rollback" strategy. The 77 percent increase in Soviet oil exports to eastern Europe in 1957 is particularly noteworthy in this regard.

If oil exports were to be the means for preserving Soviet domination of eastern Europe, they also were seen as a potential means for expanding Soviet influence in western Europe. As part of the peaceful coexistence foreign policy strategy, the Soviets mounted what a later author called their "rather spectacular oil offensive in the Capitalist World."[16] Between 1956 and 1960 Soviet oil exports to COCOM countries increased by 700 percent from 1.4 to 10 million metric tons a year. In the relative terms of market shares, the gain was from 2 percent to 6 percent of aggregate European COCOM oil imports.[17]

With an eye toward expanding this market share in western Europe, as well as continuing to meet eastern European demand, Khrushchev made the Friendship Pipeline a centerpiece of his Seven-Year Plan.[18] This 5,750-kilometer pipeline would begin in the rich oil fields of the Urals-Volga region and branch off into Poland, East Germany, Czechoslovakia, Hungary, and Soviet ports on the

FIGURE 3.1
The Friendship Crude Oil Pipeline

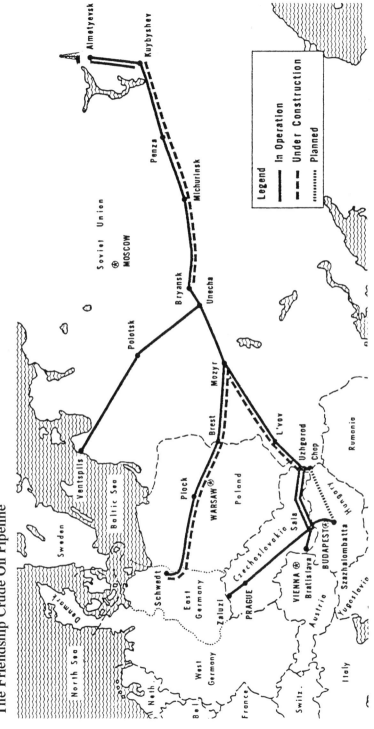

Source: Robert Ebel, *Communist Trade in Oil and Gas* (New York: Praeger, 1970), p. 65.

Black and Baltic seas (see Figure 3.1). Some of the oil would be consumed at these destinations, but much would be reexported to western Europe.

The maximum planned carrying capacity of 862,000 barrels per day required that the 1,350-kilometer trunk line between Kuybyshev and Mozyr be constructed with wide-diameter (40-inch) pipe. But despite their advances in producing some oil industry equipment such as the turbodrill, the Soviets still lacked the technological capacity to produce wide-diameter pipe. If the export capacity planned for the Friendship Pipeline was to be achieved, a source of wide-diameter pipe would have to be found.

In this context the inclusion of wide-diameter pipe in the 1958 liberalization of COCOM export controls appears anomalous. Why make available for export something for which there was evidence of Soviet need and with which the Soviets might gain political influence and other strategic advantages?

The basic pattern in the 1954 and 1958 COCOM liberalizations was that the Europeans pushed a narrow constructionist view of what exports should remain under control while the United States took a broad constructionist position. The Europeans wanted to maintain controls only on those exports that had direct military significance — as it is often put, only those that could be shot back. The Eisenhower administration no longer subscribed to the premise that virtually all exports had military significance because they allowed resources to be freed from economic tasks and transferred to the military sector. But while its new concept of "economic defense" allowed for liberalization of trade in "peaceful sectors," it still prescribed strict controls on exports, such as wide-diameter pipe, having economic applications that could be construed as being of military significance.[19] The Europeans did not deny this latter point so much as argue that the link was sufficiently indirect to be outweighed by the economic benefits gained from trade.

Recently declassified documents point to two principal reasons why the Eisenhower administration consented to the decontrol of wide-diameter pipe. First, the predominantly unidirectional flow of influence that had characterized the foreign policy dominance relationship of the early 1950s no longer prevailed. According to a National Security Council policy paper originally classified "top secret" when approved in early 1958, a principal reason why "the the United States should agree to liberalize the multilateral security controls on trade" was "facilitating accord with our allies."[20] The mounting tensions and outright conflicts within the Western alliance were of concern to Eisenhower. The 1956 Suez crisis was the most blatant instance of intra-alliance conflict. East-West trade was not the least of the other issues of disagreement. Western Europe had a generally growing interest in trade with the Soviets. Total European COCOM exports to the Soviet Union had increased from $206 million in 1954 to $409 million in 1957. Khrushchev and First Deputy Premier Anastas Mikoyan were courting European customers in a manner that would have made any bourgeois merchant proud. While drilling and refining technologies remained largely concentrated in the United States and Great Britain, most western European steel industries had developed wide-diameter pipe production capacity. And, after a decade of expansion, these steel industries were beginning to encounter problems of excess capacity and falling profits.

A second reason is revealed in a Commerce Department memorandum dated June 10, 1959. In this document a department official presented calculations allegedly showing that the United States still had a 77 percent share of total world production capacity for pipe greater than 24 inches in diameter. Moreover, the Swedish, West German, Italian, British, and French manufacturers who produced the non-American 23 percent were believed to have much of their capacity taken by the demands of the Rotterdam-Rhine, North-West and southern European pipeline projects. Therefore, the Commerce Department concluded that even if alternative suppliers were "to ship their entire annual output, the small quantity still would retard Russia's gas and oil pipeline program in its current Seven Year Plan."[21]

It soon became apparent, however, that the Commerce Department had seriously miscalculated the extent of non-American production capacity. Between the COCOM decontrol in late 1958 and the initiation of American efforts to reimpose a multilateral embargo in late 1962, the Soviet Union was able to import some 870,000 metric tons from the West. An additional 175,000 tons had been contracted for but not yet delivered.

The Soviets had concluded small contracts with Italy, Japan, and Sweden, but West Germany was the principal supplier, having an 80 percent share of the Soviet market. Following the COCOM liberalization, the Germans shipped 3,200 tons in the remainder of

1958. In 1959 exports soared to 150,000 tons, and continued to grow over the next three years to a total of 695,000 tons. The announcement on October 5, 1962, of a new agreement for an additional 163,000 tons appeared to provide the Soviets with enough wide-diameter pipe to complete the Friendship Pipeline.[22]

As the Cold War began to heat up again in mid-1961, the Kennedy administration initiated efforts to reimpose the embargo on wide-diameter pipe. Following the Vienna summit, Theodore Sorensen quotes the president as having said privately, "I did not come away with any feeling that an understanding so that we do not go over the brink would be easy to reach."[23] This feeling was reinforced the next month by the building of the Berlin Wall and the Soviet resumption of nuclear testing.

In this more militarized context the Friendship Pipeline became significant not only as an instrument for potential political influence but also for its direct impact on the conventional military balance. Sorensen notes the increasing concern that "The imbalance of ground forces that the two sides could rapidly deploy in the area was an excessive temptation to cut off access to Berlin."[24] Completion of the Friendship Pipeline would further enhance Soviet conventional capabilities by providing the means for extensive and prolonged logistical support. In arguing this perspective to the Europeans, State Department officials repeatedly cited a passage from the treatise *On Military Strategy* by Marshal V. D. Sokolovskie of the Soviet Ministry of Defense:

> In case of war pipelines can play a great role in the transport of oil and oil products to the actual theater of military action and to basic industrial regions.[25]

At minimum the American strategy was to delay completion of the pipeline past the scheduled date of early 1963. By then the Berlin crisis might have subsided, and at least the direct military significance of the pipeline would be less.

A CIA report had concluded that "disruption would be significant" if the United States could enforce a multilateral embargo on wide-diameter pipe exports. The Soviet Seven-Year Plan originally had forecast that domestic production would begin in late 1962, but the CIA predicted that the technological and quality problems would last at least through 1963 and possibly into 1965.[26]

Yet, as the October 1962 West German contract demonstrated, the Kennedy administration encountered serious difficulties in gaining the multilateral cooperation necessary for an effective embargo. It was only after a year of unsuccessful efforts and in the aftermath of the Cuban missile crisis that the United States was able to push a secret embargo resolution through NATO.

While NATO's only connection with the trade controls regime had been a peripheral one, there was some justification for this shift in the institutional forum for multilateral decision making. Article II of the North Atlantic Treaty states their member nations will "seek to eliminate conflict in their international economic policies and will encourage economic collaboration between any or all of them." Moreover, from the American perspective NATO had a number of advantages over COCOM. First, because it did not operate by the unanimity rule, agreement to control trade might be easier to achieve. Second, the defense ministries had more influence in NATO than in COCOM, and they tended to be more sympathetic to the denial strategy. Third, there was a certain moral force attached to NATO decisions that could reinforce the will of European governments to stand up to the pressures of affected interest groups.

In a November 21 secret meeting, less than a month after (in Dean Rusk's oft-quoted words) "the other guy blinked," NATO approved the following embargo resolution:

> Member countries, on their own responsibility, should, to the extent possible:
> (1) Stop deliveries of large diameter pipes (over 19") to the Soviet bloc under existing contracts;
> (2) Prevent new contracts for such deliveries.[27]

A close reading of the text of the resolution, however, reveals its ambivalence. The very fact that the resolution passed amounted to an American victory. Inclusion of existing as well as future contracts speaks to the same point. At the same time, the vague wording and rather blatant loopholes demonstrated the limits to this regulative capacity. The controls were to be imposed only "to the extent possible," and by member countries "on their own responsibility." The moral force and legality of such a resolution were precisely what a particular government chose to grant it — no more, no less.

West Germany, the country with the most to lose economically, had voted for the NATO resolution. But the matter was not settled there, because the same law that gave the executive the authority to deny export licenses also gave the Bundestag veto power. The legislature had three months in which to act. Only a majority vote of the members present was required, so long as there was a quorum.

The issue was compounded by the fact that the NATO resolution called for the renunciation of existing contracts as well as a ban on future ones. Because the October 5 contracts were signed prior to the NATO resolution, there were grounds for the Soviets and the affected German firms to claim the sanctity of existing contracts. Moreover, the 163,000 tons were valued at $28 million, which translated into handsome profits and numerous jobs.

The Soviets were not at all adverse to making sure that the trade consequences were widely known within West Germany. A secret trip to Moscow was made by executives of the three pipe manufacturers. Collateral influence was sought through other West German exporters by what an American embassy official called the "dangling of East-West trade plums before the hungry eyes of German industrialists."[28] The Soviets also appealed to German pride and nationalism. Their formal protest note claimed that "It is not pipes that matter but a major principle of relations between states." They questioned how such an action could be reconciled "with the sovereign right and State prestige of the Federal Republic," unless it was "an openly hostile act aimed at worsening relations."[29]

The coalition against the embargo developed in the Bundestag between the opposition Social Democratic Party (SPD) and the Free Democratic Party (FDP), the junior partner in the government with Adenauer's Christian Democratic Union (CDU).[30] The SPD opposed the embargo because of its deleterious effects on employment and as an overt case of American infringement on Germany's sovereign right to determine its own foreign policy. FDP opposition was based on its advocacy of bilateral German-Soviet efforts at détente separate from relations at the superpower level. Together the SPD and FDP commanded 257 of the 499 votes in the Bundestag, a clear majority. On the last day of the three-month period, debate finally was scheduled on the embargo.

Faced with certain defeat, the CDU devised an effective if less than savory strategy. The 242 CDU deputies walked out of the Bundestag, making it impossible for the quorum necessary for any vote to be achieved. The opposition political parties branded this a "blow to parliamentary democracy."[31] But without a quorum the review period expired and the embargo became the law of the land.

West German compliance with the embargo was a major victory for the United States. If the producers of wide-diameter pipe at that time were conceived of as a cartel analogous to OPEC, then West Germany's position would correspond to that of Saudi Arabia. At the same time, however, even the small producer has the potential to break the cartel if its defection sets off a chain reaction.

Great Britain was such a small producer. While no British firm had yet exported wide-diameter pipe to the Soviets, the British government qualified its vote for the NATO resolution with the statement that its interpretation of the resolution was as nonbinding. At first the United States assumed that as a nation with a major stake in the profitability of Middle Eastern oil, Britain would not act in any manner that would increase the competition from Soviet oil. But Britain also continued to be the chief critic of the overall trade controls regime. It had recently completed a new five-year trade agreement with the Soviets and, until surpassed by West Germany (in large part because of its wide-diameter pipe exports), was the leading exporter within COCOM to the Soviet Union. As American Ambassador Thomas Finletter remarked in a cable to Secretary of State Dean Rusk, Britain had "almost a perfect score of opposition to the United States . . . on all East-West trade issues."[32]

When in January 1963 the United States wanted COCOM to pass an embargo resolution in order to ensure Japanese cooperation, the British delegate announced that he would veto any such action.[33] The German foreign minister pledged German support for British membership in the EEC in an effort to get British compliance with a policy for which the German government already had paid a dear political price. This and other German appeals were resisted, and American Ambassador to London David Bruce described a later meeting between Cabinet member Edward Heath and the German ambassador as "cool if not unpleasant."[34]

In February the only known British producer of wide-diameter pipe, South Durham Steel and Iron Company, accepted a pilot contract from the Russians for 300 tons while negotiations on a larger contract continued. There was talk of orders for $70 million of British ships, steel, and pipe. Board of Trade President Frederick

Erroll told Parliament, with reference to any Soviet offer, that "We shall be prepared to consider it on its merits," unimpeded by the NATO resolution.[35]

After numerous diplomatic efforts had failed, including a personal letter to Prime Minister Harold Macmillan from President Kennedy, the State Department, in conjunction with the major American oil companies, tried to lure the British away from the Russian deal with a compensatory counteroffer. Undersecretary of State George Ball presented a proposal under which American oil companies would buy 10,000 tons of 24-inch pipe and unspecified amounts of steel plate from South Durham Steel. However, this compensatory scheme was rejected by South Durham as insufficient. An order of 50,000 tons was said to be more what it had in mind. The oil companies, which had doubts about the price and quality of South Durham's products, were not willing to go this far. At this point the idea was floated that perhaps the stick of multinational corporations' purchasing power should be tried and South Durham bids ruled out for the pipelines being planned in Britain.[36] When the pipe issue was brought up at a COCOM meeting in June, Britain again vetoed an embargo. By this time the United States had virtually given up hope of changing the British position. Rusk told Bruce to encourage the British to confine their statements to being "bland and brief without emphasizing divisive aspects among NATO countries."[37] This was a damage limitation strategy because, unlike the West Germans, the British simply were not responding to American leverage.

Ironically, no deal for wide-diameter pipe exports was consummated. One reason was that the first two Soviet wide-diameter pipe factories came on line in March 1963, giving the USSR some capacity to provide for itself much earlier than the CIA had predicted.[38] The Soviets, like the American oil companies, were unwilling to pay the high prices demanded by South Durham (now thinking it had the market cornered), and considered the quality of the British product too low.

Even without the pipe deal British exports to the Soviet Union increased substantially. While West German exports dropped over 50 percent in 1963, the British sold 11 percent more to the Soviets. In 1964 they took the additional step of breaking the long-standing prohibition on extending long-term credits to the Soviets. Over time credits would become perhaps an even more sensitive issue than transbloc energy trade.

Thus, while the immediate objective of American policy — embargoing wide-diameter pipe — was achieved, it was not without substantial opportunity costs in terms of intra-alliance tensions. Completion of the Friendship Pipeline was delayed, but by only about one year. More lasting was the exacerbation of tensions within the Western alliance over East-West trade. Twenty years later the same questions of benefits of trade, vulnerability to Soviet influence, and American policy leadership were raised again by another Soviet pipeline. And, while the United States was even more hard-line in its position, the Europeans were unified in a policy that bore greater resemblance to the British than to the West German responses to the Friendship Pipeline embargo.

BREZHNEV'S NATURAL GAS PIPELINE AND THE DEBATE IN THE WEST OVER DÉTENTE

In the early 1980s the issue is a natural gas rather than an oil pipeline. Wide-diameter pipe is again involved, but even more central to the intra-alliance conflict are exports of turbines and compressors and government-subsidized credits. Billions, rather than millions, of dollars' worth of sales and loans are at stake. Long-term energy consumption patterns will also be affected. Moreover, because in its most fundamental aspect the debate revolves around questions of international political strategy, the structure that for over 30 years has been the basis of the Western alliance is being severely tested.

In the early 1970s COCOM rules regarding energy-related exports were liberalized as part of the Nixon-Kissinger détente and the Brandt *Ostpolitik*. One of the first major deals involved West German exports of 1.2 million tons of wide-diameter pipe in exchange for Soviet natural gas and payments valued at $400 million.[39] German, French, Italian, Japanese, and American companies also helped build the 2,750-kilometer Orenburg natural gas pipeline. It was this pipeline, tapping the rich deposits in the Urals-Volga region, that made possible increased natural gas exports to both eastern and western Europe beginning in the late 1970s. By 1980, Soviet gas exports had grown from a mere 1.8 billion cubic meters (BCM) in 1970 to 24.5 BCM, and Western oil and natural gas industry exports were worth almost $3 billion.[40]

While these figures showed a burgeoning transbloc energy trade, they pale in the face of plans for the 1980s. In western Siberia the Soviets already have the world's largest gas field under production at Urengoy. One hundred fifty miles to the north and above the Arctic Circle lies the untapped "supergiant" Yamburg field, with estimated proven reserves of 2.6 trillion cubic meters. One pipeline is already partially completed, and another is planned to link these western Siberian gas fields with western Europe. If built without delays and at maximum planned carrying capacity, the western Siberian natural gas pipeline would supply 35 percent of western Europe's natural gas by 1990.

Initially, nearly every COCOM country signed on as a gas importer and/or equipment exporter and financier (Table 3.2). In terms of relative shares of natural gas and total energy markets,

TABLE 3.2
Western Europe and Soviet Natural Gas

	West Germany	France	Italy	Great Britain
Natural gas imports				
from Soviet Union				
As percentage of total gas supply				
1981	16	15	24	0
1990	25	32	35	0
As percentage of total energy supply				
1981	3	3	4	0
1990	5	6	9	0
Energy equipment exports				
to Soviet Union				
(in millions of dollars)				
1975-79 annual average	795	385	424	68
Contracts for West				
Siberian Natural Gas				
Pipeline	1200	664	890	180

Sources: U.S. Congress, Office of Technology Assessment, *Technology and Soviet Energy Availability* (Washington, D.C.: Government Printing Office, 1981), pp. 174, 370-80; and *The Economist*, July 31, 1982, p. 40.

the Soviet position in 1990 would be strongest in Italy, with 35 percent and 9 percent respectively. France and West Germany planned similar import patterns giving the Soviets 32 percent and 5 percent, and 30 percent and 5 percent.[41] Direct export earnings for all of western Europe would be close to $3 billion. Even the United States had agreed by late 1980 to allow exports of pipe-laying equipment manufactured by Caterpillar and the rotors for 25-megawatt gas turbines, of which General Electric (GE) was the world's leading producer. GE's contracts were actually with three European firms — Nuovo Pignone of Italy, John Brown Engineering of Britain, and AEG-Kanis of West Germany — that would use the rotors to manufacture 125 finished compressor stations. GE stood also to profit from a contract for 40 rotors held by the French company Alsthom-Atlantique, which produced rotors under license from GE.

During the Carter administration American policy had zigzagged between tight controls and liberalization. In May 1979, Dresser Industries was granted a controversial license to export rock drill bits and to construct a turnkey state-of-the-art factory. A few months later the license was suspended in protest over the trials and imprisonment of human rights dissidents Alexander Ginzburg and Anatoly Scharansky. Soon thereafter, the suspension was lifted as policy "zigged" back toward liberalization. Over 50 licenses for energy-related exports that had been held up were granted in January 1979. Total energy-related exports increased more than 50 percent over 1978, to $238 million.[42] With administration support Congress passed the Export Administration Act of 1979. With statements such as "The restriction of exports can have serious adverse effects on the balance of payments and domestic employment," it sounded more like a bill to promote than to control exports.

Then came the Soviet invasion of Afghanistan and another "zag." Energy exports were put under total embargo. The Dresser license was revoked (although, according to company officials, the bulk of the exports had already been made) and Caterpillar's license application for its pipeline equipment was initially rejected in January 1980.

The Europeans' response to Afghanistan fell far short of what would have been expected if they had shared Jimmy Carter's per-ception of the greatest threat to world peace since World War II. In most high-technology areas they did cooperate with the American position that no exceptions be made to existing COCOM controls. However, the one exception on which they insisted to this no-exceptions policy was in the export of spare parts for oil and gas pipelines. Outside high-technology sectors cooperation was even less. While total American exports to the Soviet Union fell by 54 percent, European increases ranged from Britain's 67 percent to West Germany's 32 percent.[43]

Ronald Reagan came into office breathing fire, but the Europeans were far more interested in the heat and light promised by the western Siberian pipeline. Reagan presented his analysis of the negative strategic implications of the pipeline at the 1981 Ottawa summit. No changes in European transbloc energy trade policy resulted. Interest rates were juggled and pledged imports slightly scaled down, but these adjustments were commercially rather than politically motivated. Initial export deliveries were made and import plans were firmed up.

About two weeks after the proclamation of martial law in Poland on December 13, 1981, Reagan took additional steps to block the western Siberia natural gas pipeline. American exports related to the pipeline were embargoed, and efforts initiated to gain support for a multilateral embargo. Caterpillar, which initially had its license application rejected because of Afghanistan and then had it granted by the Commerce Department in August 1981, now had the license suspended. General Electric had already exported some rotors to Europe, but in January 1982 a license application for $175 million in exports was not renewed. This was the first step in applying export controls on an extraterritorial basis. The real targets were the European firms holding the contracts for the finished turbines and compressor stations. The next step, to block production under an American license by the French company Alsthom-Atlantique, was discussed but left temporarily in abeyance.

In contrast with the November 1962 NATO oil pipeline embargo resolution, little concrete collective action came out of the January 1982 NATO foreign ministers' meeting. The communiqué issued January 11 did condemn the Soviet Union for "its active support for the subsequent systematic suppression" in Poland. Specific economic sanctions were levied against Poland — suspension of export credits other than for food, embargo of certain exports, unwillingness to automatically reschedule debts. Against the Russians, however, sanctions were threatened but not enacted:

> Soviet actions towards Poland make it necessary for the Allies to
> *examine* the course of future economic and commercial relations. . . .
> The Allies will also *reflect* on longer-term East-West economic relations,
> particularly energy. . . . [44]

Whatever credibility the threats to examine and reflect may have
had was further diluted by the statement that appeared twice: that
the NATO resolution was nonbinding and that "Each of the allies
will act in accordance with its own situation and laws."[45] Shortly
thereafter, the British foreign secretary, the French foreign minister,
and the German minister of economics indicated that in accordance
with their situations and their laws, they would "honor contracts."[46]

For nearly six months the Reagan administration contemplated,
threatened, and "leaked," but did not take further definite action.
The internal debate pitted Secretary of Defense Caspar Weinberger
against Secretary of State Alexander Haig. Weinberger sought not
only to block the pipeline-related efforts but also to restrict loans
and subsidized credits as part of an economic warfare strategy that
transcended the immediate crisis in Poland.[47] Haig argued against
this strategy on the basis of its likely inefficacy against the Russians
and its likely exacerbation of tensions with U.S. allies.

After the Versailles summit provided little more than a vague
pledge from the allies "to pursue a prudent and diversified economic
approach to the U.S.S.R. and Eastern Europe, consistent with our
political and security interests,"[48] President Reagan resorted to
the extreme action of invoking the full extraterritorial reach of
unilateral American export controls. On June 18 he suddenly
announced that the United States would definitely enforce its export
controls against foreign manufacturers using American-made parts,
regardless of whether contracts were signed prior to the December
1981 promulgation of the first set of regulations. In addition, the
decision was made to claim jurisdiction over foreign manufacturers
producing under license from an American corporation.

This action so infuriated Alexander Haig that he resigned, and
so incensed the leaders of western Europe that they displayed
an uncommon unity in their responses. French President François
Mitterrand ordered French companies not to comply, and his foreign
minister spoke of a "progressive divorce" because "We no longer
speak the same language."[49] West German Chancellor Helmut
Schmidt refuted the basic premise that Europe would become

vulnerable to Soviet political influence and pledged, "The pipeline will be built."[50] Even Reagan's fellow anti-Communist hard-liner Prime Minister Margaret Thatcher argued that "The question is whether one very powerful nation can prevent existing contracts being fulfilled," and pledged to order British companies to proceed with their exports.[51]

During the summer and fall of 1982 the pipeline dispute brought relations within the Atlantic Alliance to a new nadir. The French, British, West German, and Italian governments took legal action to compel their companies, including subsidiaries of U.S.-based corporations, to honor export contracts. The Reagan administration responded by threatening to invoke the full range of penalties authorized by American law — 10-year prison sentences for officers of offending companies, fines up to $100,000 per infraction, and denial of all trading privileges in the United States.

The first flash point came in late August. A cargo ship set sail from the French port of LeHavre loaded with the first installment of pipeline equipment. Less than an hour after the word reached Washington, the Commerce Department issued a denial order barring Dresser France and Creusot-Loire from all trade in the United States. Over the next few weeks this contemporary version of an old western shoot-out was replayed against the British firm John Brown Engineering, Italy's Nuovo Pignone and West Germany's AEG-Kanis.

The new American Secretary of State, George Shultz, managed to convince the president to limit the countersanctions to trade in energy equipment and technology. But the fervor with which the policy was enforced stripped this compromise of any salutary effects. Assistant Secretary of Commerce Lawrence J. Brady, an ardent critic of East-West trade, requested (rules of commercial confidentiality prevented him from requiring) reports from 39 American manufacturers of energy equipment concerning all exports by them and their subsidiaries to all destinations over the past seven years. In October, the U.S. Customs Service seized a $3 million shipment of gas turbine parts ordered by Nuovo Pignone from General Electric. Although the equipment was said to be for use in Algeria, its export was prohibited by the denial order.

Increasingly, though, President Reagan was forced to acknowledge the negative consequences that his policy was having on Western unity and, ultimately, on the strength and credibility of the American deterrent against the Soviet Union. *The New York Times* editorialized against "pipeline machismo," stressing that "the only possible beneficiary of the confrontation is the Soviet Union."[52] Helmut Kohl's pledge to honor contracts and his chastizing of Reagan's willingness to sell grain yet embargo energy equipment, demonstrated that German interests, rather than Helmut Schmidt's stubbornness, were at the root of German policy. Secretary of State Shultz avoided the theatrics of his predecessor but worked persistently and quietly for a change in American policy.

On November 13 the lifting of the countersanctions against European companies was announced. President Reagan claimed that the sanctions no longer were necessary because "substantial agreement on a plan of action" had been reached.[53] Yet there was little in the joint communiqué to corroborate this claim. A pledge was made not to sign new natural gas import contracts until a study of potential political consequences was completed. But with oil prices falling and conservation programs cutting into the growth in consumption there was little commercial motivation for additional Soviet gas. Other study groups were established under NATO, OECD, and COCOM auspices. That an agreement to talk and study was not necessarily an agreement for collective action was stressed by French Foreign Minister Claude Cheysson. While affirming French support for the accord he stated that "decisions on what to do about the information . . . would have to be taken by governments, based on their own views of their national interests."[54] Reports of new talks concerning the building of an additional pipeline spur to Greece and of bids tendered by the French and Germans for the Soviets' latest project, a $1.5 billion pipeline from the Astrakhan gas fields on the northern shore of the Caspian Sea, provided further evidence of the continuing European commitment to transbloc energy trade.

THE TWO PIPELINES COMPARED: THE POLITICAL AND ECONOMIC CONDITIONS FOR LEVERAGE MAXIMIZATION

From the weak NATO and Versailles resolutions to the firm opposition in Europe to the American claim of extraterritorial application of its export controls, the resistance to American leverage in 1982 resembles the British opposition, and contrasts markedly with the West German cooperation, of 1962-63. These distinct patterns of behavior both within and across the two cases lend support to an emphasis on *foreign policy dominance* and *convergent economic interests* as the political and economic conditions for the maximization of *leverage*. The evidence presented in the case studies points to direct relationships between American leverage and the extent to which power, prestige, and policy have put the United States in a position to set the agenda of ends and select the means for its allies' foreign policy, on the one hand, and the extent to which economic interests have been shared, on the other.

In 1962-63 the United States held a much more dominant position over West German foreign policy than over British foreign policy for two reasons. First, American political prestige was enhanced in West Germany and damaged in Great Britain by related foreign policy issues. President John Kennedy had taken and held a firm stand on Berlin, which for symbolic as well as substantive reasons was of fundamental importance to the Adenauer government and the West German people. Since the earliest postwar days there had been no more powerful demonstration of American prestige among the European people than the adulation that greeted Kennedy's "Ich bin ein Berliner" speech in June 1963.[55] Adenauer and the CDU could soar on the crest of this wave in the face of strong domestic opposition to the embargo. Moreover, as Angela Stent argues, the embargo was perceived as a test of *Westpolitik* with respect both to the counterpoint of *Ostpolitik* and to Gaullism. In the context of Charles de Gaulle's challenge to the United States and his rebuff of the British, Adenauer's signing of the Franco-German treaty of cooperation in January 1963 was interpreted among conservatives at home as well as abroad as "an anti-American act because it emphasized the desire of Germany and of France for greater independence from the United States."[56] The Bundesrat would not ratify the treaty without adding an understanding to the resolution of endorsement that the treaty did not constitute a shift away from a U.S.-oriented foreign policy. As the CDU parliamentary whip argued during the embargo debate, Germany could not "call on NATO for one's protection on one side and ignore its clear decisions on the other."[57]

In contrast, American political prestige in Britain was damaged by two other issues. One was the Skybolt missile affair, in which both national pride and Prime Minister Macmillan's prestige suffered serious wounds. The norms of the special relationship had been violated; whether because of Washington's bureaucratic politics (as claimed) or because of the junior partner mentality, the damaging effect on bilateral relations was the same. The second issue was the inability of the United States to help Britain become a member of the Common Market. While the United States may have won the Cuban missile crisis, it clearly lost against de Gaulle on this issue.

A second reason for the variations in American leverage involved differences in the degree of consensus over ends and means on the specific issue of trade controls strategy. At least since Stalin's death, Britain had argued for trade liberalization in all sectors other than those with direct military significance as a more effective means of deterring Soviet aggression. Winston Churchill, whose anti-Communist credentials were impeccable, laid out the Brittish strategy in a speech in February 1954:

> The more the two great divisions of the world mingle in the healthy and fertile activities of commerce, the greater is the counterpoise to purely military calculations. Other thoughts take up their place in the minds of men.[58]

As part of its extended period of American tutelage, West Germany had been a steady supporter of the COCOM trade controls regime. Adenauer was firm in resisting Soviet efforts to win political concessions while negotiating the 1958 and 1960 trade treaties. He berated a Krupp executive who went to Moscow for trade talks without first clearing the visit with Bonn. For the most part, his trade policy demonstrated consensus with the means of export controls as well as the end of containing the Russians. In fact, he was highly critical of the October 1963 American wheat sale to the Soviet Union.[59]

An even more striking contrast in the elements of the foreign policy relationship is evident in a comparison of the early 1960s with the early 1980s. American prestige was soaring in West Germany and damaged in Great Britain then; today it is badly battered throughout Europe. The U.S. role in Vietnam; the embarrassment and hypocrisy of Watergate and related scandals (CIA-gate, Lockheed-gate, Korea-gate); and the failed leadership of Jimmy Carter were even more deleterious to American prestige than to American power. For French President François Mitterrand, who initially gave unusually strong support to the tough overall Reagan approach, the embargo came to be part of "the insupportable attitude of American political and economic domination."[60] For German Chancellor Helmut Schmidt, both the substance of the embargo policy and the unilateral manner of enactment caused comparisons with the neutron bomb affair, the Afghanistan and Iranian sanctions, and American failures on arms control. On all of these issues European leaders, notably Helmut Schmidt, had borne heavy domestic political costs for decisions made in Washington (and, in the case of the neutron bomb, unmade and then made again).

Nor is there any longer much consensus on either the ends or the means of the trade controls strategy. As the ends have been redefined by the Reagan administration from inducing Soviet good behavior to a new and expanded version of the old rollback doctrine, whatever common ground remained has been rapidly eroding. Such a strategy not only is in tension with European economic interests but also contradicts the dominant European view of how international economic relations can be most functional in achieving international political stability. The Reagan administration's tendency to ignore differences over strategy only adds to the discord. Moreover, the discussions at Ottawa in 1981 and at Versailles in 1982 were marked by repeated attempts by President Reagan to keep the trade and credit controls issue inside the Poland-Afghanistan-Soviet Union issue area. European leaders, on the other hand, insisted on a high American interest rates-American grain sales framework.

The extent of American influence also has been strongly influenced by European nations' calculations of economic interests. For both West Germany and Great Britain the Friendship Pipeline presented mixed economic incentives, although for different reasons. Overall trade with the Soviet Union was not particularly important to either country in absolute terms. Even after increasing from $164 million in 1958 to $394 million in 1962, German trade with the Soviet Union still amounted to only 1.6 percent of its total trade. For Britain the percentage was roughly the same. Yet the basic export orientation of both countries' economies meant that growth and prosperity were tied to continually expanding export markets. Trade accounted for 32.8 percent of the British GNP and 28 percent of the West German GNP, compared with only 6.6 percent of the American GNP.

The major divergence between West German and American economic interests stemmed from their contrasting positions in the international oil economy. West Germany was an oil consumer and the United States an oil producer, with the basic defining characteristic being the degree of control over energy resources either by virtue of indigenous endowment or by ownership or control of foreign oil resources. While it was rational economic behavior for an oil producer to support a policy intended to limit the capabilities of another producer nation, it also was rational for a consumer nation to oppose such a policy.

Accordingly, part of the West German interest in the Friendship Pipeline was economic in nature. Since the Suez crisis of 1956 there had been a growing concern among European oil consumer nations that excessive dependence on Middle Eastern oil did not provide sufficient security of supply. An internal Standard Oil of New Jersey memorandum acknowledged that European "governments and the public want assurances that will give a greater sense of security."[61] A report by the Organization for European Economic Cooperation (OEEC) recommended "the line of achieving a reasonable dispersal of our commitments."[62] Because it would diversify their import portfolios, Soviet oil became more attractive to European oil consumer nations such as West Germany.

Amid outcries from the Anglo-American major oil companies, the Soviets made their oil even more attractive by cutting its price. The average price paid by West Germany to the Russians was reported to be $1.15 per barrel, well below the average price of $1.50 for Persian Gulf oil.[63] As oil jumped from 6.7 percent (1955) to 19.7 percent (1960) of total energy consumption in West Germany, and imports rose 211 percent, an inexpensive supply of oil was becoming more and more important. Since oil accounted for a large portion of the costs of production of manufactured goods, low-priced Soviet oil offered the consumer nations an advantage comparable with that guaranteed to American industry by government oil import quotas and price controls.[64] Consequently, German imports of Soviet oil had increased from a mere 5,000 metric tons in 1955 to over 2 million metric tons in 1960. With the efficient means of distribution to be provided by the Friendship Pipeline, there would be added economic incentives for an oil consumer nation to increase purchases of Soviet oil.

In 1962-63, however, the divergence of interests between European oil consumer nations and the American oil producer was not as acute as it would be in the 1970s and 1980s. The major oil companies both cut their prices and offered other incentives to customers to counteract the price-based attractiveness of Soviet oil. But the critical factor was that American foreign policy dominance was great enough to overcome whatever economic incentives remained.

For Britain the principal economic incentive for refusing to cooperate with the overall American approach to transbloc trade was cyclical rather than structural. Unemployment, while still only 1.5 percent, had increased from 265,912 to 479,713 in a year. The trade deficit was $2.1 billion, highest in the industrial world, and the pound was on the verge of devaluation. In opposing the embargo the British delegate to COCOM had cited the "current special difficulties" in the British economy.[65] A riot of unemployed workers in front of Big Ben on the day that American Undersecretary of State George Ball was meeting with Prime Minister Macmillan dramatized the problem. As the *New York Times* stated in its report of the incident and the failure of the Ball negotiations, Britain had a tremendous "need for all the business she can get these days."[66] After the defeat of Britain's bid for membership in the EEC, this feeling was reflected in Board of Trade President Erroll's musing that the Soviet Union as a trade partner could be "no worse . . . than our closest friends."[67]

Yet while Britain developed its transbloc trade in numerous sectors, its sectoral position as an oil producer nation (through the British Petroleum and Shell Oil companies in the so-called "Seven Sisters" cartel) pulled against the other motivations for trade within the energy sector. Competition from Soviet oil was particularly unwelcome in the tight market conditions of the late 1950s and early 1960s. Prices were falling at the same time that profits were being squeezed by the escalating demands of host governments. The British in particular had been hurt by the nationalization of oil companies in Iran, and more recently by General Kassim's coup and nationalization in Iraq. In addition, and quite ironically, it was Soviet competition that spurred the major oil companies to cut posted prices in August 1960 without consulting the host governments. This decision was the final precipitant of the September 1960 Baghdad Conference at which Iraq, Iran, Saudi Arabia, Kuwait, and Venezuela formed an organization called the Organization of Petroleum Exporting Countries (OPEC).

The ambivalence of British economic interests helps explain its defection from embargo diplomacy yet its de facto cooperation. Its quasi-independent foreign policy position and its macroeconomic problems, especially with a national election about a year away, contributed to its position of opposition. Its status as an oil producer nation, however, militated against a practice of opposition, at least with respect to oil industry exports.

In the current case, however, the divergence of economic interests is much more pronounced. With trade representing an average of 56 percent of GNP in the four major European countries, growth has become even more tightly linked to trade. While trade has increased to 17 percent of the American GNP, this still amounts to much less structural openness than in Europe.

With Europe mired in its worst recession since the Great Depression, the cyclical forces against any further losses of jobs, profits, and export earnings are quite strong. Unemployment in West Germany, only 3.8 percent in 1979, reached 5.5 percent in 1981 and 8.2 percent in mid-1982. British unemployment of 11.3 percent in 1981 ignited the worst urban riots that country has known in this century. In mid-1982 it stood at 12.4 percent. The Socialist government of France, pledged to provide jobs for its supporters, has seen unemployment rise from 1.64 million at the time of Mitterrand's victory to 2 million in January 1982.[68] While it is difficult to determine precisely the number of jobs associated with the pipeline, in the current economic climate it is both a politically and an economically significant number.

The pipeline also may mean the difference between life and death for a number of major private and state-owned corporations. In early August 1982, AEG-Telefunken, the giant German electronics firm, became the country's largest bankruptcy victim in the postwar period. Its AEG-Kanis subsidiary was expected to earn $320 million from the sale of 47 compressor stations to the Soviets, a contract that a company spokesman said "was to have guaranteed capacity utilization at Kanis for the next two years."[69] But Kanis' compressors require GE's rotors, which were under U.S. embargo.

Similarly, the German steel firm Mannesmann has been counting on its 1.2 million metric tons of wide-diameter (56 inches) pipe exports to recover from a 70 percent drop in production in 1981.[70] Its pipe exports are not subject to American extraterritoriality, but stand to be jeopardized if the entire transaction collapses or runs into major delays. The other principal supplier of pipe is the Italian firm Finsider, which the *New York Times* described as "the troubled steel unit of the Institute for Industrial Reconstruction, a state holding company."[71] Nuovo Pignone, another state-owned company facing severe excess capacity, holds a $470 million contract for which it needs GE rotors.

The Reagan administration's extraordinarily poor sense of timing has heightened the domestic political reverberations of the economic stakes in Europe. One of the reasons the Adenauer government was able to absorb the political opposition to its 1962-63 embargo was that the issue was handled deftly by the Kennedy administration. Quite in contrast was the Reagan administration's imposition of sanctions a few weeks after a summit meant to communicate alliance solidarity and a few weeks before announcing continued American grain sales. The distinction between grain and the pipeline in terms of their strategic significance, whether valid or invalid, is absolutely irrelevant to the fact that the grain sales have exacerbated the divergence of economic interests at the cyclical level.

The deterioration of the position of energy consumer nations since 1973 has caused even greater divergence at the sectoral level. (The fact that Great Britain, an energy producer nation, has not contracted for any natural gas imports is consistent with the argument about the policy impact of a nation's position in the structure of the international energy economy.) Since the first OPEC embargo and price increases western European nations have tried to reduce their dependence on OPEC through conservation, alternative fuels, and alternative suppliers. As a percentage of total energy consumption, natural gas increased from 10 percent in 1973 to 18 percent in 1981. West Germany's distribution among different sources was fairly typical, with 37 percent of its gas coming from the Dutch, 30 percent from domestic sources, 18 percent from the Russians, and 15 percent from Norway.[72]

Nevertheless, West Germany was still dependent on OPEC for 31 percent of its total energy supply. France and Italy had even higher OPEC dependencies of 38 percent and 51 percent, respectively. Although oil prices have leveled off and even eroded recently, there is little confidence that at some point OPEC will not jack prices up again. There is even less confidence that the supply of OPEC oil will not be interrupted. One of the ironies of the present situation is that just as the Ayatollah Khomeini spurred a Cold

War renewal in the United States, he increased the incentives in Europe for transbloc energy trade. For the Europeans it is difficult to accept the implication of the American argument that the Ayatollah is a more reliable supplier than Brezhnev. While Europeans are not so naive as to place total confidence in the Soviets, they see the greatest security in diversification of their energy portfolio. So long as contingency plans for management of energy supplies under crisis conditions are developed as planned, the net security effect of increased imports from the Soviet Union is likely to be positive.

Thus, the overall divergence of interests has eroded the basic economic condition for the maximization of American leverage at the same time that the politico-strategic conditions creating foreign policy dominance have been diminished. The United States may insist that the issue is strategic and not economic, but for Europe transbloc energy trade policy is a function more of economic interests – and Middle East regional politics – than of superpower politics.

CONCLUSION: AMERICAN TRADE CONTROL POLICY IN THE 1980S

In conclusion, the principal policy implications that follow from this analysis must be emphasized. It has been established that the economic coercion strategy of denying the Soviets the benefits of trade is now severely constrained by the political will and economic capacity of the Europeans to act as substitute trade partners. The political and economic conditions that once maximized American leverage now militate against it. Foreign policy dominance is less and economic interests, especially in the energy sector, are greatly divergent.[73] Therefore, unless other tactics are employed for overriding the potential international constraints, the American economic coercion strategy is not likely to have either significant economic impact or even a chance of some political influence.

The Reagan administration's June 18, 1982, decision to claim the full scope of extraterritorial application of unilateral American export controls constituted an effort to develop such alternative tactics. Dissatisfied with the recalcitrance of its friends, the United States imposed its will on them – for their own good, of course.

In effect, the United States was taking the significant step from leverage through persuasion to leverage through punishment. The pressures exerted on West Germany and Great Britain in 1962-63 were largely through quiet diplomacy, and stopped well short of retaliatory threats or actions. Efforts to exert leverage in this matter are akin to Richard Neustadt's classic conception of presidential power in American domestic politics.[74] Like a nation that is the leader of an alliance, a president is enmeshed in relationships that have elements of conflict but are less Hobbesian than Lockeian. Accordingly, persuasion and other forms of nonconfrontational pressure are the key instrumentalities. Elements such as prestige, consensus on ends and means of policy, bargaining advantages through issue area linkages, and convergent economic interests are more important to the lead actor than are strict power endowments.

Even leverage through punishment may not always overcome insufficiencies in the resources of persuasion. If they do it is only at the risk of altering the nature of the relationship. When punitive measures are introduced, efforts to exert leverage over allies come to resemble coercion of adversaries. The relationship may not actually become adversarial, but it does stand to lose the nonadversarial nature that could be counted on to constrain both the lead actor's tactics and the fallout to other dimensions of the relationship. This is especially true when there are shifts toward confrontation in other issue areas, as is at present the case with respect to nuclear arms control, the Middle East, steel and other sectors of trade, and "domestic" economic policies such as interest rates.

The cry that "the end is nigh" for the Western alliance has been heard too often for that to be the final message of this discussion. Nor do the fallacies of current policy in any way make the converse of unfettered trade between East and West any less fallacious in its own right. Trade between adversaries is inherently political, and therefore cannot be cleanly delinked from the overall foreign policy goals of containment and deterrence even during times of détente. The Russians should not be permitted to have their trade and interventionism too. Nor does it make much business sense to compete one capitalist against the other in offering concessionary terms of trade.

It is essential to carve out a third option other than laissez faire or strict embargo approaches. For whatever its appeal to gut emotions against "trading with the enemy" or its functionality for demonstrating a vote-getting ideological position (especially when combined with liberal grain trade), the traditional American embargo strategy has and is causing levels of intra-alliance tension that diminish from the overall credibility of the Western deterrent. As Henry Kissinger wrote in an effort to carve out a third option between the "to trade" and "not to trade" poles, "The most important message would be that the industrial democracies propose to speak with the East with one voice."[7][5] In an era in which the political and economic conditions that once maximized American leverage have eroded, it is even more urgent that unilateral and ideological tendencies be replaced by a more strategic view in which the fulfillment of goals vital to the national interest takes precedence over the purity of the ideology.

NOTES

1. Congressional testimony of November 12, 1981; in *Defense 82*, February 1982, pp. 16-19.

2. U.S. Congress, Senate, Committee on the Judiciary, Subcommittee to Investigate the Administration of the Internal Security Act and Other Internal Security Laws, *Soviet Oil in East-West Trade*, Hearings, 87th Cong., 2d sess., July 3, 1962, p. 1.

3. The best sources on the creation and first decade of the Western trade controls regime are Gunnar Adler-Karlsson, *Western Economic Warfare, 1947-67* (Stockholm: Almqvist and Wiksell, 1968); Suchati Chuthasmit, "The Experience of the United States and Its Allies in Controlling Trade with the Red Bloc" (Ph.D. diss., Fletcher School of Law and Diplomacy, Tufts University, 1961); Theodore Osgood, "East-West Trade Controls and Economic Warfare" (Ph.D. diss., Yale University, 1957); and Harold J. Berman and John R. Garson, "The United States Export Controls — Past, Present and Future," *Columbia Law Review* 67 (May 1967), pp. 791-890.

4. George W. Baer, "Sanctions and Security: The League of Nations and the Italian-Ethiopian War, 1935-36," *International Organization* 27 (Spring 1973): 165-80.

5. For a thorough review of competing definitions of power and influence in the international relations literature, as well as an interesting application to arms sales, see Ariel Levite and Athanassios Platias, *Small States' Dependence on Arms Imports: Consequences, Alternatives and Choices*, Cornell University Peace Studies Program, Occasional Paper Series (Ithaca, N.Y.: Cornell University Peace Studies Program, 1983).

6. Marina von Neumann Whitman, *The United States Investment Guaranty Program and Private Foreign Investment* (Princeton: Princeton University Press, 1959) and *Government Risk Sharing in Private Investment* (Princeton: Princeton University Press, 1965).

7. Heinrich Hassmann, *Oil in the Soviet Union* (Princeton: Princeton University Press, 1953), p. 55.

8. Robert E. Ebel, *Communist Trade in Oil and Gas* (New York: Praeger, 1970), p. 35.

9. Department of State, *First Semiannual Report of the Administrator of the Mutual Defense Assistance Control Act to the Congress (Battle Act Report)* (Washington, D.C.: Government Printing Office, 1951), p. 43.

10. Report to the Secretary of the Interior and Petroleum Administrator for Defense to the National Security Council, "National Security Problems Concerning Free World Petroleum Demand and Potential Supplies" (December 8, 1952), Harry S. Truman Presidential Library, Papers of Harry S. Trumen, PSF, p. 3.

11. The question of vulnerability of the target nation is related to, but outside the immediate concern of, this chapter. There remains a great deal of work to be done in developing a theory of the conditions under which a target nation will be economically, and especially politically, vulnerable to economic coercion. On this subject see Peter Blau, *Exchange and Power in Social Life* (New York: Wiley, 1964) pp. 367-84; James Barber, "Economic Sanctions as a Policy Instrument," *International Affairs* 55 (July 1979) pp. 378-416; John Galtung, "On the Effects of International Economic Sanctions, with Examples from the Case of Rhodesia," *World Politics* 19 (April 1967); Klaus Knorr, *The Power of Nations* (New York: Basic Books, 1975), ch. 6; and Peter Wallensteen, "Characteristics of Economic Sanctions," *Journal of Peace Research* 3 (1968), pp. 248-67.

12. Central Intelligence Agency, Office of Reports and Estimates, "USSR Petroleum Industry," (January 5, 1950), Harry S. Truman Presidential Library, Papers of Harry S. Truman, PSF, p. 6.

13. Report of Secretary of Interior . . . to National Security Council, "National Security Problems," p. 17.

14. "The production of crude oil in 1965 may reach to as much as 265 million tons or 25 million tons (10%) in excess of plan." For an extremely detailed analysis of the Soviet oil industry in the early 1960s, see the two-volume study by the National Petroleum Council (NPC), *Impact of Oil Exports from the Soviet Bloc* (Washington, D.C.: NPC, 1962). This quotation is from vol. II, p. 10.

15. On the turbodrill see NPC, *Impact of Soviet Oil*, vol. II, pp. 81-90; and Robert Campbell, *The Economics of Soviet Oil and Gas* (Baltimore: Johns Hopkins University Press, 1968), pp. 108-120.

16. Josef Wilczynski, *The Economics and Politics of East-West Trade* (New York: Praeger, 1969), p. 259.

17. NPC, *Impact of Soviet Oil*, vol. II, p. 447.

18. For a detailed discussion of the Friendship Pipeline as well as the overall Soviet pipeline system and future plans, see NPC, *Impact of Soviet Oil*, vol. II, pp. 185-217.

19. See the declassified documents NSC 5704/3, "U.S. Economic Defense Policy" (September 16, 1957), and NSC 5810, "Basic National Security Policy," (April 15, 1958), National Archives, Modern Military section.

20. NSC 5810, "Basic National Security Policy," p. 18.

21. U.S. Department of Commerce, memorandum for the record, "East-West Trade," (June 10, 1959), Dwight D. Eisenhower Presidential Library, Joseph Rand, Records: 1954-61.

22. Memorandum, Ambassador Timberlake to Secretary of State Rusk, "Large Diameter Pipe Shipments to the USSR" (March 21, 1963), John F. Kennedy Presidential Library, National Security Files, box 223.

23. Theodore C. Sorensen, *Kennedy* (New York: Harper and Row, 1965), p. 618.

24. Ibid., p. 662.

25. Department of State telegram from Tubby to Rusk (April 30, 1963), John F. Kennedy Presidential Library, National Security Files, box 223.

26. Central Intelligence Agency, Office of Research and Reports, "Estimated Impact of Western Economic Sanctions Against the Sino-Soviet Bloc," RR EP 61-47 (July 16, 1961), Carrollton Declassified Document Index microfiche, p. 2.

27. Department of State, "Large Diameter Pipe" (March 25, 1963), John F. Kennedy Presidential Library, National Security Files, box 223.

28. Telegram, American Embassy in Bonn to Secretary Rusk (January 9, 1963), John F. Kennedy Presidential Library, National Security Files, box 223.

29. *New York Times*, April 7, 1963, p. 28.

30. The details of the West German response are drawn from the excellent account in Angela Stent, *From Embargo to Ostpolitik* (New York: Cambridge University Press, 1981), pp. 93-126.

31. Ibid., p. 107.

32. Telegram, Ambassador Finletter to Secretary Rusk (April 29, 1963), John F. Kennedy Library, National Security Files, box 223.

33. Telegram, Ambassador Bruce to Rusk (January 29, 1963). Box 223, National Security Files.

34. Telegram, Ambassador Bruce to Rusk (May 17, 1963). Box 223, National Security Files.

35. Cited in memorandum from William H. Brubeck, State Department, to McGeorge Bundy (February 13, 1963), John F. Kennedy Presidential Library, Country Files, box 171.

36. Telegram, Undersecretary Ball to Ambassador Bruce (March 19, 1963); memorandum from Secretary Rusk (March 23, 1963); telegram, Ambassador Bruce to Rusk (March 25, 1963); telegram, Ambassador Finletter to Rusk, (April 29, 1963). All are from Box 223, National Security Files.

37. Telegram, Secretary Rusk to Ambassador Bruce (May 17, 1963). Box 223, National Security Files.

38. *New York Times*, March 27, 1963, p. 9.

39. Congressional Office of Technology Assessment (OTA), *Technology and Soviet Energy Availability* (Washington, D.C.: U.S. Government Printing Office, 1981), p. 358.

40. Ibid., pp. 352, 172.

41. Ibid., pp. 373-77.

42. Gloria Duffy, "Adding to Soviet Energy Problems," *New York Times*, March 8, 1980, Op-Ed page; OTA, *Technology and Soviet Energy*, p. 174.

43. OTA, *Technology and Soviet Energy*, p. 379.

44. Text reprinted in *New York Times*, January 12, 1982, p. A9. Emphasis added.

45. Ibid.

46. *New York Times*, July 23, 1982, p. A6.

47. One of the most explicit statements of this new version of an economic warfare strategy accompanied the presentation of the new defense budget in January 1982. See *Annual Report to the Congress of the Secretary of Defense FY 1983* (Washington, D.C.: U.S. Government Printing Office, 1982), esp. sec. I, pp. 22-23, and sec. II, pp. 26-32.

48. Text reprinted in *New York Times*, June 7, 1982, p. D6.

49. *Newsweek*, August 2, 1982, p. 37.

50. *The Economist*, June 26, 1982, pp. 52-53.

51. *New York Times*, July 2, 1982, pp. A1, A4.

52. *New York Times*, September 1, 1982, p. A22.

53. *New York Times*, November 14, 1982, p. 24.

54. At the last minute France had withdrawn from the accord announced on November 13. They did not want the Americans to claim that the counter-sanctions were lifted only after the Europeans had made concessions. The Gaullist impulse for resisting any semblance of American domination seemed to collide with the Reagan penchant for ideological consistency. The matter was cleared up during Secretary of State Shultz's trip to Paris in December, although not to the point where the French were willing to let things stand without Cheysson's "clarification." See the *New York Times*, December 15, 1982, p. A13.

55. Sorensen, *Kennedy*, pp. 676-78.

56. Stent, *Embargo to Ostpolitik*, pp. 95-96.

57. *New York Times*, March 16, 1963, p. 3.

58. Adler-Karlsson, *Western Economic Warfare*, p. 91.

59. Stent, *Embargo to Ostpolitik*, pp. 20-92, 121-24.

60. James O. Goldsborough, *New York Times*, July 20, 1982, p. A23.

61. Cited in Robert Engler, *The Politics of Oil* (Chicago: University of Chicago Press, 1961), pp. 188-89.

62. OEEC, *Europe's Need for Oil: Implications and Lessons of the Suez Crisis* (Paris: OEEC, 1958), p. 44.

63. On oil prices see M. A. Adelman, *The World Petroleum Market* (Baltimore: Johns Hopkins University Press, 1972), pp. 183, 410; and NPC, *Impact of of Soviet Oil*, vol. I, p. 83. On energy consumption patterns see United Nations, *World Energy Supplies, 1955-58* (New York: U.N. Statistical Office, 1959), pp. 16, 96, and *1958-61* (New York: U.N. Statistical Office, 1962), pp. 21, 92.

64. The High Authority of the European Coal and Steel Community, *Memorandum on Energy Policy* (Brussels: Publications Department of the European Communities, 1962), p. 7.

65. Telegram, Paris Embassy to State Department (June 20, 1963), John F. Kennedy Presidential Library, Country Files, box 171.

66. *New York Times*, April 1, 1963, p. 60.

67. Michael P. Gehlen, "The Politics of Soviet Foreign Trade," *The Western Political Quarterly* 18 (March 1965): 110.

68. All unemployment figures are drawn from United Nations, *Monthly Bulletin of Statistics*, July 1982, pp. 17, 20.

69. *Wall Street Journal*, January 19, 1982, p. 32.

70. *New York Times*, May 30, 1982, p. F7.

71. *New York Times*, July 25, 1982, p. 1

72. Miriam Karr and Roger W. Robinson, Jr., "Soviet Gas: Risk or Reward?" *The Washington Quarterly* 4 (Autumn 1981): 8.

73. Robert J. Lieber, "Cohesion and Disruption in the Western Alliance," in Daniel Yergin and Martin Hillenbrand, eds., *Global Insecurity* (Boston: Houghton Mifflin, 1982), pp. 320-48.

74. Richard E. Neustadt, *Presidential Power* (New York: Wiley, 1960).

75. Henry A. Kissinger, "Trading with the Russians," *The New Republic*, June 2, 1982, p. 15.

71-103

4

ENERGY TRADE RELATIONS BETWEEN THE FEDERAL REPUBLIC OF GERMANY AND THE USSR

Reimund Seidelmann

INTRODUCTION

International energy relations are not just a matter of economics; they have important political consequences as well. These result from the distribution of resources, production, and consumption in the world energy economy. Political power is shaped not only by the volume and value of energy trade but also by the fact that the uninterrupted availability of energy is a prerequisite for development, industrialization, and improved living standards. Energy shortages are a potential threat to modern industrialized societies, since their productivity and political legitimization are based on high consumption standards. Thus energy exports can be used as an economic and political weapon against nations that depend on energy imports. Examples can be found in the price increases of the 1970s, the competition in the market for nuclear power plants, and changes in the Middle East policies of the West.

For Western industrialized countries dependent on foreign energy supplies, this linkage between economics and politics has gained special importance in recent years. First, these countries had to overcome the economic consequences of the two oil-price shocks in 1973-74 and 1979-80. They also had to adapt to changes in relations between oil-producing and oil-consuming countries, and to respond to threats by Arab countries to use the "oil weapon." In addition, they had to react to developments in East-West relations. New U.S. policies led to reconsideration of East-West trade and of the implications of energy imports from the USSR.

The U.S. grain embargo against the USSR, U.S. demands for tighter control over Western exports to the USSR, and the idea of using the economic and financial dependencies of eastern Europe to prevent Soviet intervention in Poland indicate the current relevance of these problems.

In such a framework, energy trade relations between the Federal Republic of Germany (FRG) and the USSR are of special importance. First, the FRG is the most important Western trading partner of the USSR. Second, the gas pipeline deal of 1981 will increase energy imports from the USSR substantially. Third, the ongoing West German policy of détente is based on economic cooperation between East and West. Fourth, the energy policies of the FRG, a highly industrialized country that depends heavily on energy imports, are directed toward the reduction of economic dependence and its political consequences. Therefore, it is important to determine whether West German-Soviet energy trade leads the FRG into economic dependency, vulnerability, and "Finlandization" or — as its government claims — whether it leads to an overall reduction of dependency by balancing risks, creating economic interdependencies, and increasing Soviet interests in future détente.

THE ENERGY POLICY PROFILE OF THE FRG

Energy Production and Consumption

The FRG possesses limited energy resources, yet it has had a high and growing need for energy (see Table 4.1). The limitation of domestic resources is twofold. First, the resources are limited in variety. Second, they are limited in volume. Deposits of hard and brown coal are extensive, those of natural gas are limited, and those of oil are insignificant (see Table 4.2). Water, solar, wind, and other alternative energy resources do not play a major role in the domestic energy output.

Though the economic development of the 1970s shows a shift to technology-intensive production and engineering, which leads

TABLE 4.1
Primary Energy Consumption

($ = 2.4 DM)

Year	Real GNP (billion DM)	Growth Real GNP (percent)	Primary Energy Consumption (mil./tons coal equiv.)	Growth of Primary Energy Consumption (percent/year)	Oil as Percent of Primary Energy Consumption	Hard Coal as Percent of Primary Energy Consumption	Brown Coal as Percent of Primary Energy Consumption	Natural Gas as Percent of Primary Energy Consumption	Nuclear Energy as Percent of Primary Energy Consumption	Import of Primary Energy as Percent of Primary Energy Consumption
1970	679		311		53.1	28.7	9.1	5.4	0.6	65
1971	702	3.4	312	0.3	54.7	26.6	8.6	7.1	0.6	66
1972	727	3.6	327	4.8	55.4	23.6	8.7	8.6	0.9	67
1973	763	5.0	352	7.6	55.2	22.2	8.7	10.2	1.0	68
1974	766	0.4	343	-2.6	51.5	22.6	9.6	12.7	1.1	67
1975	752	-1.8	326	-5.0	52.1	19.1	9.9	14.1	2.0	67
1976	792	5.3	349	7.0	52.9	19.1	10.2	14.0	2.1	69
1977	815	2.9	342	2.0	52.1	18.0	9.4	14.9	3.2	70

TABLE 4.1, continued

Year	Real GNP (billion DM)	Growth Real GNP (percent)	Primary Energy Consumption (mil./tons coal equiv.)	Growth of Primary Energy Consumption (percent/year)	Oil as Percent of Primary Energy Consumption	Hard Coal as Percent of Primary Energy Consumption	Brown Coal as Percent of Primary Energy Consumption	Natural Gas as Percent of Primary Energy Consumption	Nuclear Energy as Percent of Primary Energy Consumption	Import of Primary Energy as Percent of Primary Energy Consumption
1978	844	3.6	357	4.4	52.3	17.8	9.2	15.5	3.0	68
1979	878	4.5	367	2.8	50.7	18.6	9.3	16.2	3.4	71
1980	898	1.8	352	−4.0	48.0	21.1	10.3	16.3	3.7	70
1985		3.5		1.9-3.0	46.2	15.5	9.9	18.2	10.3	84
1990		3.5		1.9-3.0	42.6	15.1	7.3	16.9	15.7	82
2000					27.0	17.0	6.7	16.0	27.0	67

Sources: The figures for 1985, 1990, and 2000 are estimates derived from the FRG government energy program (second version).

to a relative reduction in energy demand, the high industrialization[1] of West Germany continues to create an enormous energy demand. The FRG's steel, chemical, and heavy machinery industries require large amounts of energy. Countries like the FRG also need vast supplies of energy for private consumption. Despite the demands from various ecological or "green" movements, an increase in the standard of living is connected with an increase in energy consumption. Although price increases led to a reduction of private consumption in certain areas in 1980 and 1981 — the consumption of oil-dependent products has decreased by 10 percent[2] — an increase in industrial and private energy consumption is foreseeable.

There have been substantial improvements in energy conservation. However, the estimated yearly increase in primary energy consumption is likely to be between 1.9 percent and 3.0 percent during the 1980s and 1990s.[3] While West German energy demand has grown, domestic energy production has declined.[4]

The overall West German energy picture varies among specific types of energy resources. In hard coal the FRG has an abundance of resources. Production of hard coal throughout the 1970s was higher than domestic consumption, even though it decreased by 21 percent from 1970 to 1980. In 1979 the FRG exported 15 million tons of coal, the major source of its energy exports. This

TABLE 4.2
FRG Domestic Energy Resources (Proven)

Resource	*Amount*
Hard coal (1979)	44,000 million tons
Brown coal (1979)	55,000 million tons
Natural gas (1975)	235 billion cubic meters + 330 billion cubic meters (probably proven)
Oil (1979)	45 million tons
Natural uranium	4,000 tons

Source: United Nations, Economic Commission for Europe, *Energy Reserves and Supplies in the ECE Region* (New York: United Nations, 1979).

abundance is likely to continue into the distant future, since proven resources of recoverable hard coal amount to about 44 billion tons (see Table 4.2). This means that on the basis of the relatively high level of production in 1973, coal will not be depleted for roughly 185 years. However, it must be added that the most accessible reserves have already been exploited, so that the cost of future coal extraction may increase. Hard coal, 45 percent of which is used in steel and electricity production, is the energy source for roughly 30 percent of all electricity generated in the FRG.

In brown coal both domestic consumption and production increased by 21 percent between 1970 and 1980. Reserves of brown coal are even larger than those of hard coal, but face the same problem of increasing extraction costs. Ninety-four percent of brown coal is used for the production of electricity, providing 26 percent of the FRG's total electricity needs. Hard and brown coal together provided the FRG with almost 60 percent of its electricity requirements and 37 percent of its primary energy consumption.

The amount of energy supplied by gas in the FRG changed dramatically in the 1970s – and these changes are likely to continue throughout the 1980s. Consumption jumped from 32.0 to 61.3 billion cubic meters between 1970 and 1980, an increase of 92 percent. This led to an increase in imports, which rose from 22 percent of gas consumption in 1970 to 69 percent in 1980. Forty-seven percent of total gas consumption is used in the production of electricity, which makes up one-fifth of the energy needs for the country's electricity production.

The FRG contains only tiny deposits of crude petroleum, and there are no significant offshore reserves. Domestic production dropped from 8 million tons in 1970 to 5 million tons in 1980. If new deposits are not discovered, domestic reserves will be depleted by the mid- to late 1980s. Consumption of oil dropped from 118 million tons in 1973 to 94 million tons in 1975; imports decreased by 10 percent in 1980 and by 19 percent in 1981. Oil is used for heating, transportation, and industrial production. In 1980 oil represented 48 percent of West German primary energy consumption. Since 96 percent of it had to be imported, oil is the major source of dependency in the FRG's energy balance.

The FRG currently imports all enriched uranium for its nuclear power plants. In 1980 the share of nuclear energy in total primary energy consumption was, at 3.7 percent, relatively small, but the government expects that nuclear power, which generated 11.8 percent of all electricity in 1981, will expand dramatically by the end of this century, at which time nuclear energy could have the same share in primary energy consumption as oil (27 percent). At the moment, however, there are uncertainties over new plant construction.[5] If the present plans for construction are realized in time, the FRG could produce all enriched uranium needed for its power plants by 1990.

Water-powered plants are limited in number, and generated only 5.1 percent of the FRG's electricity in 1980. Other alternative power plants are relatively unimportant, constituting only 3.7 percent of the electricity produced in 1980. In sum, the West German energy economy is, and will be, based on traditional sources: domestic coal, imported oil, imported gas, and — in the future — nuclear energy.

Energy Policies

Because of West Germany's natural endowments, hard and brown coal were traditionally its major sources of energy. From the beginning of German industrialization until the 1960s, coal had formed the basis for German industrial might. However, as an energy resource, coal lost prominence during the 1960s, when cheap oil conquered the German market as a result of the government's open-door policies. Unable to compete with oil, but still producing at former levels, the West German coal industry entered a period of overproduction. Market pressure forced the mining companies to concentrate and to establish the Ruhrkohle AG, in which the government plays a major role. This unusual state intervention was necessitated by the link between cheap coal and cheap steel, and by the political influence of the Ruhr's trade unions and industries.[6] The West German coal industry survived only because of this state intervention.

In the early 1970s this policy changed as a result of the Arab oil embargo and its consequences. First, the West German market had to cope with the quadrupling of the price of oil, which at the time provided more than 50 percent of the country's primary energy needs (see Table 4.1). By March 1981 the price of oil had jumped to 619 DM/ton from 84 DM in 1973, although the DM had gained against the U.S. dollar, in which oil is priced. Second, this contributed to an overall import price inflation of 14.2 percent for 1980-81, whereas export prices rose by only 5.7 percent in the same period. Out of a domestic inflation rate of 5.6 percent for 1980, between 0.5 percent and 0.75 percent can be traced to the oil price increases. Third, the decline in GNP growth due to oil price increases was approximately 0.5 percent in 1979 and 2.0 percent in 1980, which translates into a loss of 150,000 jobs. Fourth, energy import expenditures in 1979 led to the first balance-of-payments deficit in the history of the Federal Republic.[7] Half of this "negative swing" (−9.6 billion DM in 1979 and −29.1 billion DM in 1980) stems from the oil bill.[8] In 1972 the share of net energy imports of all imports was 9.5 percent, but in 1980 it was 22.7 percent.[9] Fifth, the new political importance of the OPEC countries contributed to a reevaluation of the FRG's Middle East policy, including relaxed relations with the PLO.

The West German government could not proceed in the 1970s and 1980s with the same free-market energy policies that had characterized the 1960s. Oil price increases threatened the country's growth rate and its position in the world economy. The FRG's energy policies were brought into harmony with those of other industrial countries at the world economic summit meetings and adjusted within the guidelines of the 1980 proposals of the Council of Energy Ministers of the European Communities.[10] They are based on the principles of reduction, conservation, diversification, and substitution. The European Communities' (EC) guidelines recommend that by 1990 oil not exceed 40 percent of any country's primary energy consumption. The 1980 statistics for the FRG showed a decline in the share of oil in the country's primary energy consumption to 48 percent. In 1981 oil imports were further reduced by 19 percent. These decreases were in part due to the process of supply and demand, but also to increased taxes on gasoline and other incentives to reduce oil consumption in electricity production, industry, heating, and transportation. Furthermore, conservation technologies and other energy-saving measures were widely introduced.[11] These were intended to break the link between economic growth and growth in energy consumption, in order to fulfill the EC guidelines of a relation of 0.7 between the two.

Conservation has been supplemented by the substitution of domestic energy sources for imported energy. Hard and brown coal

FIGURE 4.1
Development of Consumption of Energy in the FRG

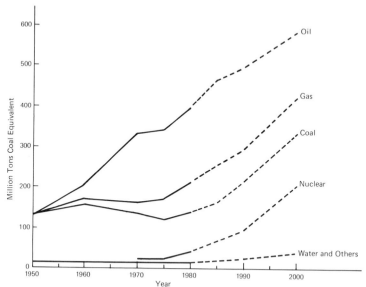

Source: Based on the FRG government energy program (second version).

have been designated among the major energy sources for the future (see Table 4.1 and Figure 4.1). In addition, nuclear energy is intended to substitute for oil, especially in the production of electricity. Although government forecasts indicate that nuclear energy will provide as much as 27 percent of primary energy needs in the year 2000, the ecological movement has delayed the nuclear construction program and brought the Social Democrat-Liberal coalition government to a compromise solution.[12] Present nuclear energy policy calls for a "policy of options," aimed at constructing only a limited number of power plants but continuing with the development of nuclear energy technology. Natural gas is the third type of energy that has attracted increasing attention. As a clean, relatively cheap, and politically uncontroversial source of energy, it has enjoyed increased use in recent years. The present policy is summarized by the following statement: "Our political objectives are and will be: a shift away from oil, economical and rationalized use of energy, priority of domestic coal, and limited development of nuclear energy."[13]

Although domestic energy sources are playing an increasingly important role, the FRG is and will remain one of the largest net energy importers in the industrialized world. It cannot choose between domestic and foreign energy sources, but only between the various sources of imported energy. Threatened by economic and political pressures, the FRG thus must diversify its energy consumption as much as possible. Diversification encourages development of the domestic coal industry and helps to promote imports from allied or EC countries,[14] such as North Sea oil from Great Britain and Norway and natural gas from Norway and the Netherlands. Diversification further allows West Germany to coordinate its energy imports with the nation's foreign policy objectives (see Table 4.3). One such goal might be to import energy from those high-absorber countries that are able and willing to use earnings from energy exports directly for the purchase of goods and services from the FRG.

TABLE 4.3
Diversification of FRG Energy Imports in 1980

	Hard Coal		*Natural Gas*		*Crude Oil*		*Enriched Uranium*
Share of primary energy consumption (percent)		21.1		16.3		48.0	3.7
Imports as percent of consumption		9.3		69.3		96.0	100
Main exporting countries and their share (in percent) of FRG imports	USA	18	Nether-		Saudi		Niger 29
	UK	16	lands	37	Arabia	25	USA 22
	Poland	16	USSR	17	Libya	15	Canada 16
	Rep. S.		Norway	16	UK	15	Rep. S.
	Africa	10			Nigeria	11	Africa 14
					Algeria	7	Argen-
					Egypt	6	tina 6
					Iran	6	
					USSR	3	
					Norway	3	

Note: Polish coal exports to the FRG (19 million in 1980) were partially reexported. In 1979 the USSR provided 28.5 percent of all enriched uranium of the FRG. FRG imports of refined oil products are not counted because they can be replaced easily — the FRG refinery capacity is high.
Sources: Statistisches Bundesamt; *Jahresberichte der Bundesregierung.*

The idea of a "West-East-South cooperation in energy policies"[1][5] is based on the FRG's need to import energy and to export industrial goods and services. Such cooperation should seek to smooth out price fluctuations and to avert sudden interruptions in energy supplies by integrating the economies of the energy-exporting countries into the Western-dominated world economy. By establishing the necessary interdependencies between energy exporters and energy importers, this West-East-South cooperation should lead to an internationally controlled world energy system. This cooperation, in conjunction with a national policy of diversification, reduction, conservation, and substitution, would provide the best conditions for securing permanent, stable, cheap, and adequate energy imports and for expanding markets for West German industrial exports. A ranking of countries exporting energy to the FRG in 1980 shows the distribution of the FRG's import sources:[1][6]

Saudi Arabia	12 percent of FRG primary energy consumption
United Kingdom	7 percent
Libya	7 percent
Nigeria	5 percent
Netherlands	4 percent
USSR	3 percent
Norway	3 percent
Algeria	3 percent
Egypt	2 percent
Iran	2 percent
USA	1 percent
Niger	1 percent
Rep. of South Africa	1 percent
Canada	1 percent

In terms of political groupings OPEC accounts for 36 percent of FRG primary energy consumption, the EC for 11 percent, Western countries (EC and NATO) for 16 percent, and Eastern countries for 3 percent. Compared with the situation in 1970, diversification has attained considerable results. In analyzing energy imports from the USSR, these figures have to be kept in mind.

ENERGY IMPORTS FROM THE USSR

Energy Imports

The FRG imports crude oil, refined oil products,[17] natural gas, enriched uranium, and hard coal from the Soviet Union. Whereas crude oil and hard coal have been imported from the USSR since about 1970, natural gas and enriched uranium imports began only after 1973-74. This means that in the first half of the 1970s energy imports from the USSR were relatively unimportant. Crude oil imports varied between 2.5 percent and 3.5 percent of all FRG petroleum imports (see Table 4.4). In the second half of the decade these percentages did not change significantly. Meanwhile hard coal imports from the USSR varied between 1.8 percent and 4.0 percent, far less than the 18 percent of hard coal imports from the United States in 1980 (see Table 4.3). Although the volume of imported crude oil from the Soviet Union actually declined from 35 million tons in 1970 to 28 million tons in 1980, Soviet earnings from crude oil exports to the FRG jumped from 173 million DM in 1970 to 1,346 million DM in 1980. Hard coal and crude oil imports from the USSR are not essential for the energy demands of the FRG, but the hard currency generated from such sales may well be essential to the Soviet Union.

Imports of enriched uranium from the USSR started with 146 tons in 1974 and ended abruptly in 1979 at their peak of 722 tons. The Soviet share of all enriched uranium imports varied between 5.4 percent in 1975 and 34.5 percent in 1978. In 1974, 1978, and 1979 the USSR was the most important supplier of West Germany's enriched uranium needs. However, because of the relative unimportance of nuclear energy in FRG primary energy consumption, these were relatively modest. Enriched uranium imports from the USSR were initiated as a reaction to problems in the supply from the United States. In the competition over the South American nuclear investment market, U.S. suppliers seemed to use the dependency of the FRG on U.S. imports of enriched uranium as a means of preventing the German nuclear industry from entering Latin American markets.[18] In order to alleviate these pressures and avoid price increases, the FRG began to import from the USSR. However, the wisdom of such a switch was brought into question when the price of Soviet enriched uranium began to increase. In 1980 the

TABLE 4.4
Energy Imports from all sources and from the USSR 1970-80

	Crude Oil			Natural Gas			Enriched Uranium			Hard Coal		
	Imports as Percent of Consumption	Imports in Million Tons	Imports from USSR as Percent of All Imports	Imports as Percent of Consumption	Imports in Billion Cubic Meters	Imports from USSR as Percent of All Imports	Imports as Percent of Consumption	Imports in Tons	Imports from USSR as Percent of All Imports	Imports as Percent of Consumption	Imports in Million Tons	Imports from USSR as Percent of All Imports
1970	93.0	98.8	3.5	22.3	7.3	0	0	0	0	9.1	8.8	0.4
1971	93.1	100.2	3.3	29.4	15.0	0	100	604	0	7.8	7.3	0.4
1972	93.7	102.6	2.8	36.7	20.6	0	100	657	0	8.1	6.9	0.5
1973	94.4	110.5	2.5	44.8	16.0	no data	100	697	0	8.3	6.5	1.5
1974	94.3	102.5	2.9	53.0	22.9	no data	96.0	647	22.6	7.0	5.6	4.4
1975	93.9	88.4	3.5	59.1	26.9	11.8	97.1	1,996	5.4	8.7	6.1	2.3

TABLE 4.4, continued

	Crude Oil			Natural Gas			Enriched Uranium			Hard Coal		
	Imports as Percent of Consumption	Imports in Million Tons	Imports from USSR as Percent of All Imports	Imports as Percent of Consumption	Imports in Billion Cubic Meters	Imports from USSR as Percent of All Imports	Imports as Percent of Consumption	Imports in Tons	Imports from USSR as Percent of All Imports	Imports as Percent of Consumption	Imports in Million Tons	Imports from USSR as Percent of All Imports
1976	94.7	97.7	3.4	60.5	28.8	13.6	97.0	1,256	16.8	8.2	5.6	4.0
1977	94.7	96.3	3.0	63.2	31.8	15.8	99.0	1,467	34.3	8.6	6.1	2.5
1978	94.9	94.4	3.0	63.5	34.8	24.6	97.5	1,659	34.5	8.6	6.4	1.8
1979	95.7	107.4	3.4	67.4	40.7	no data	100	2,537	28.5	10.8	7.7	3.8
1980	96.0	96.9	2.9	69.3	61.3	17.0	100	2,775	0	9.3	9.0	2.2

Note: Detailed gas import figures are confidential. Therefore, only those figures are given that were disclosed by official government sources.

Sources: Statistisches Bundesamt; FRG government sources.

amount of enriched uranium that had formerly come from the USSR was replaced by imports from Niger, with which the FRG had forged a link in 1978.

There are at least three options for West German nuclear power development. The first is to proceed with the development of re-cycling and fast-breeder industries, which would lead to self-suf-fiency of uranium supply by 1990. The second is to rely on the present import profile (Niger, United States, Canada, Republic of South Africa), with its negative effects on the balance of payments, and hope that Niger can be played off against U.S. and Canadian firms in order to avoid sudden price increases or supply cutoffs. The third, and the most unlikely option, is to import enriched uranium once again from the Soviet Union or develop the small European sources. It is the first option that would best serve West German interests, since it would lead to self-sufficiency in an energy source that is likely to experience tremendous growth at least until 2000, at which time nuclear energy should account for 27 percent of the FRG's primary energy consumption. It would lessen the FRG's dependency on other sources of energy, reduce energy import costs, and create opportunities for high domestic investment.

Imports of natural gas from the USSR started in 1973 and have continued to grow in absolute terms. Cooperation between the German Ruhrgas AG and the Soviet Soyuzgasexport started in 1969. After the Austrian-USSR deal of 1968, in which pipe was sold in exchange for natural gas, the following contracts were made:

1970   3 billion cubic meters per year (from October 1973 on)

1972   additional 4 billion cubic meters per year

1973   additional 4 billion cubic meters per year

1981[19]   additional 10.5 billion cubic meters per year (from 1984 on)

After energy imports from Norway started in 1977, and imports from the Netherlands continued to increase, the share of imports from the USSR fell from its peak of 24.6 percent of all natural gas imports in 1978 to 17 percent in 1980. If the present import profile remains constant, the 1981 gas contract will mean an increase, in relative terms, of imports from the Soviet Union to 30 percent of all FRG gas supplies in 1984-85. However, present energy policies aim to increase imports of natural gas from Norway and the Netherlands. In addition, the FRG may start to import from Algeria in the next few years. This means that the 30 percent share for Soviet imports in the German supply of natural gas in 1984-85 is a maximum estimate. The actual figures in later years probably will be much smaller.

In contrast with energy imports from some other countries, Soviet natural gas exports to the FRG create an interdependency, since the FRG depends on Soviet energy imports and the USSR depends on West German industrial exports. This mutual dependence is reflected in the conditions of the contracts. All gas import contracts are so-called compensation contracts.[20] Pipelines and pumping stations, including the technology needed to construct them, are financed by private credits[21] through bank consortia, which are guaranteed — as are all other export credits — by the state-backed Hermes Fund.[22]

Credits and interest are repaid with the earnings from the natural gas transported through these pipelines. In the case of the 1981 gas pipeline deal, the USSR will receive credits until 1984 toward the construction of pipelines, pumping stations, and the transfer of technology, all of which will drastically increase its foreign debt. The higher the interest and debt are, the greater the Soviet interest in exporting its gas in order to repay its loans. Furthermore, the pipeline systems are built in single sections. As soon as one section is finished, gas is exported, and then the next section is built. The 1981 deal calls for the construction of only one pipeline in the first phase, and — after gas exports are under way — a parallel pipeline to double transport capacity in the second phase. This step-by-step or section-by-section strategy reduces the risks for the FRG and encourages the USSR not to break the contract by holding sections of pipeline as "hostage" against gas deliveries.

In the 1970s the USSR proved to be a reliable energy supplier for the FRG.[23] However, if the USSR did restrict its gas exports for the purpose of achieving political advantage, the consequences would be much less grave than a comparable measure undertaken by OPEC. Dependence on gas imports not only is limited, but has not previously led to economic and political vulnerability. Contracts between Ruhrgas AG and its German customers are "interruptable"[24] — that is, customers, such as power plants, are prepared to deal with a cutoff of supplies by shifting to other types of energy or other supplier countries when the situation warrants. For this purpose, buffer stocks of natural gas are maintained and enlarged in order to provide sufficient time for conversion. As a further precaution, most Western supplier contracts foresee the possibility of emergency increase in supplies from other sources in order to fill the gap opened by Soviet cuts.

Even if all these measures were to come to naught, it must be kept in mind that the uses of natural gas are divided in the following way: 50 percent is used for electricity production, 25 percent for private households, and 25 percent for industrial use. The transportation network allows the German gas suppliers to reduce household consumption drastically and to keep up industrial and power plant consumption in case of a Soviet cutback, which means that a Soviet cutback would harm neither industrial nor electricity production, but only private, nonvital consumption. If explained in an adequate political way, this would not lead to major loss of mass support for the government in power, as the experiences with the drastic measures during the first oil shortage showed. Therefore, the FRG could react with flexibility and would be able to minimize the effects and duration of a Soviet cutback — even if the USSR were to capture a 30 percent share of all West German gas imports.

The German interest in the gas pipeline deal with the USSR is a matter not only of prudent energy policy,[25] but also one of fundamental economic interest. The deal creates orders for German firms in a time of economic difficulties and growing unemployment (see Table 4.5).[26] It can be expected that in 1982 Soviet orders to German contractors will amount to between 1.5 billion DM and 2 billion DM.[27] Although only 1.8 percent of all employed Germans are dependent on orders from eastern Europe, both government and industry are interested in keeping unemployment at the lowest possible level. In addition, the USSR is regarded as a high-absorber country, which means that most of its export earnings will return to the FRG or to other Western countries in the form of orders for new equipment, investment goods, and technology transfers.

New orders could both revitalize German-Soviet bilateral trade and secure the FRG's position as the most important Western trading partner of the USSR. Because 73.2 percent of Soviet exports to the FRG in 1980 consisted of energy and energy products, the export earnings of the USSR have increased drastically in recent years.

TABLE 4.5
FRG-USSR Trade, 1970-80

Year	FRG Nominal GNP in Billion DM	FRG Imports in Billion DM	FRG Imports as Percent of GNP	FRG Imports from USSR in Million DM	FRG Imports from USSR as Percent of All Imports	FRG Exports in Billion DM	FRG Exports as Percent of GNP	FRG Exports to USSR in Million DM	FRG Exports to USSR as Percent of All Exports
1970	679	110	16.1	1,254	1.1	125	18.5	1,546	1.2
1971	756	120	15.9	1,257	1.1	136	18.0	1,608	1.2
1972	827	129	15.6	1,386	1.1	149	18.0	2,295	1.5
1973	920	145	15.8	1,993	1.4	178	19.4	3,114	1.7
1974	987	180	18.2	3,269	1.8	231	23.4	4,774	2.1
1975	1,030	184	17.9	3,240	1.8	222	21.5	6,948	3.1

TABLE 4.5, continued

Year	FRG Nominal GNP in Billion DM	FRG Imports in Billion DM	FRG Imports as Percent of GNP	FRG Imports from USSR in Million DM	FRG Imports from USSR as Percent of All Imports	FRG Exports in Million DM	FRG Exports as Percent of GNP	FRG Exports to USSR in Million DM	FRG Exports to USSR as Percent of All Exports
1976	1,123	222	19.8	4,357	2.0	257	22.8	6,755	2.6
1977	1,201	235	19.6	4,561	1.9	274	22.7	6,451	2.4
1978	1,291	244	18.9	5,438	2.2	285	22.1	6,301	2.2
1979	1,400	292	20.9	7,381	2.5	315	22.5	6,624	2.1
1980	1,498	341	22.8	7,411	2.2	350	23.4	7,943	2.3

Source: Statistisches Bundesamt.

Soviet terms of trade showed an overall net increase of 5.5 percent per year during the period 1975-79. Against Western countries the terms of trade rose 47 percent[28] in the same period. Therefore, after years of a negative trade balance with the FRG, the USSR exported a value of 7.4 billion DM in 1979 but imported a value of only 6.6 billion DM. At the end of 1980 Soviet debts to the FRG were about 16 billion DM.[29] The 1981 gas pipeline deal will provide the USSR with additional yearly earnings of 6.5 billion DM from the FRG (on the basis of 1981 prices). However, most of these earnings have to be used to repay credits and interest for the equipment delivered. Finally, in connection with increasing Soviet export earnings another interest has to be considered, that of the eastern European countries that show worsening trends in their current and capital accounts. Their present debts to the West are estimated at $70 billion for 1982. Political and economic considerations are forcing the USSR to guarantee or to repay many of these debts indirectly, so that growing export earnings return to Western countries not only as a result of new industrial orders but also as loan repayments.

Both exports from and imports to the USSR should not be overestimated. In spite of the growing export orientation of the FRG (exports formed 23.4 percent of GNP in 1980), exports to the USSR remained small, only 2.3 percent of total exports. Although the new gas pipeline deal may double the volume of the total bilateral trade after 1984-85, the Soviet market will remain of limited importance. With the exception of some firms that are oriented toward Eastern markets, the West German economy could quite easily overcome a loss of many of those markets. The 2.2 percent of imports in 1980 from eastern Europe are, with the exception of energy, negligible in both quantity and quality.

West German-Soviet trade relations are asymmetric in economic terms. Whereas the FRG exports investment goods and technology, the USSR exports raw materials and especially energy. Imports from and exports to the Soviet Union are of limited relevance to the FRG, whereas the Soviets regard this commerce as vital to their economic health. The FRG is their most important Western trading partner, and the role of West German imports in Soviet industrialization plans cannot be underestimated.[30]

Soviet Interests in Energy Cooperation

The USSR shows a significant interest in economic cooperation with the FRG for a variety of reasons. A fundamental interest in economic cooperation and limited integration into the Western-dominated world economy can be found in Soviet positions concerning the North-South dialogue, Soviet economic policy toward that dialogue in the framework of COMECON, and Soviet trade policies toward the Western countries and the Third World. The USSR, although propagating "socialist internationalism," acts in the tradition of classical power politics. In spite of the antagonistic ideologies, economic cooperation with the Western states has been increasing in the fields of industry, energy, raw materials, and agriculture. This goal can be found, for example, in the Five-Year-Plan for 1981-85, in which the USSR officially recognizes East-West trade as an integral part of the plan to improve production and to stimulate economic growth. Trade with Western countries will increase by 4 percent, according to the plan, and future investments will be financed partially by export earnings. In addition to direct trade with Western countries, the indirect trade via the COMECON countries must also be considered. The USSR imports manufactured goods from east European countries that use Western technology or components. This practice, which is counted as internal bloc trade, limits the outflow of hard currencies.

The recent prominence of East-West trade for the USSR is a result of severe economic problems. According to Western sources, the Soviet GNP showed real growth rates of 5 percent between 1960 and 1970, of 4 percent between 1970 and 1975, and of 2.5 percent between 1975 and 1980. This decline is due to decreased capital efficiency, low growth in employment, a slowdown in energy and raw material production, and a high debt ratio to the West. The Soviet economic system has not been able to manage efficiently the transition from extensive to intensive types of growth, nor has it been able efficiently to develop energy production and high-technology industries. Hopes of imitating the Japanese model – replacing imported technology and goods with sophisticated domestic techniques – have failed. Even realistic planning is not implemented. In 1980 production was only 85 percent of the amount called for in the plan, and energy production totaled only 90 percent of the planned amount. Efforts to achieve reforms in pricing, linkages between earnings and productivity, and improved central planning are not likely to change the overall trends because these most recent schemes are not directed at the structural causes of the nation's economic weaknesses.

But the necessity to increase economic and financial assistance to COMECON countries, the pressure to assist Communist Third World countries, and the competition with Western worldwide economic and financial assistance programs force the USSR to seek increased growth. In addition, domestic demands for better living standards, higher agricultural yields, and improved public services further increase the need for growth. Finally, the heavy military burden caused by the arms race aggravates economic problems. Indeed, the Soviet growth rate of 2 percent per year in the period of the 1981-85 plan can be realized only if imports from the West provide the necessary investment goods, management skills, and technology. This dependence on imports from the West is different from the FRG's dependence on imports from the USSR. The USSR's cannot be diversified or substituted. They are not short-term or medium-term dependencies, but long-term and structural dependencies. Even to keep up the productivity in those sectors that are heavily dependent on Western technology and investment, the USSR needs steady trade with Western countries.

An example of the structural problems in the Soviet economy is the energy production and extraction sector (see Table 4.6). With the exception of natural gas production, which entails a high degree of cooperation with the West and especially with the FRG, even the moderate figures of the plan could not be met. The energy production plan, mainly oriented toward domestic demand, is based on imports of investment goods and services, to be paid for with additional extracted energy. In this sector Western imports are of vital importance. After more than a decade of economic cooperation with the Western countries and especially with the FRG, the USSR has been unable to bridge the technical and industrial gap. It has not been able to substitute for Western technology and for highly sophisticated industrial goods in general. In order to avoid becoming a net importer, the USSR energy sector cannot proceed without Western help.

Soviet elites must fear the USSR's structural dependence on Western imports. The original idea of "paying" for Western imports with semifinished or even consumer goods has proved illusory. This and the increase in energy prices have led to their concentrating on energy exports. Export revenues helped to overcome the trade deficit and at the same time to secure the needed assistance for the extension of Soviet energy production. The more energy the USSR can supply, the more it can balance its dependence on Western imports by the FRG's dependence on energy imports.

Comparing the different nature of Soviet and West German import dependence, roughly one-fourth of the 2 percent growth rate planned for the 1980s in the USSR will result from direct or indirect imports from the West. In the energy sector, not only present growth rates but also the actual production of natural gas

TABLE 4.6
Planned and Real Energy Production in the USSR

Year	Coal in Million Tons	Coal, Change from Previous Year in Percent	Crude Oil In Million Tons	Crude Oil, Change from Previous Year in Percent	Natural Gas in Billion Cubic Meters	Natural Gas, Change from Previous Year in Percent
1976	711.5		519.7		321.0	
1977	722.1	0.9	545.8	4.8	346.0	7.8
1978	723.6	0.0	571.5	4.5	372.2	7.6
1979	718.7	−0.1	585.6	2.5	406.6	9.2
1980	716.4	0.0	603.0	3.0	435.0	7.0
1980 plan	745.0		606.0		435.0	
1981 plan	738.0	3.0	610.0	1.2	458.0	5.3
1985 plan	770-800	7.5-11.7	620-645	2.8-7.0	600-640	37.9-47.1

Sources: United Nations, Economic Commission for Europe; Proceedings of Congress of Communist Party of Soviet Union.

depend on Western technology, spare parts, and investment goods and services. While the Soviet Union could endure stagnation or even a decrease in private energy consumption if it had to, there could not be sufficient growth in the energy sector without Western help. Underproduction would mean using scarce hard currency to buy on the world market.

Soviet imports from the FRG and other Western countries cannot be easily substituted or diversified. This is another difference in the Soviet dependence on the FRG and the West — those products and services that the USSR needs most for its industrialization are produced only in a limited number of Western countries. Whereas the FRG can diversify and substitute its energy imports from the USSR and its exports to the USSR, the Soviet ability to withstand a united Western policy of similar economic and trade strategies is much more limited. A cutoff of Soviet energy to the FRG and other western European countries and the closure of the Soviet market to Western exports would harm the FRG and other trading partners only to a limited extent and only for a limited time. A cutoff of Western exports to the USSR would stall its growth prospects by hampering energy production and the ability to generate hard currencies for industrial imports. Increasing West German energy imports have reduced, but not done away with, the Soviet net dependency. The FRG has the possibility of reducing its dependence vis-à-vis the USSR, but the USSR may not be able to gain greater independence from the West.

Political Aspects

The FRG's détente policy is based on a strategic mixture of cooperation in political, economic, and cultural affairs, on the one hand, and assured deterrence in the military field, on the other.[31] In other words, the present strategy is a combination of conflict and cooperation. In this context economic cooperation must be of a structural type — that is, long-term and irreversible. Irreversibility, stability, and reliability can best be attained by the establishment of a mutual long-term dependence, which does not represent serious risks for West German national security. Compensation deals, as described above, are an ideal instrument for building such interdependence.

Economic cooperation of this kind serves different political purposes. First, it assures the political will to cooperated by creating "détente lobbies" in both countries. Those industries or political factions profiting from the economic cooperation will work for the continuation and extension of the détente process in order to increase the political possibilities for further and greater economic cooperation. In domestic conflicts over the distribution of resources among different sectors, each "détente lobby" can argue that economic cooperation proves the other's will to avoid war, and competes with the demands of opposing military-industrial elites for higher defense expenditures.

Second, economic cooperation of this kind serves integration and the cause of peace. Integration of the USSR and eastern European countries into the structures and interdependencies of the world market, which is clearly dominated by the Western industrialized countries, and into an asymmetric East-West cooperation, in which the Western countries have a considerable net power advantage, means establishing a network of economic advantages. These advantages function politically: in case of cooperation they can be expanded, in case of noncooperation they can be limited or even lost. Such a strategy, which concentrates on economic incentives, is neither new nor untried. It can be found in the policies of U.S. governments in the 1960s and 1970s, and in the policies of European governments in the 1970s.

In addition, it has been part of the North-South and Middle East policies of the western European countries for a decade. It proved successful in central Europe, where the formerly belligerent and militarily oriented Germanies were integrated into NATO/EC and Warsaw Treaty Organization/COMECON. But integration works against military conflicts only if it provides advantages to those countries that are integrated. This means that the integrators have to share advantages and responsibilities in order to bring about peace. In the specific case of East-West economic cooperation this is not a major problem. Because of the complementary export profiles and the different levels of industrialization, cooperation is not a zero-sum, but a variable-sum game. Economic cooperation creates additional growth opportunities not only for one's own economy but for one's partner's economy as well.

Third, economic cooperation serves political negotiating purposes. Economic cooperation of a certain amount and quality, such as in the case of the FRG's trade with the USSR, can be used in case of conflict. The threat to limit or to cut off existing economic cooperation is more effective than the threat not to start economic cooperation. Existing cooperation therefore can be used as a bargaining chip.

In analyzing present East-West relations, one must remember that cooperation is only one component; conflict is the other. Even in the FRG's negotiating strategy, cooperation and conflict are combined, although the conflict component functions as an ultima ratio. Conflict threatens the already proved benefits from this cooperation with the West. Cooperation offers current or future advantages, if adequate response is given. Economic cooperation enables one to combine a policy of incentives with the threat of sanctions. It is assumed, for example, that this combination of economic threats and incentives played a major role in Soviet policy toward Poland. Any German government would have substantially reduced and probably ended its economic cooperation with the USSR as a reaction to direct military intervention.[32] The present détente concept cannot tolerate any Soviet military intervention or belligerent behavior in Europe.

The 1981 gas pipeline deal has, from the viewpoint of the FRG, two additional concrete political aspects that should not be underestimated. First, the 1981 deals have led to a breakthrough on the Berlin question, one of the most vulnerable and problematic points in the foreign policy of the FRG. Though the agreement of the allies has brought a certain stabilization of the status and security of West Berlin, the West German détente policy toward the East failed, until 1981, to obtain from eastern Europe or from the USSR the recognition of West Berlin as a de facto part of the FRG. The Berlin question became the major problem of West Germany's Ostpolitik in the 1970s, because east European governments refused to negotiate agreements with an FRG that included West Berlin. A West German-Soviet electricity-nuclear power plant deal ran aground in the 1970s because the West Germans wanted to include a supply of electricity for West Berlin. However, the 1981 gas pipeline deal explicitly agrees to deliver natural gas to West Berlin, as the November 1981 communiqué of Brezhnev's visit to Bonn acknowledged. This is not only a matter of energy supply for West Berlin but also a major diplomatic breakthrough in the FRG'S *Ostpolitik*.

The second new aspect in the 1981 gas pipeline deal is the fact that it involves a network of bilateral arrangements between the USSR and the FRG, France, Belgium, the Netherlands, Italy, and Austria. It is thus a major west European multilateral attempt at energy cooperation, most of which has been bilateral until now. Because of the pipeline and its distribution system, any cutoff would hurt all customers simultaneously and unite them against the USSR.

Limitation and Control of Energy Imports

The summit meeting at Ottawa in 1981 brought the political debate over East-West trade to the formal attention of West European governments and especially to that of the FRG. Demands to improve NATO's COCOM (Consultative Group Coordinating Committee) and to strike a balance between economic interests, on the one hand, and security risks, limitation of the freedom of action toward the USSR, and economic dependence, on the other hand, were written into the summit communiqué. Subsequently the Reagan administration tried to persuade the west Europeans not to sign the gas pipeline deal. But no west European government nor major opposition party supported the U.S. position.

From the European perspective, a number of arguments in favor of the energy imports from the USSR were brought forward:

1. Increased gas imports from the USSR reduce dependence and vulnerability vis-à-vis Arab oil imports.

2. Oil and coal imports from the USSR are relatively low. Imports of enriched uranium ended in 1980. Imports of Soviet natural gas may provide as much as 30 percent of gas imports by the late 1980s, but while they create a certain dependence, they produce little economic or political vulnerability.

3. A cutoff of the gas supply would stop all further assistance to the USSR's extraction and transport facilities. Therefore the USSR would be hurt in its energy production, its general growth policies, and its ability to buy energy on the world market.

4. The gas pipeline and the subsequent energy deals maintain the USSR as a net exporter in the energy field (without these measures, the USSR could become a net importer). This avoids

competition and discourages the Soviets from taking the risk of military measures to secure scarce oil supplies.

5. Soviet gas export earnings return directly to Soviet customers. These take the form of energy development investments, industrial investments, agricultural purchases, and amortization of eastern European debts.

6. Economic cooperation in the energy field serves integration. It also acts as a bargaining chip in East-West relations.

Arguments that these energy imports create vulnerability can be countered, although it cannot be denied that a limited, short-term dependence is created. The argument has been made that Western exports to the USSR enable the Soviet Union to increase its military expenditures indirectly, since without Western assistance the growth rate and the quality of growth would be considerably lower. Even agricultural exports to the USSR enable its government to neglect investment in agriculture in order to direct investment toward the military sector. These arguments have a certain validity. The idea that détente, and especially economic cooperation, might weaken Soviet military elites proved wrong – at least (and clearly) in the case of the SS-20 buildup.

But it must be questioned whether economic sanctions – even if they hurt the USSR – would change the influence of the military elites on foreign policy and decisions about the distribution of resources. On the contrary, sanctions might stabilize government elites, which could blame economic mistakes on the West and its aggressive policies. In a number of cases, the strategy of economic sanctions against the USSR has proved completely insufficient or ineffective. The last U.S. grain embargo is an example. Soviet techniques for domestic repression remain extensive, and the Soviet ability to impose a reduction of the standard of living without suffering a crisis of political legitimation is much more developed than in Western countries. Moreover, Soviet and eastern European governments are willing to resist economic threats from the West.[33]

If there is one strategy for peaceful integration and for political "good behavior" that can work, it is a strategy that combines politics with economics, and incentives with the threat of sanctions. Such a strategy of conditioned cooperation must include the threat of imposing sanctions at any time and in an effective way. But it must also offer incentives. The positive use of economic instruments, especially in a case where the USSR needs economic cooperation for structural purposes, can be accepted more easily and is more attractive to political and economic elites than the negative use of sanctions.

However, vital interests have to be respected and cannot be traded off by economic means. A strategic mix of political, military, and economic instruments allows one to act flexibly in response to every challenge and conflict, but only if adequate capacity is built up. In the case of an economic instrument this means that a strong economic link would have already been established and have proved attractive in quality and quantity. The higher the Eastern interest in supporting and increasing economic cooperation with the West and the more attractive its outcomes are, the more the USSR might be willing to cooperate in the political and military spheres. It is obvious that the use of economic instruments for political purposes has preconditions — namely, primacy of politics over foreign economic cooperation and a clear and predictable government control policy — but this is not to say that economic instruments are powerless.

In the specific FRG-USSR case, additional considerations limit the applicability of arguments against the latest gas pipeline deal. First, in the 1960s the FRG experienced a COCOM embargo on the export of pipe to the USSR. The measure applied to the Federal Republic but not to other west European countries. In turn, the latter took over the West German contracts.[34] Second, offers to replace gas imports from the USSR with coal imports from the United States — which would be more expensive and contrary to diversification goals and ecological considerations — led to the impression that U.S. political arguments against the energy imports from the USSR were made mainly to promote the sale of coal. Third, the reliability of Soviet energy supplies was compared with the problems with U.S. deliveries of enriched uranium during the 1970s. Fourth, U.S. demands to limit economic cooperation with the USSR seemed to contradict its own trade policy. The lifting of the grain embargo is a case in point. After lifting of the embargo, the United States in 1980 exported $938 million worth of corn and wheat, and $269 million in machinery and transport equipment. These figures exclude a Soviet order to the American firm of International Harvester for agricultural machinery worth $250 million, which was halted by U.S. sanctions against the USSR.[35] In addition, competition between U.S. and West German firms in the Soviet market remains a commercial fact of life. Finally, the Bonn government and its opposition were of the opinion that energy imports from the USSR and West German exports to the USSR did not have much military relevance or significance for national security.[36]

Comparing the advantages in energy, industry, and détente that the FRG would gain against the limited risk of dependency, the Bonn government decided to follow its national interests together with the other western European nations involved in the 1981 deal. However, the maintenance by these governments of alliance policy in the European strategic military field suggests that fears of weakness, lack of common Atlantic interests, or even "Finlandization" are exaggerated.[37]

NOTES

Data in this chapter are from the files of the Statistisches Bundesamt (Statistical Federal Office). Data from other sources are checked against these data. Figures without footnotes come from Statistisches Bundesamt or *Jahresberichte der Bundesregierung* (Yearly Reports of the Federal Government), which are based on data from the Statistisches Bundesamt. More details, data, and methodological remarks are given in Reimund Seidelmann, "Die sowjetischen Energieimporte in die Bundesrepublik Deutschland, Abhängigkeit oder politische Zusammenarbeit," *Beiträge zue Konfliktforschung* (1982): no. 1, 27-66.

1. In 1980, 45 percent of all employed persons were in the industrial sector. Only 6 percent were employed in the agricultural sector. Concerning the disproportionate industrial employment, it has to kept in mind that in 1980, 23.4 percent of GNP came from exports.

2. On average, figures for the different sectors vary.

3. Governmental estimates for energy-saving potential are as follows: industry, 1973-2000, 21-25 percent; private consumption, 1973-2000, 13-25 percent.

4. In coal, however, this trend may be reversed in the next few years.

5. The major German parties (CDU, SPD, FDP) support the development of nuclear energy. Therefore, the demands of ecological movements for limitation of growth, priority of ecology, and a halt to nuclear energy development have little chance for political realization.

6. The Ruhr is the region of coal extraction. Originally steel production needed large amounts of coal, so it was historically located there.

7. Estimates from the Deutsche Bundesbank (German Central Bank).

8. Experts expect a positive balance of payments for 1983 and the following years.

9. Estimates from the Deutsche Bundesbank.

10. See *Jahresbericht der Bunderegierung 1980* (Yearly Report of the Federal Government)

11. A good example of such policies is the plan to use power plants for the production of both electricity and home heating. This leads to a better use of energy inputs and reduces emissions from the traditional individual heating of houses.

12. A Christian Democrat government would not change this policy fundamentally, although it might make limited compromises with the ecological movement.

13. Chancellor Schmidt, statement in the Deutsche Bundestag (German Federal House of Parliament), November 11, 1980.

14. Which can be classified as high absorber countries.

15. Foreign Minister Hans-Dietrich Genscher (Liberal), statement in the Deutsche Bundestag, November 26, 1980.

16. Calculations based on data from the Statistisches Bundesamt.

17. In 1980 the refined oil products from the USSR accounted for about 10 percent of all relevant imports. Refined oil product imports for the FRG show high variation. The general trend is to refine oil in the FRG itself. Therefore, refined oil product imports do not play a major role in comparison with crude oil imports.

18. One of the major points of conflict was the FRG-Brazil deal.

19. Signed in November 1981, shortly before the visit of Leonid Brezhnev to Bonn.

20. Between 15 and 20 percent of all FRG-USSR contracts are compensation contracts — that is, investment goods are paid for with energy or consumption goods. The FRG government tries to limit the number of compensation contracts but favors them in the case of energy.

21. The 1981 figures are 0.6 billion DM Soviet deposit, 1.2 billion DM credits from contractors, 2.2 billion credit from Ausfuhrkreditanstalt.

22. Helmut Schmidt, in a statement in the Deutsche Bundestag, February 28, 1980, mentioned that especially on credit guarantees for FRG-USSR deals, the Hermes Fund makes a substantial profit. There is no single case in the bilateral trade relations where the fund had to pay the guaranteed sum.

23. In the past there was not a single case of cutoffs or squeezing directed against Germany for political reasons.

24. This is part of the arrangement under which the government agreed to the deal.

25. The import prices (1980) are 0.05 DM/kwh for oil and 0.03 DM/kwh for natural gas. In addition, a complicated index system creates delays between oil and other energy price increases and gas price increases, to keep gas imports from the Soviet Union at an attractively low price.

26. The orders for pipelines will amount to 6 billion DM. Pipelines are produced by Mannesmann, which has a monopoly on large special pipelines.

27. The deal started with yearly contracts.

28. Data from United Nations, Economic Commission for Europe, and FRG government sources.

29. Estimates from Deutsche Bundesbank.

30. In this respect my evaluation differs in part from that of Angela Stent, for example, in "The USSR and Germany," *Problems of Communism*, September/October 1981, pp. 1-24. For more details, see Reimund Seidelmann, *Die Entspannungspolitik der Bundesrepublik Deutschland* (Frankfurt: Campus, 1982); and Deutsche gesellschaft für Friedens und Konfliktforschung, *Jahrbuch zur Entspannungspolitik in Europa* (Baden-Baden: Nomos, 1980).

31. In detail see Reimund Seidelmann, *Die Entspannungspolitik der Bundesrepublik Deutschland*. This political concept is expressed in NATO's Harmel Report (1967) as well as NATO's declaration of Bonn (1982).

32. Though the FRG government has avoided much public discussion about its reaction to an intervention, its minister of economy made it clear that economic cooperation could not be kept in such a case. See *Wirtschaftswoche* 35, no. 39 (1981): 18.

33. See Georgij A. Arbatov, *Der sowjetische Standpunkt. Ober die Westpolitik der UdSSR* (Munich: 1981); and, for the GDR case, Institut fur Internationale Beziehungen/Institut fur Internationale Politik und Wirtschaft, *Sozialismus und Entspannung* (Berlin: 1980).

34. See Kurt Tudyka, "Gesellschaftliche Interessen und auswärtige Beziehunger. Das Röhrenembargo," *Politische Vierteljahresschraft* 10, Sonderheft (1969): 205-23.

35. A detailed analysis of U.S. economic policies toward the USSR, with specific attention to the arguments for sanctions against the USSR, is presented by Hanns-Dieter Jacobsen, "Die Ostwirtschaftspolitik der Reagan-Administration," paper for Stiftung Wissenschaft und Politik, Ebenhausen, 1982.

36. Minister for Economy Otto Graf Lambsdorff, in *Wirtschaftswoche* 35, no. 39 (1981): 18-20, about the idea to give COCOM control over all deals that exceed 100 million: "This is not a reasonable approach. The reasonable approach must lie in security policy considerations. Selling cabbage for 100 million is not relevant for COCOM."

37. A realistic U.S. view is presented in *NATO Today: The Alliance in Evolution*, a report to the Committee on Foreign Relations, U.S. Senate, 97th Cong., 2nd Sess., April 1982.

REFERENCES

Bundesministerium fur Wirtschaft. *Der deutsche Osthandel 1980*. Bonn: The Ministry, 1980.

——. *Der deutsche Osthandel 1981*. Bonn: The Ministry, 1981.

Bundesregierung. *Jahresberichte*. Bonn: 1976-80.

Communist Party of the Soviet Union. "The 26th Congress of the Communist Party of the Soviet Union," *Information Bulletin* special iss. 19 (1981).

Deutsche Bundesbank. *Monatsberichte*, 1977-81.

——. *Pressemitteilungen*, 1977-81.

Deutsche Bundestag, *Verhandlungen und Unterlagen*, January 23, 1980; February 28, 1980; November 26, 1980; December 12, 1980; January 29, 1981.

Sowjetunion '81, Verlagsbeilage zum *Vorwärts* no. 48 of November 19, 1981.

Statistisches Bundesamt, *Jahrbücher* 1970-80.

United Nations. *Yearbook of World Energy Statistics 1979*. New York: United Nations, 1981.

United Nations, Economic Commission for Europe. *Energy Reserves and Supplies in the ECE Region*. New York: United Nations, 1979.

————. *Economic Survey for Europe in 1980*. New York: United Nations, 1981.

Wirtschaftswoche 35, no. 39 (1981): 16-18.

5

ENERGY AND
SOVIET FOREIGN POLICY

Nils Andrén

THE OVERRIDING IMPORTANCE OF ENERGY

Energy is both an instrument and a condition of Soviet foreign policy. This observation applies to domestic resources as well as to resources outside the Soviet Union.

Domestic energy provides the basis for the modern Soviet economy. The Soviet Union is rich in all kinds of energy resources. They are necessary not only for domestic growth but also for financing vital imports — ranging from coarse grain to refined technology — and for exercising influence abroad. More than half the Soviets' hard currency imports are paid for by oil exports.

Outside energy resources are also important. They are a potential resource for the needs of domestic consumption — if it would become desirable or necessary for the Soviet Union to become a major importer of oil. They can also be used in a traditional game of power politics. To be able to control, to influence, or just to disturb the international flow of oil may be a useful weapon in the ongoing tug-of-war between East and West.

Indirectly, the Soviet Union has already influenced the energy battle focused on the Middle East. By counter-balancing the influence of the Western and former colonial powers, the Soviet Union has contributed to conditions favorable for the growth of Arab nationalism and for the economic and political emancipation of the oil-producing states.

The major theme of this chapter is the possible effects of serious Soviet oil shortages. In one sense it provides a long-range perspective, since the general energy and oil situation is basically more secure for the Soviet Union than for its rivals in the West. The USSR is the largest producer of oil in the world. So far, its production has exceeded its consumption by a wide margin. The Soviet Union also excavates the world's largest tonnage of coal (although with less energy content than American coal). In addition, according to the current Five-Year Plan, it will soon be the world's largest producer of natural gas.

In a short-term perspective the energy vulnerability of the Soviet Union stems from its vital dependence on oil exports, both for political reasons and for the foreign trade balance. Oil and gas surpluses constitute necessary assets both for enforcing cohesion in the Soviet bloc and for purchasing the products of high technology from the oil-hungry industrial countries in the West. In 1979 these exports (measured in energy equivalents) amounted to approximately 15 percent of total Soviet energy.

THE SOVIET ASSESSMENT

This general evaluation is confirmed by statements from leading Soviet politicians. Energy was one of the major themes in the late President Brezhnev's address to the Communist Party Congress in 1981, reflecting both the difficulties and ambitions of Soviet efforts.

> An expressed condition for accomplishing all the economic tasks . . . is the development of heavy industry. This applies in particular to its basic branches, and, first and foremost, to fuel and power. . . . The task of improving the structure of the fuel and power budget is becoming even more topical. It is necessary to reduce the share of oil as fuel, to replace it by gas and coal, and to expand the nuclear power industry, including fast nuclear reactors, more rapidly. And, of course, the march of events calls for a continued quest for fundamentally new energy resources, and this includes laying the foundation of a nuclear fusion power industry.

West Siberia was singled out by Brezhnev as the hope for the future, containing "such gigantic resources that it can for many years meet the country's domestic and export needs, including export to capitalist countries." As for oil, "There are enormous possibilities in increasing its extraction rate from the oil fields," but with a condition: "A new approach is evidently needed in the extracting industries. They already absorb a lion's share of capital investments, yet the demand for raw materials and energy will increase." At the same time economy will be of the essence: "Very much can be done by improving engines and switching road transport to diesel and gas."

The needs of the defense and space industries generally enjoy the highest priority in the field of science and technology. Yet Brezhnev, in his speech to the 1981 congress, repeatedly emphasized the importance of assigning resources of high technology and "big science" to the field of energy. He maintained that

> The success of the national economy as a whole will depend in large measure on making the extracting industries more efficient. The road to this runs through accelerating scientific and technological progress.

And again,

> The country is badly in need of having "big science" — in addition to working on fundamental problems, concentrating efforts in a larger measure on solving key economic problems and on discoveries which could bring about truly revolutionary changes in production.

Formally this statement is related to all branches of the national economy. However, by implication it is particularly important for energy production.

Add to this the energy visions of Nikolay Tikhonov at the same Communist Party Congress. It has almost the ring of the early Utopian socialist authors in Russia:

> Electric power production is to be increased chiefly by using nuclear fuel, hydropower sources, and coal in the eastern areas of the country. It is planned that in 1981-85 nuclear and hydropower plants will account for more than 70 percent of the rise in electric power production, and in the European part of the country they already account for almost the entire production increase. Big thermal power projects

are to be based on cheap coal mined by open-cast techniques in the Kansk-Achinsk and Ekibastuz coal fields. In the coming years it is proposed to initiate a fundamentally new trend in the centralized heat supplies of big cities, namely, to build several big nuclear heat provision stations, each of which would be able to assure dependable heat supplies to a city of many thousands of inhabitants without polluting the environment.

These authoritative political statements may be supplemented with the more recent views of a leading Soviet academician, A. P. Alexandrov, president of the USSR Academy of Sciences (as quoted in *Soviet Analyst*, May 19, 1982). He is reported to have been less optimistic than Brezhnev and official spokesmen of the Oil Ministry who had underlined the significance of the vast amounts of gas and oil in western Siberia. He argued that the older oil fields were approaching exhaustion and that oil was too valuable an asset to burn. Rather, it should be preserved for use as a raw material in the chemical industry.

MARKETS AND POLITICS[1]

Soviet energy markets can be subdivided into three groups: the home market, eastern Europe and other socialist countries (state trading countries), and capitalist (hard currency) countries. The distribution of oil among the major Soviet markets since 1970, and the prospects until 1985, are shown in Table 5.1.

The three oil markets of the Soviet Union are all important in relation to fundamental Soviet goals.

- Economic growth, in order to increase the living standard of the people, to ensure a high level of investments, and not least to fulfill the second goal.

- Maintenance of the military resources necessary for a super-power (with a seemingly incurable inferiority complex that, not least in the field of oil technology, seems to be completely justified).

- Preservation of a reliable buffer zone on the western border; this is a goal for which, in view of the historical experiences of the Soviet Union, no price can be regarded as too high.

TABLE 5.1
Actual and Projected Soviet Production and Consumption of Crude Oil and Exports of Oil and Oil Products
(CTN 21 + 22), 1970-85
(million metric tons)

Year	Production	Consumption	Net Exports	Exports to				Imports from LDC's
				CMEA-6	OCPE's	MDC's	LDC's	
1970	353.0	260.7	92.3	40.293	10.192	41.567	3.748	3.500
1971	377.1	277.1	100.0	44.742	10.622	45.627	4.109	5.100
1972	400.4	301.2	99.2	48.924	11.284	42.960	3.832	7.827
1973	429.0	320.9	105.1	55.237	12.429	47.704	2.930	13.179
1974	458.9	347.1	111.8	58.699	13.015	41.527	2.934	4.390
1975	490.8	366.9	123.9	63.276	14.381	47.978	4.716	6.499
1976	519.7	377.6	142.1	68.375	15.537	59.980	4.622	6.425
1977	545.8	(391.6)	(154.2)	(72.805)	(16.550)	(65.659)	(5.742)	(6.556)
1978	571.5	(414.8)	(156.7)	(76.502)	(17.380)	(66.509)	(5.013)	(8.709)

109

TABLE 5.1, Continued

| Year | Production | | | Consumption | | | Net Exports | | | Exports to | | | | | | | | | | | Imports from LDC's |
| | | | | | | | | | | CMEA-6 | | | OCPE's | | | MDC's | | | LDC's | | | |
	L^1	M^2	H^3	L	M	H	L	M	H	L	M	H	L	M	H	L	M	H	L^4	M^4	H^4	H^4
1979	585	585	585	432	432	432	153	153	153	80	80	80	18	18	18	57	57	57	-2	-2	-2	-2
1980	595	598	600	449	449	449	146	149	151	80	81	82	17	18	18	53	53	53	-4	-3	-2	-2
1981	585	598	610	449	455	460	136	143	150	80	82	84	16	18	19	46	47	49	-6	-4	-2	-2
1982	565	593	620	449	460	472	116	133	148	80	83	86	15	18	19	29	37	45	-8	-5	-2	-2
1983	545	588	630	449	467	484	96	121	146	80	84	89	14	18	20	12	25	39	-10	-6	-2	-2
1984	525	582	640	449	472	496	76	110	144	80	85	91	13	18	20	0	14	35	-17	-7	-2	-2
1985	505	578	650	449	478	508	56	100	142	80	86	93	12	18	21	0	4	30	-36	-8	-2	-2

[1] Low.
[2] Medium.
[3] High.
[4] Net exports.

Source: Joint Economic Committee, East European Assessment, 2, 97th Cong., 1st Sess., p. 555.

All these factors have a clear relevance for Soviet foreign policy and national security. A growing shortage of oil might increase the difficulty of realizing these goals. The dependence of the east European countries on the Soviet Union for their energy needs is an instrument to maintain the reliability of these client states. Hence, Soviet oil resources are crucial for preserving bloc stability. This stability is a precondition not only for bloc security but also for any form of détente with the external world. Without confidence in the strength or invulnerability of its own system, no superpower is likely to reembark on a genuine course of détente.

The foreign policy relevance of energy is directly related to the size and significance of exports to foreign markets. Indirectly, the satisfaction of the domestic market might also influence the "actor capability" of the Soviet Union; reductions in domestic energy supply might lower both the efficiency of the system and the loyalty of its members. It is, however, generally understood that the repressive Soviet system is less vulnerable to domestic demands and discontents than the open Western systems — at least up to a point that does not now appear to be within reach.

Oil is also a highly important asset in trade with the West. However, natural gas will soon become more important than oil for the balance of payments of the Soviet Union. This fact is well understood by the major parties in the conflict over the future of the Soviet gas pipeline to Western Europe.

In a wider security policy perspective, the oil and energy problems of both power blocs are very important. An increase in the demands for the same resource would lead to sharper competition and greater risks of conflict. A growing dependence on a resource in an unstable, restless part of the world may — for both blocs — constitute a temptation to strengthen their own political, economic, or military control of this resource, or to anticipate efforts by the other side to do so.

The vital importance assigned to these problems has, in recent years, been emphasized by a number of events, such as the Soviet invasion of Afghanistan, the U.S./NATO concentration of naval forces around the Persian Gulf, and the American long-range Rapid Deployment Force program. Add to this also the steady efforts by both superpowers to recruit reliable friends in the Middle East.

UNCERTAINTIES AND PROBLEMS

The importance of energy for the Soviet Union is clear. However, estimates concerning future Soviet energy supply are rather uncertain, particularly in relation to oil. During recent years many pessimistic estimates have been published. So far the most gloomy predictions concerning reductions in production have not been fulfilled. However, the targets envisioned in the Soviet Five-Year Plan have not been reached, and the signals of warning are evident. Not only Western intelligence estimates are involved but also Soviet ones as well. For the Soviet Union oil may constitute a serious "window of vulnerability." But the statistical data available are shaky.

Soviet oil production in 1981 almost reached its target of 610 million tons. However, this represented a reduction of the previous target by 20 million tons, and actual production was only a slight improvement on the 1980 figure of 603 million tons. Some Western experts predict that production of oil may actually fall during the late 1980s through the early 1990s.

The problems of Soviet oil production are partly ascribed to shortcomings in planning, production, and infrastructure. Traditionally the responsibility for planning is shared among the Ministry of Construction, the Ministry of Oil Production, the Soviet Academy of Sciences, the State Planning Committee (GOSPLAN), the State Committee of Science and Technology, and the Council of Ministers. There is an obvious lack of coherence.

These factors have been operating for some time. Recent difficulties may be assigned to special reasons. Output from the more accessible fields has begun to decline more quickly than planners were able to foresee. Newer and more remote fields in western Siberia, where an increase of about 25 percent in the first part of the 1980s was envisaged, have proved difficult to exploit. These deposits are smaller than believed. Most of them are situated in swamp areas. The infrastructure is insufficient. Roads, housing, power distribution, and pipelines lag behind plans, and the recruitment of workers is difficult.

Add to this the technological worries that are besetting the Soviet oil industry. Exploration in western Siberia must be undertaken at depths down to five kilometers. Soviet equipment has so far been inadequate for work of this magnitude. The drills in current use are designed to work only down to about three kilometers. Western oil companies are technologically still far ahead.

THE KEY ROLE OF THE WEST

Any restrictions on the export of oil technology to the Soviet Union is, hence, likely to delay the necessary expansion of its oil industry. However, experience from the defense and space sectors indicates that Soviet research and industry should be capable of redressing the situation. Yet if the assessment, often quoted in the West, that Soviet technology in general is more than 25 years old is true, it would take an enormous effort to offset major restrictions on technology transfer. In view of the uncertain messages concerning three major factors — energy resources, extraction techniques, and consumption needs — the cautious assumption regarding the Soviet oil problem may be that oil production may stagnate, and possibly diminish, within the next few years.

Even if the Soviet Union commands resources to counter such a development, it nevertheless may not be possible to avoid it altogether. The decisive influence may partly lie in the hands of the Western industrial nations. If the Soviet Union were to expand its imports of technology (both knowledge and equipment) from the leading oil nations in the West, it could in all likelihood be able to overcome major difficulties.

But there are important political problems involved. If these states increase their technology exports to the USSR, they may thus assist the Soviet Union to overcome deficiencies in oil production. They may also contribute both to international stability and to the strength and options of the Soviet Union.

Hence the Western antagonists could well be the first line of defense for securing an adequate output from the Soviet oil industry. It is, however, far from certain that the Western industrial states would give a higher priority to stabilizing the present international structure than to weakening the Soviet system, particularly if this could be done merely by doing nothing.

BEST-CASE ANALYSIS

If the Soviet Union should have to, or would prefer to, face its oil crisis alone, it would. not be without the means to mitigate its effects. Should its oil production be so far below its targets that basic political goals were threatened a number of steps could be taken to avoid a catastrophic situation. The inadequacy of oil production could be compensated for in different ways. Oil has substitutes, primarily natural gas, which is abundant in the Soviet Union and for which there are likely to be new uses.

Not so long ago it seemed plausible to believe that increased oil prices on the export market would substantially offset any decline in Soviet oil production. Recent developments and predictions make this appear less certain. There are also other commodities, such as gas and gold, that might help to balance the economic consequences of a reduction in the quantities of oil exported, or a total discontinuation of oil exports. Recent experience indicates, however, that – because of the sensitivity of gold prices to changes in world market supply – heavy reliance on gold export is to some extent a counterproductive solution.

Improvements in agriculture would also be an efficient means of improving the Soviet external trade balance. This may be illustrated by the fact that the failure of the 1981 harvest cost the Russians some $6 billion for imported grain from the West. For 1982 the grain crop will again be far below its target. On the whole, Soviet agriculture is unlikely to achieve most of the output goals set for 1981-85 – not even with the help of occasional bumper harvests.[2] Indeed, experience so far indicates that it will be difficult for the Soviets to achieve long-range improvements in the agricultural industry that could make them independent of imported grain.

To what extent it would be possible to compensate for the economic effects of inadequate oil production would depend greatly on factors outside the Soviet bloc. The decisive factors would be the Western industrialized states and the major OPEC countries.

WORSE-CASE ANALYSIS

The preceding analysis is, on the whole, a list of highly uncertain developments that could offset the effects of an unfavorable and not wholly unlikely development in the Soviet oil business. It is possible, but far from certain, that the Western powers will help the Soviet Union. The controversy over the gas pipeline reveals both a strong west European interest in major energy deals with the Soviet Union and profound fears of the present American administration concerning the possible consequences of increased dependence on Soviet resources.

It is possible that the NATO-affiliated industrial West, and particularly the United States, might find it in their interest to put pressure on the Soviet Union by refusing to alleviate its economic difficulties. The present reaction in the West – particularly in the United States – to the Polish crisis adds, at least in part, to the credibility of such a scenario. Much depends on the durability of Western economic sanctions. (The current case indicates that western Europe, especially in times of economic difficulties, is unlikely to endure the domestic strain of abstaining from an expanding Soviet market.) Regardless of plausibility, however, such a scenario inevitably raises the question of how the Soviet Union would react if the Western or other correctives of an unfavorable oil balance did not materialize or failed to solve the problems.

When ambitions and resources do not agree, one possibility is to reduce the ambitions. Such reductions could apply to one of the major goals, or affect them all. These goals relate to the standard of consumption, military strength, and relations with eastern Europe. We will look at these three possible areas from the point of view both of the West and of the Soviet Union. The first aspect is relevant, in view of the fact that the Western industrialized states may considerably influence the course of events in the Soviet Union. The West ought to decide whether the likely effects of not assisting the Soviet Union – such as less stability and predictability, with the possibility of a greater inclination to resort to violent methods – would be greater than the risks involved in providing economic or technological assistance.

From the Western point of view, the desirability of Soviet abandonment of the goal of increasing the living standard depends on long-range Western objectives. If Western policy is focused on breaking up the Soviet system, or at least on creating difficulties for its progress, social crisis and domestic instability in the Soviet Union might be regarded as a positive development. However, if the West, or at least some major countries in the West, wants to maintain the goals of détente and rely on economic instruments to realize them, a Soviet energy crisis could in the long run mean both economic and political difficulties for the West.

If a very dangerous international instability is regarded to be a likely consequence, and if the West is not prepared to accept the risks involved in such a development, it is obvious that the Western countries would be wise to avoid an aggressive economic and technological foreign policy. Recently, this problem has been very real in relation to the major gas pipeline deal.

The pipeline issue has also revealed that the conflict between western European economic interests and American strategic fears constitutes a threat to Western cohesion. It is, then, a Scylla-Charybdis situation for the West. To abandon policies of energy cooperation with the Soviet Union would create economic diffi-culties – likely to be politically destabilizing – in both East and West. However, to continue the plans might threaten the cohesion of the Western system. Both policies would be likely to have a harmful impact on East-West relations.

The only possible solution to this dilemma seems to be a formula by which East-West energy cooperation may continue in forms that keep Soviet possibilities for mischief within limits that are strict enough to remove or reduce American apprehensions.

If the reliability of the Soviet *cordon sanitaire* in Eastern Europe could not be supported by economic means, tighter military control might be the only alternative. The political inconveniences of such a course would be obvious. Formal occupation instead of the cos-metic equality of the Warsaw Pact and COMECON would hardly help to restore a lost energy balance. Occupation might reduce the need for energy, but not abolish more than a fraction of it. It would also reduce satellite abilities to find alternatives in the open, hard-currency market, and hence put the total burden on the USSR. Further, the substitution of physical coercion for reliability based on loyalty and community of interest (to the extent that such a situation may have existed at all) might increase the risks of war in central Europe.

From the point of view of the Western powers, a reduction of Soviet ambitions to expand a strong military apparatus would be an ideal solution. The wish to force the Soviet Union into a position of necessary arms limitation might also make the Western powers encourage the development of a critical situation in the Soviet Union rather than alleviate its internal difficulties. This is, however, not a very plausible scenario. It is not likely that the Soviet Union would give up the ambition to develop and retain a strong military organization. Military power is still the only real basis for its super-power status. The most likely Soviet response to an oil shortage is to seek other ways out of a critical situation, rather than give up vital national goals. The choice of alternatives is likely to depend on how critical the situation is perceived to be. It may only appear to involve a possible threat, but it may also be perceived as a manifest danger.

IS THERE A CASE FOR A SOVIET TAKE-OVER BID?

The critical question is in which situation the Soviet Union would be tempted to take direct control of oil sources in the Middle East. It is clear that such a step would constitute a deadly threat to a majority of countries in western Europe and to Japan.

The Soviet Union is probably aware of the extremely dangerous consequences of such a desperate step. So far, its attitude toward conflicts in the Middle East has been remarkably cautious – with the exception of the invasion of Afghanistan. It is, then, plausible to assume that a crisis would have to be very severe before such steps were considered. It should, however, also be kept in mind that the Soviet Union – whether or not it is aggressive and expansive in its basic attitude – rarely hesitates to take a chance if the prize is high but the price is assumed to be reasonable.

We might begin with a scenario in which the threat is clearly perceived but not supposed to be imminent. It is by and large a situation very similar to the present one. In this scenario there is still enough oil for the Soviet Union to provide for its major needs domestically, in the east European countries, and on the hard-currency export markets, and there is perhaps a clear possibility that future shortages in oil exports might have satisfactory substitutes in coming gas production. At least the hope of maintaining future hard currency earnings by means of gas exports might serve as a moderating influence on aggressive Soviet behavior. It is, hence, difficult to imagine that the Soviet Union would meet a situation of this kind by open military attempts to conquer oil sources – for example, in west Asia, the Middle East, and the Persian Gulf area. This does not, of course, rule out that the Soviet Union would continue its attempts to gain influence by less dramatic steps in oil-rich areas, insofar as it is possible to do so by means other than direct military intervention.

However, the possibility cannot be completely ruled out that a crisis might be perceived to be imminent and desperate, with little or no realistic hope of improvement. Such a situation might mean, for example, that all, or almost all, oil export to the West had disappeared and no adequate compensation had been found by selling other products. Gold prices might be too low and gas exports insufficient. The dependence of the Soviet Union on the West would be very small, and this might also reduce the USSR's concern for maintaining or restoring good relations with the Western markets. In such a situation the possibilities for the Soviet Union to have recourse to military force, for example, in order to acquire control of new sources of oil might be greater.

THE GAS CONTROVERSY

These scenarios bring the role of gas into focus. Gas is an important supplement that, together with nuclear power, will reduce the need to burn oil in the future. The Five-Year Plan (1981-85) for gas is impressive. It is planned to construct some 20,000 kilometers of pipelines served by 232 compressor stations. This building program is far beyond the capacity of Soviet industry, which, in this field too, has been criticized as slow and insufficient. Hence, help is needed from the industrial West, and agreements have been concluded with industries in a number of west European states that will receive future gas deliveries. The gas deal is also important to western Europe in a period of unemployment and to lessen its vulnerability to a future oil crisis.

The problem is whether the project is so big that it will have an impact on the political balance in Europe, and between the power blocs. This prospect raised fears that the United States transformed into practical policies. Until November 1982, the Reagan administration sought to stop or limit the building of the pipeline for transporting gas from the Soviet Union to western Europe.

This attitude would have created difficulties for the Soviet Union if it could have seriously impaired the pipeline project. However, the most severe problems arose in respect to intra-NATO relations. The irritation was clearly and unambiguously voiced in Bonn and Paris, as well as in London. Insofar as a major objective of Soviet foreign policy has been to encourage splits between the United States and its NATO allies, the European consequences of Reagan's gas policy were to the benefit of the Soviet Union — very valuable in a situation when a number of other factors operated to its disadvantage, especially Afghanistan and Poland.

In the summer and fall of 1982, European governments prohibited compliance with the U.S. embargo on the provision of equipment and technology. This threatened a widening rift between the United States and western Europe, and in December, the United States retreated from its adamant position. Both commercial interests and politicians have voiced criticism against using unilateral, compulsory export restrictions for political purposes.

Much of the problem depended on fears that the Soviet Union would, at some time in the future, be able to pressure or blackmail its customers in western Europe, when the project had been completed.

Here also a number of scenarios should be tested. We may exclude the open war scenario, when all peaceful interactions are discontinued. In a protracted struggle the loss of an important energy resource would of course be a serious disadvantage.

For all scenarios the size of energy dependence is a crucial variable. However, gas deliveries will in no way constitute a Soviet monopoly or even predominant role as gas supplier. The Federal Republic of Germany is the key area in the gas deal. The West Germans are expected to depend for 30 percent of their total gas consumption on the Soviet deliveries.

This has raised a number of questions. Is 30 percent a dangerous dependence? President Reagan seemed to think so, but former Chanceller Schmidt said no: "It diversifies the risks inherent in our energy supplies." If the limit is acceptable, is it certain to remain restricted? This is an important question, but to west Europeans whether the Soviets will be able to live up to their undertaking may be a more important question.

Another important question is whether the Soviet need for Western technology and industrial goods will ever be lower than the Western need for Soviet gas. So far, the answer is clearly to the advantage of the West. The future consequences of a gas and pipeline deal depend on a number of political, economic, and technological factors that can hardly be assessed today. Generally, there has been a tendency in many quarters to exaggerate the usefulness of energy as an instrument of political pressure and blackmail. The possibilities of restricting consumption have been underestimated, as have the energy resources available on a global basis.

Without underwriting the belief (expressed in *Sovietskaya Rossiya*, May 11, 1982) that "one should doubtless not be surprised should the United States one fine day 'discover' in the pipes of the gas main Russian soldiers sneaking into Western Europe," it seems nevertheless obvious that the American attitude has been based on uncertain and probably exaggerated fears.

Given the nature of Soviet energy problems, the pipeline to the West and the gas deal seem to be economically and politically stabilizing factors that may postpone or reduce an energy crisis in the USSR. For those in the West who prefer stability to instability, this is a positive factor; for those who, on balance, prefer measures, that might contribute to undermining the Soviet system, the final evaluation may go in the opposite direction.

CONCLUSIONS

The essence of the arguments here is that, given a reduction of Soviet ability to produce oil, the future Soviet energy situation may depend on Western behavior to a large extent. The quarrel over American high-technology compressor equipment for the Soviet Euopean gas pipeline has been a clear illustration.

However, this is not the whole truth of the interbloc oil balance. It obviously is equally true that the Soviet Union may influence the access of the West to vital energy resources. The so-called Carter Doctrine was formulated in clear recognition of such a possibility. The frantic American preparations to improve a military rapid deployment capability point in the same direction. The Soviet Union enjoys geographical strategic advantages in the Middle East.

The major part of this analysis has been based on the rather uncertain assumption that the Soviet Union would be faced with a situation in which oil resources are insufficient to meet the requirements imposed by its major domestic and external political goals. Yet so far the Soviet Union has muddled through its energy problems with some success.

In a serious oil shortage scenario it is very unlikely that the Soviet Union would rush into solutions involving any serious danger of a major war. The declarations at the 1981 Communist Party Congress indicate an awareness of the problems and of the steps desirable to cope with them: expansion and diversification of energy production.

However, if these policies — with or without Western assistance — prove inadequate, the prospects might be grim. The alternatives would be either to adjust consumption to the resources available or to take some action in order to get better access to external resources. Both solutions could endanger the fulfillment of basic domestic and external political goals.

What if the Soviet energy situation were to worsen? Past experience seems to indicate that domestic consumption is flexible. How much it could be restricted would depend on the situation prevailing at the time. Yet it would be difficult for the Soviets to pay hard currency for imports of oil. To abstain from importing grain could create internal problems, and to refrain from high-technology goods would reduce the pace of industrial development, not least in such favored branches as defense and the exploration of outer space. In eastern Europe the Soviet military might increase its strength in order to anticipate problems arising if Soviet energy supplies were reduced. In any case, the last thing that the Soviet Union would be likely to reduce is its military power.

If power alone, not energy and economics, were to constitute the major instrument of assuring control of eastern Europe, the role of the military would be increased, possibly with implications for the Soviet state. In the long run the Roman consolation may not be enough: *Oderint dum metuant* (Let them hate, if only they fear). Increased Soviet military preoccupation with controlling the eastern European clients might reduce Soviet capability of undertaking other interventions. It is, however, also beyond any doubt that it would create a most unfavorable atmosphere in Europe for future détente policies.

NOTES

1. The material in this section on the Soviet markets and their significance for security policy follow a pattern elaborated by Erik Moberg in *Sovjet, oljemakt med problem* (Soviet, Oil Power with Problems) (Stockholm: Centralförbundet Folk och Försvar, 1980).

2. Cf. K. E. Wädekin, "Soviet Agriculture's Dependence on the West," *Foreign Affairs* (Spring 1982), vol. 60, pp. 882-903.

6

OIL AND SECURITY IN THE MIDDLE EAST: THE FRENCH-IRAQI CASE

Guy de Carmoy

Franco-Iraqi relations were put in the limelight on June 7, 1981, when Israeli F-16 planes destroyed the Iraqi nuclear research reactor installed by France. These relations should be analyzed in the wider geopolitical context of the Middle East and of the changing position of Iraq in this area. France, which since 1967 had pursued a pro-Arab policy, was eager to supply Iraq with civilian and military equipment in payment for its oil imports, which had increased in volume and in price since 1973. In 1975 it signed a nuclear cooperation agreement. As the reactor was nearing completion, Israel launched a campaign to arouse Western public opinion against the deal, then undertook a preemptive action. Israel was condemned by the UN Security Council. The larger issue of the value of the nuclear safeguards provided by the Nonproliferation Treaty (NPT) was once more debated while tension in the Middle East increased and Iraqi oil supplies to France fell to a trickle in the wake of the Iraq-Iran war.

EUROPE AND THE MIDDLE EAST

In an industrial system based on growing consumption of primary energy, the supply of oil is essential to economic viability,

123

and therefore to security. Thus the defense of Europe is linked to the political balance of its main oil-supplying area, the Persian Gulf states, even though the Middle East is outside the geographical limits of the Atlantic Alliance. This situation induced several European states to establish lasting relations with the oil-producing countries.

The nature of these relations changed when concessionary arrangements were dismantled through nationalization. Bilateral agreements between sovereign states replaced concession contracts. Higher oil prices entailed trade deficits for which the oil-importing countries tried to compensate through the sale of arms and equipment. Conversely, the oil-producing countries were eager to develop an industrial base and to protect themselves against the encroachments of their neighbors in an area where superpower rivalry and the continuing Arab-Israeli conflict created tension and insecurity even during the periods between recurring local wars. Purchases of equipment and arms required government decisions because they were part of an economic development plan or of a defense policy program.

Direct oil exports by OPEC national companies accounted for 50 percent of their total exports in 1980. Supplies to the major oil companies decreased as a consequence. Among the key OPEC exporters, Iraq sold the largest proportion of its oil on a government level (60 percent), followed by Libya (30 percent).[1] Consumer governments involved in direct oil purchases were mostly Mediterranean countries with strong state-owned oil companies, notably France, Italy, and Spain.

The lasting Arab-Israeli conflict and intra-Arab rivalries were the major causes of the quantitative and qualitative increases in arms purchases by the Middle East countries. In 1977-80 Middle East arms imports accounted for 32 percent of world imports of major weapons and for 43 percent of imports of major weapons in the Third World. The United States (43.3 percent), and the Soviet Union (27.4 percent) were the main suppliers, followed by France (10.8 percent), Italy (4.0 percent), Britain (3.7 percent), and West Germany (3.0 percent).[2] Six Middle East countries topped the list of arms purchasers during that period: Iran, Saudi Arabia, Jordan, Syria, Iraq, and Libya. The United States had set the example by its huge arms deals with Iran (up to the revolution) and with Saudi Arabia. Israel was also a major purchaser of American arms.

IRAQ AND ITS MIDDLE EAST RELATIONS SINCE 1968

The Baathist regime came to power in 1968 under the leadership of Ahmed Hassan al-Bakr and Saddam Hussein. Iraq's inclination to involve itself in fighting with Israel was limited by the protracted campaign to suppress the Kurdish rebellion and by border disputes with Iran, Kuwait, and Syria. Iraqi forces were not heavily committed in the 1967 and 1973 wars. Since 1968 Iraq has been militarily dependent upon the Soviet Union. Military aid culminated with the 1972 Treaty of Friendship and Cooperation.[3] In December 1977, one month after Anwar Sadat's spectacular visit to Israel, Iraq took part in the Tripoli conference of the Arab countries, opposing any rapprochement with Israel. But Iraq, owing to its disputes with Syria, refused to join the latter and the other signatories of the Front of Steadfastness and Confrontation: Algeria, Libya, and South Yemen.[4] In November 1978, Iraq and Syria were reconciled at the Baghdad conference that condemned the Camp David agreements — a short-lived reconciliation that was broken in 1979. In 1978 the fight by the Baath against the Iraqi Communist Party was a factor in the cooling of Soviet-Iraqi relations. Despite the Iraq-Iran treaty of 1975, the Baathist government, a minority Sunni Muslim regime, was concerned about the rise to power of the fundamentalist Shia regime in Iran after the fall of the shah. Saddam Hussein launched a war against Iran in October 1980. Iraq has been supported in this fight by the conservative Persian Gulf states and opposed by the Soviet backed regimes, notably by Syria, which in 1980 signed a Treaty of Friendship and Cooperation with the Soviet Union. Following the outbreak of the war, the Soviet Union stopped its arms deliveries to Iraq. A certain disengagement ensued. Nonetheless Iraq, while trading with the United States and being fascinated with its technology, did not reestablish diplomatic relations. An attitude of nonalignment certainly suits the policy of President Saddam Hussein, who succeeded Fidel Castro in November 1982 as chairman of the Conference of Nonaligned Nations.[5]

Iraq's proved oil reserves rank sixth in the world, far behind Saudi Arabia, Kuwait, and Iran but close to the reserves of the Soviet Union and of the United States. Prospects for the extension of potential reserves are favorable. Prior to nationalization in 1972, Iraqi oil was exploited by the Iraq Petroleum Company (IPC), the capital stock of which was shared jointly by British, American, and French major oil companies, the French share being 23.7 percent. After nationalization, the Iraqi government pursued a policy of maximizing oil revenues. Production rose from 99 million tons (m.t.) in 1973 to a maximum of 168 m.t. in 1979. It fell back to 138 m.t. in 1980 after the start of the war against Iran. The fall was much more drastic – to 45 m.t. – in 1981, curtailing the supplies to Iraq's traditional clients in Europe and especially to France.

THE FRENCH QUEST FOR OIL

Since the Six Day War in 1967, France had engaged in an openly pro-Arab policy. One of its first actions was to lift the ban on delivery of arms to Iraq in 1968. France quickly accepted the decision on IPC nationalization, and on June 18, 1972, signed a ten-year agreement with Iraq under which Compagnie Française des Pétroles (CFP) was entitled to buy 23.75 percent of the production of the former IPC fields. Thus the French retained privileged access to Iraqi oil and the Iraqis acquired French goodwill. Saddam Hussein, in an interview in *Le Monde* on June 20, 1972, stated that he wanted to see Iraq's relations with France raised to the level of those with the Soviet Union.[6] In 1973, Iraq was France's second supplier of oil after Saudi Arabia, with 13.8 percent of French imports. In 1980 the proportion was raised to 21.6 percent (23.8 m.t.), with the same ranking. In 1981 it fell to 2.5 percent because of the Iraq-Iran war. The share of Saudi Arabia increased accordingly, from 35.4 percent to 50 percent.

An extensive economic and technical agreement was signed between France and Iraq in March 1974. In the military sector, during 1977-80 France sold 60 Mirage F-1 planes, about 100 helicopters of various types, defense systems, radar, and missiles. Negotiations are under way for the delivery of several units of the Mirage 2000. In the civilian sector, France reaped an important contract for the construction of the new Baghdad airport. It built steel, aluminum, and cement plants. In 1978 and in 1979, France was the third-ranked exporter of civilian equipment to Iraq after West Germany and Japan.[7] Total military and civilian contracts with Iraq signed in 1980 reached 26.3 billion francs.[8] French exports included the delivery of the controversial nuclear research reactor.

THE NUCLEAR RESEARCH CONTRACT

In October 1969, Iraq ratified the NPT and agreed in 1972 to submit to the control of the International Atomic Energy Agency (IAEA). In November 1975, Iraq signed a nuclear cooperation agreement with France a few months after signing one of the same type with the Soviet Union. By 1981-82 France was to deliver a nuclear research center comprising a 70-megawatt reactor named Osiraq derived from the Osiris reactor at Saclay, France, and an 800-megawatt Isis power reactor. The research center at Tamuz, near Baghdad, was to accommodate up to 600 engineers and technicians. Iraqi engineers would be trained in France. The contract provided that the materials, equipment, facilities, and the fissile materials produced should not be used for military purposes.[9] The reactor was of the swimming pool type, all equipment being immediately visible. It was to be fueled with uranium enriched at 93 percent. Deliveries were programmed to correspond to the needs of the reactor. On their arrival in Iraq the nuclear fuels were irradiated; they were therefore handled at a distance and not usable as material for a bomb. A first delivery of 12 kilograms of enriched uranium took place in September 1980, too small a quantity for a bomb.[10] Early in 1976, Italy signed an agreement with Iraq concerning the chemistry of uranium and of the transuraniums. A contract of February 1978 provided for the delivery of four laboratories, including a "hot cell" for the extraction of limited quantities of plutonium.

Two motives come to mind for the Iraqi nuclear contract: knowledge and defense. Developing countries want to raise their scientific, technical, and industrial base. One purpose of the reactor was for Iraq to become, over time, the scientific center of the Arab world. "Iraq as an ambitious and rich developing country certainly wanted nuclear technology for its own sake."[11] The Iraqi rejection in 1979 of a French offer to replace enriched uranium with "Caramel," a feebly enriched fissile material unusable for military purposes, could at the time be seen as suspicious. So might the purchase from Italy of a "hot cell." In any event, within a matter of years the country would have hundreds of highly trained technicians able to launch a military project without external assistance.

ISRAEL'S PUBLIC OPINION CAMPAIGN AND PREEMPTIVE BOMBINGS

In July 1980, Israel started an extensive campaign to arouse public opinion in western Europe and in the United States against the Franco-Iraqi deal. This followed two actions generally attributed to Israeli agents. In April 1979 several unidentified men blew up the core of one of the reactors intended for Iraq at the assembly site near Toulon, France. In June 1980, one of Iraq's leading nuclear scientists, Egyptian-born Yahia el-Meshad, was found beaten to death in his Paris hotel room. In August 1980, Foreign Minister Yitzhak Shamir expressed Israel's profound concern over the nuclear agreement. Was it a warning that "the Israelis might launch a preemptive strike against Baghdad's nuclear installations"?[12]

The French Ministry of Foreign Affairs issued a statement on July 29, 1980, underlining the precautions inserted in the contract with Iraq and observing that most research reactors in the world were operated on enriched uranium.[13] Previously the ministry had published a list of 34 countries that so far had imported 78 research reactors of the same type as Osiraq, most of them of American construction. The list included "sensitive" countries such as South Africa, South Korea, India, Iran, Pakistan, and Israel.[14]

The controversy called attention to Israel's own nuclear capability and to its refusal to sign the NPT. French aid was instrumental in setting up Israel's secret nuclear facility at Demona in the 1960s. According to a 1974 CIA report made public in 1978, Israel had then produced nuclear weapons. Former Israeli President Ephraim Katzir was quoted as saying to visiting science writers in 1974 that Israel had "the potential to produce atomic weapons."[15]

Israel took delivery of the first American F-16 fighter bombers in the spring of 1980. Thus Osiraq came within the range of Israel's air force. The decision to bomb the Iraqi plant was taken in October 1980, after the Israelis failed to persuade the French government to discontinue its association with Iraq. The actual bombing of the Iraqi research center took place on June 7, 1981, and was successful. The American AWACS radar planes in use in Saudi Arabia did not detect the overflight of the Israeli bombers. The Soviet-supplied missiles and interceptors located in Iraq failed to respond to the attack. Prime Minister Begin claimed that the raid had been "literally a survival operation."

The fundamental question then was whether Iraq had an opera-
tional nuclear capability at the time. The director of the IAEA,
Sigvard Eklund, said that recent on-site inspections had shown no
misuse of nuclear materials by Iraq, and on June 9 issued an official
statement condemning the Israeli raid. In agency circles, it was
mentioned that the Iraqis would not have been able to manufacture
an atomic bomb for at least a decade.[16] On June 11, the Commissariat
à l'Energie Atomique in Paris issued a communiqué stating that the
research and development program at Tamuz was implemented
jointly by the French and foreign teams. Assuming a breach of their
commitments, the Iraqis would not have been able to produce
significant quantities of fissile material for military use because the
French would have cut the supply of enriched uranium. According
to the research contract, French cooperation was to be pursued on
site until 1989 – a provision that had been kept secret.[17] Last,
Iraq had no plane nor missile capable of launching a bomb.

CONDEMNATION OF ISRAEL BY THE UN SECURITY COUNCIL

President François Mitterrand, in an interview on June 18, 1981,
with the *Washington Post*, condemned the Israeli raid. He had pro-
tested the 1975 contract. He ignored the existence of the provision
on continuous French cooperation. He felt that "no demonstration
had been made of a possible diversion by Iraq of nuclear technology
for military purposes." He stressed that he was a friend of Israel
and reminded the interviewer that he was the only French statesman
who headed a major political party to have approved the Camp
David accords. He asked for condemnation of the raid by the UN
Security Council.[18] The French representative to the council stated
that it was not by ignoring the guarantees offered by the international community "that Israel would be recognized by its neighbors as a trustworthy partner."[19]

By a unanimous vote on June 19, the Security Council condemned
Israel for an outright violation of the UN Charter. It considered the
attack as a serious threat to the system of guarantees of the IAEA,
which were the basis of the NPT, and asked Israel to place its own
nuclear facilities under the control of the IAEA. Last, the council
recognized the inalienable right of Iraq and of all other developing
states to launch nuclear development programs in order to expand
their economy and their industry for peaceful purposes.[20] No
sanctions were imposed on Israel.

SITUATION IN THE MIDDLE EAST AFTER THE BOMBING

In a few lines *The Economist* encapsulated the international scope of the June 7 air raid:

> A state [Iraq] which has subjected itself to NPT safeguards, and was still apparently observing the rules, has been attacked by another state [Israel] which has rejected the Treaty and is thought to be well on the way to the bomb — and the second state claimed that the first had been posing a nuclear threat at it.

The journal then observed that this will not encourage adherence to NPT or wholehearted compliance with its safeguard system. Non-NPT countries (India, Pakistan, South Africa) may be confirmed in their belief that the treaty cannot offer them any security, and signatories of the treaty such as Libya and Syria may reconsider their position.[21]

As a matter of fact, the nuclear potential for civilian and military use is increasing in the Middle East. In 1975 Libya bought a research reactor from the Soviet Union, and later a power plant. It is making substantial purchases of uranium from Niger as a stockpile. Egypt embarked on a massive uranium research project with the help of West Germany. Since its ratification of the NPT in 1981, Egypt has ordered nuclear power stations from Germany, France, and the United States. Britain supplied a research center for Cairo University. Saudi Arabia laid plans for a research center to be supplied by the United States. Pakistan is reported to have built an enrichment plant and a reprocessing plant.[22] It probably is well on the way to mastering the atom bomb in its efforts to emulate India.

In the aftermath of the bombing, Iraq raised the nuclear stakes. On June 23, Saddam Hussein called on all the peace- and security-loving states to help the Arabs acquire the atom bomb in order to face the bomb the Israelis already had. On June 28 he reiterated his call for an Arab nuclear weapon so as to deter Israel from the use of its own weapon and to establish a nuclear balance between the adversaries. The Israelis were quick to pick up Hussein's statement as an avowal and as a justification for the raid.[23]

PROSPECTS FOR FRENCH-IRAQI RELATIONS

The Israeli bombing strained French-Iraqi relations. The debate centered on the conditions of the reconstruction of the Tamuz reactor. The French position was based on two principles: the right of Third World countries to nuclear technology and the installation of adequate safeguards against military use. President Mitterrand stressed the point in his June 18, 1981, statement. Saddam Hussein was asking France to adopt a clearer position; if France was not prepared to rebuild the reactor, then Iraq would approach other countries.[24] In the course of his September visit to Saudi Arabia, President Mitterrand indicated that France agreed in principle to the reconstruction, which was to be financed by Saudi Arabia.[25] But the French insisted on supplying the future reactor with the low-grade "Caramel" fuel that the Iraqis had refused in 1979. A break in the negotiations would destroy French credibility with Iraq and other Arab states, leading to the cancellation of military contracts. An acquiescence to Iraq's request for enriched uranium would destroy the new friendship for Israel proclaimed by the French president. Cynics observe that there is no separation between the materials, the facilities, and the know-how necessary to make bombs and those necessary to produce electricity. Nuclear capacity relies essentially on the training of a sufficiently large team of technicians. There is agreement on one point: the future plant should be built deep enough underground to be protected from a possible air attack. But the setback of Iraq in its war against Iran is postponing the reconstruction issue.

THE NPT AND THE ATLANTIC ALLIANCE

The attack of June 7, 1981, drew the attention of public opinion to the risks of proliferation and the fragility of the safeguards, and raised doubts about the ability of the IAEA to detect a diversion of fissile materials.

The sound implementation of the NPT is a security factor for the Atlantic Alliance. Various member countries are of necessity involved in the dual and interlocking aspects of nuclear energy: the possession of nuclear weapons and prevention of their use, on the one hand, and the development and use of nuclear-generated electricity and the export of nuclear technology, on the other hand.

Three alliance member states possess nuclear weapons: the United States and Britain, which were the promoters of the NPT, and France, which did not sign the treaty but stated its intention to apply its provisions regarding relations with nonnuclear countries.

Four member states are exporters of nuclear technology: the United States, Canada, France, and West Germany.

The American policy regarding the production and export of such technology for civilian use has differed from that of the European countries. In 1977, President Carter convened the Conference on International Fuel Cycle Evaluation to assess the impact on proliferation of the development of the breeder reactor and of the setting up of plants for the reprocessing of irradiated fuels. The conference concluded in 1980 that such equipment would contribute to meeting the energy needs of the industrialized countries and to reducing their dependence on imported oil. The 1980 economic summit at Venice endorsed this statement. Thus the American non-proliferation policy was no longer an obstacle to the development of the breeder and of reprocessing plants in Europe. In 1981 President Reagan took a position in favor of the resumption of both technologies in the United States.

Caution remained in order regarding the acquisition by developing countries of civilian nuclear technologies considered a possible means to a nuclear weapons option and to the spread of the "plutonium economy." Negotiations between the United States and its allies led to de facto arrangements according to which Germany could engage in nuclear cooperation with Brazil and Argentina, and France with South Africa and Iraq, provided the safeguard rules were observed.

All the members of the Atlantic Alliance have a direct interest in preventing nuclear weapons proliferation in the Middle East because of the security of vital oil imports from the area to western Europe and, to a lesser extent, to the United States. The danger of a nuclear war developing out of the conflicts in the Middle East could have a medium-term effect on the economic security of the Atlantic Alliance far more than did local conventional wars. It is therefore more urgent than ever that the United States come to grips with the Arab-Israeli conflict, the root of which is the Palestinian question.

NOTES

1. IFRI, *Ramsès 1981, Le second choc pétrolier* (Paris: IFRI, 1981), p. 59.

2. *SIPRI Yearbook 1981*, pp. 106, 179.

3. Claudia Wright, "Iraq, New Power in the Middle East," *Foreign Affairs*, Winter 1979-80, p. 263.

4. J. C. Hurewitz, "Arab Regional Politics and the Dispute with Israel," in Robert O. Friedman, ed., *World Politics and the Arab Israeli Conflict* (New York: Pergamon Press, 1979), p. 122.

5. Philippe Rondot, "L'Irak: Une puissance régionale en devenir," *Politique étrangère* 3 (1980): 650.

6. Edith Penrose and E. F. Penrose, *Iraq, International Relations and National Development* (London: Ernest Benn Boulder Westview Press, 1978), pp. 433-35.

7. J. M. Quatrepoint, "L'Irak a pris la place qu'occupair l'Iran dans le commerce extérieur de l'Europe et du Japon," *Le Monde*, April 3, 1980.

8. "L'Irak deviendrait le premier client de Paris au Proche Orient," *Le Monde*, October 3, 1981.

9. Xavier Weeger, "Les relations nucléaires franco-irakiennes," *Le Monde*, July 31, 1980.

10. "Paris a récemment livré à Bagdad une première charge d'uranium très enrichi," *Le Monde*, September 26, 1980.

11. Richard Johns, "Lengthening List of Nuclear Powers," *Financial Times*, June 10, 1980.

12. "Fallout from a Nuclear Deal," *Newsweek*, August 11, 1980.

13. *Le Monde*, July 31, 1980.

14. Charles Hargrove, "France Rejects Criticism of Its Nuclear Pact with Iraq," *The Times*, July 18, 1980.

15. Edward Cody, "French-Iraqi Deal Spurs Israeli Nuclear Planning," *International Herald Tribune*, July 23, 1980.

16. Joseph Fitchett, "France Condemns Attack, Sees Effect on Relations," *International Herald Tribune*, July 10, 1981.

17. "L'Irak a-t-il violé le Traité de Non-Prolifération nucléaire? *Le Monde*, June 13, 1981.

18. "M. Mitterrand condamne à nouveau l'attaque israélienne mais s'oppose à des sanctions," *Le Monde*, June 19, 1981.

19. "La France demande la condamnation du raid israélien," *Le Monde*, July 17, 1981.

20. "Le Conseil de Sécurité a 'vigoureusement condamné' le raid israélien sur Tamuz," *Le Monde*, June 21, 1981.

21. "Nearer a Multinuclear World," *The Economist*, June 13, 1981.

22. Judith Perera, "Pandora's Box," *The Middle East*, August 1981.

23. Francois Cornu, "Jerusalem: Un aveu," *Le Monde*, June 25, 1981; Edward Cody, "Iraq's Hussein Seeks Better U.S. Relations," *International Herald Tribune*, June 30, 1981.

24. Michel Bolé-Richard, "Les suites du raid israélien sur Tamuz," *Le Monde*, June 21, 1981.

25. Paul Joly, "Les Saoudiens ont aimé la franchise de Mitterrand," *France Soir*, September 29, 1981.

7

MEXICAN OIL AND THE WESTERN ALLIANCE

Edward F. Wonder

INTRODUCTION

The recent discovery of Mexico by oil consumers and oil analysts alike has drawn attention to the energy, economic, and political implications of growing Mexican oil production. The first question asked, as it is every time a new source of oil appears on the scene, was all too familiar, and all too misleading. Will this be the straw to break the OPEC back? This scenario of a new supply source as deus ex machina dominated the initial reactions in the United States to the announcement of large oil discoveries in Mexico in the mid-1970s. Not only was there a "new Saudi Arabia," but it very conveniently was located in Uncle Sam's back yard, and thus would be a new river of oil, separate from the OPEC system and politically very secure.[1]

The prospect of all that oil just south of the border spawned a host of proposals from U.S. commentators and politicians for the establishment of a North American common market or accord, or at the least a U.S.-Mexican special relationship in which some sort of package deal, trading off between energy, trade, and immigration, could be struck so that the United States would be assured a secure supply of oil. For those advocating such an approach, and then-candidate Ronald Reagan at least raised the idea, there were as many, if not more, attacking this concept as insensitive to the realities of oil politics in Mexico, and even as undesirable from the standpoint of broader U.S. foreign policy interests.

This latter argument was intriguing, because its proponents maintained that special relationships involving oil were counter-productive, and specifically that a U.S.-Mexican special relation-ship would send all the wrong signals to U.S. allies and adversaries. At best, the United States would appear to be leaving its less ad-vantaged allies to fend for themselves in securing their oil supply, and might thus drive them deeper into the arms of Persian Gulf and North African states. At worst, it might tempt the Soviet Union into believing the United States would no longer resist Soviet en-croachment in the Persian Gulf, since that region would no longer be so crucial to U.S. energy security.

The broader underlying issue — the potentially divisive impact on the Western alliance of a competition for access to oil via special relationships with particular supplier states — was not a new one. Secretary of State Henry Kissinger, in several speeches and inter-views in the wake of the October 1973 embargo, had warned that if the West did not recognize its interdependence, the alliance could disintegrate in the face of rivalries "in which each region will try to maximize its own special advantages," leading to inevitable tests of strength.[2] Eight years later, in the spring of 1982, amid renewed talk of OPEC's imminent collapse, falling oil prices, and a world-wide oil glut, Kissinger's remarks seem a bit anachronistic. None-theless, the theme of competition for oil that he articulated continues to influence the debate on oil and foreign policy. Its relevance to Mexico merits examination.

Despite the growing number of studies on Mexican oil policy, and U.S.-Mexican energy relations, relatively little attention has been paid to the alliance context of Mexican oil. The importance of this broader context stems from a number of factors. Several European countries, Japan, and Canada have signed sizable oil contracts with Mexico, and are actively seeking investment and export opportunities in Mexico. Moreover, many of these countries find themselves aligned with Mexico, or at least more sympathetic to the Mexican rather than the U.S. perspective, on how to deal with economic, political, and security problems in Central America. By the same token, while one must be careful not to overstate the argument, the existence of significant oil resources in the region has clearly affected both U.S. perceptions of the stakes involved in the region and the diplomatic assertiveness of Mexico, and has influenced Mexico's role in regional and even transatlantic maneuvering over Central America.

The discussion here of Mexican oil and the Atlantic Alliance is a very preliminary one, and is intended to raise questions as much as to answer them. Clearly, given the challenges and opportunities that oil poses for Mexican political and economic development, the contribution Mexican oil exports can make to diversifying international oil trade, the problems of integrating an industrializing country like Mexico into the international trade regime, and the potential dangers lurking in Central America, the questions are worthy of much more extensive consideration than can be attempted here.

Several areas of inquiry frame this analysis. Insofar as the competition/special relationship thesis implies that consumer states can influence suppliers' policies, one must ask what the principal determinants of Mexican oil production and export policy are. How susceptible to consumer state influence is that policy? Second, how significant is Mexican oil for the energy needs of the United States and those of its allies? What is the global significance of that supply? Third, what form has consumer state competition taken in regard to Mexico, and what problems, if any, does it pose for the alliance? Finally, how does Mexican oil figure, directly or indirectly, in the diplomatic dynamics of Western responses to Central American and Caribbean affairs?

MEXICO'S OIL POLICY: SOURCES AND CONSTRAINTS

Almost nine years have passed since the discoveries near Villahermosa in 1972 ushered in the modern era of Mexican oil. Almost six decades have come and gone since Mexico's first and short-lived rise to world oil prominence in the 1920s. The nationalization of the oil industry in 1938, which assured oil a central place in Mexican politics, occurred over 40 years ago. Oil production in Mexico is thus not a new phenomenon. Only its discovery by oil analysts is new.

Mexico, thanks to the Iranian revolution and Iran-Iraq war, climbed in 1981 into fourth place among world crude producers, with oil production averaging 2.38 million barrels per day (mbd) for the year. Oil exports averaged 1.1 mbd in 1981. Both figures were below their respective targets for 1981, a result of slumping world demand. The percentage increase in production and exports over the previous year was less than that achieved in 1980. This short-term setback in no way detracts from Mexico's significance for world oil, however.

Official Mexican figures place total hydrocarbon resources at approximately 250 billion barrels of oil equivalent, with proven reserves at least 72 billion barrels of oil equivalent and another 80 billion barrels of probable (somewhat less assured than proven) reserves. Much of the expectation that Mexico was another Saudi Arabia may have stemmed from a confusion of Mexican total potential resources with Saudi reserves. The rapid increase in Mexican estimates — in 1973 reserves were put at 5.4 billion barrels — may have encouraged analysts to overlook this point.

These estimates must be interpreted carefully, and viewed with caution. First, Mexican figures combine oil and gas in a ratio of 65:35 oil to gas, so that oil accounts for two-thirds of the total. Moreover, the conversion ratio of gas to barrels-of-oil-equivalent used by Petroleos Mexicanos (PEMEX) may overstate the oil portion of the total by 20 percent. There are also questions regarding what is included in the reserve category, though drill data have ultimately supported reserve claims. Very importantly, over 110 billion barrels of the above resource total are located in the Chicontepec field, which presents very difficult reservoir characteristics and low productivity per well, and thus high development costs. As a result, this area should be considered quite apart from the rest. Nonetheless, the extremely high productivity of wells in the Bay of Campeche and the steady flow in Chiapas and Tabasco, the first area of major discoveries in the 1970s, are indicative of the richness of Mexican oil fields. While there is some disagreement over the accuracy of Mexican reserve claims (both sides of the question are argued — that the claims are inflated, and that they are consciously deflated), the experience to date with new discoveries, and the potential for huge structures offshore, make the question about Mexico not whether it will be a major oil actor, but how great a one.

One factor frequently overlooked is the quality of the oil. Mexico exports two blends — one called Isthmus, produced by blending crudes produced onshore, and an offshore blend called

Maya. While the former is of fairly high quality (although not of North Sea or Nigerian standards), the latter most assuredly is not, and requires expensive refining technology to process it into products more marketable and valuable than the large quantities of heavy fuel oil produced in refineries without this upgrading equipment. Maya has posed considerable problems for refiners, and how much Maya is exported relative to Isthmus is a particularly sensitive point in oil dealings with Mexico.

The significance of the previous points is not solely technical. Indeed, although in recent years the regularity with which reserve additions have been announced has kept world attention riveted on Mexico, often overlooked is the fact that publicizing these additions serves various political and economic ends.[3] These include maintaining the confidence of the international financial community in Mexico's creditworthiness, bolstering PEMEX's power in the bureaucracy, justifying politically the government's production and export program in the face of conservationist and nationalist sentiments, and increasing Mexican bargaining leverage vis-à-vis industrialized consumer states. It was no coincidence that major discoveries were revealed in 1976 and 1977, when the newly installed Lopez Portillo government had to restore the confidence of domestic business leaders, the International Monetary Fund (IMF), and other creditors in the government's ability to curb inflation, end capital flight, and reduce excessive external borrowing. Thus, the timing of announcements of new discoveries may not be without an element of calculation.

Economics and Politics of Oil

One can view the foregoing technical factors as establishing both opportunities and underlying constraints on what is physically possible in oil production. Economic and social factors, however, have exerted a determining influence on actual Mexican policy. Disequilibrium in the external sector of the Mexican economy, domestic inflation, and the revenue needs of industrialization and economic development have been especially important. Oil market conditions are also becoming more important. Among these, the external sector of the economy has been particularly important.[4] Problems in the external sector encouraged the expansion of production and exports in the first years of the Lopez Portillo government, because the economic strategy of the preceding Echeverria government, which depended heavily on external borrowing and on an expansionary monetary policy, had resulted in a rising external public debt, high inflation, and a serious current account deficit, leading to imposition of an austerity program by the IMF in 1977. Oil exports offered a means of rectifying this situation and relieving IMF pressure on Mexican economic policy. A six-year plan for oil and gas announced in 1976 called for almost tripling production, with half of this output to be exported.

The external sector of the economy remains a crucial factor in policy making for oil, and is perhaps becoming even more important in the depressed oil market of 1982. Rapidly growing oil export revenues have been a primary source of funds for an economic development strategy that has stressed heavy industrialization requiring large volumes of capital goods, many of which must be imported. Whatever cannot be paid for with foreign exchange from oil exports must be financed with foreign borrowing.

The relationship between the two can be seen in recent developments. Foreign borrowing requirements have risen considerably in 1982 as oil export revenues have fallen below projected levels. In 1980 PEMEX had projected oil revenues for 1982 at the level of $27 billion. The Banco de Mexico, in early 1982, estimated they might reach $13 billion, less than in 1981.[5] This creates added pressure for more borrowing.

Mexico has the second largest external debt among the industrializing states; it exceeds $70 billion, and is steadily rising. The ratio of external debt service to exports fell from 53 percent in 1978 to 29 percent in 1980, but has begun to rise as foreign borrowing has expanded. In real terms, the value of manufactured exports is falling, while the share of oil and gas export revenues has risen to over 70 percent of all export revenues. Moreover, PEMEX is a major foreign borrower and the source of almost 45 percent of expenditures in the state-affiliated sector of the economy. Oil also supplies over 22 percent of total public sector revenues.[6]

This relative dependence on oil revenues is a source of concern within Mexico's ruling circles. Whether Mexico is in danger of becoming too dependent on oil revenues, as have other major oil exporters, is a matter of continuing debate. President Lopez Portillo went out of his way in his September 1981 State of the Union

Address to stress that Mexico was not becoming a "petrolized" economy.[7] The "petrolization" argument has been used by critics of rapid expansion of production and exports.

Inflation is a growing problem in Mexico, which, like other oil exporters, has discovered that the short-run impact of rapid expansion of oil production can be inflationary because of the cost of required capital goods and bottlenecks in the economy.[8] The official Mexican inflation rate had been 30 percent through 1981, and higher in the oil-producing areas, but the rate of increase in the Mexican consumer price index in the first quarter of 1982 was equivalent to 60 percent on an annual basis. Inflation created pressures to devalue the peso, as Mexico did in early 1982, but this is a very sensitive step politically, in part because of the impact of devaluation on the cost of food imports and real wages. Domestic politics impede efforts to fight inflation, while oil exports tend to contribute to inflation. (For example, the economic "austerity" plan accompanying the devaluation contained wage hikes of up to 40 percent for some workers.) The potential trade-offs between reducing inflation and maintaining an economic growth rate sufficiently high to please political factions place Mexico in a difficult situation.

The third factor, foreign borrowing, has already been introduced. Mexico borrowed over $18 billion in 1981, almost $6 billion greater than anticipated at the start of the year as a result of falling oil revenues in the second half of the year. Greater dependence on foreign debt increases Mexican vulnerability to world economic trends, and imposes on Mexico a requirement to maintain the confidence of its creditors. A steady flow of oil export revenues is one of the principal means of doing so.

Oil revenues are of critical importance to Mexico's economic development. Oil is seen as Mexico's chance to make the leap to industrialization. The pace and financial requirements of economic development, and not reserve size or export demand, will have a much greater impact on oil and gas policy. Mexico's economic development strategy emphasizes indicative planning and the identification of zones of opportunity and target industrial sectors. What complicates the implementation of this strategy, however, is a planning horizon effectively limited to six years (the president's term of office), a bureaucratic structure that confuses lines of responsibility and hierarchy, and a shifting of priorities between capital-intensive industry, subsidized by low domestic energy prices, and agriculture, where output has lagged and poverty and the maldistribution of income are particularly evident.[9]

Both the National Industrial Development Plan, announced in 1979, and the Global Development Plan (1980) make clear that a steady flow of oil export revenues is crucial to Mexican economic development strategy. The two plans, coming at different times and prepared by different ministries, have different emphases and policy priorities. The former is highly specific as to individual industrial sectors to be developed. The latter is much more general, and emphasizes exports of manufactured goods and revival of agriculture. Together, the two plans identify two broad themes that affect oil strategy: sector-specific negotiation of oil for investment packages with oil-consuming states; and diversification of trade and investment patterns in order to reduce Mexican vulnerability to fluctuations in the U.S. economy. Oil is important to both, because it provides Mexico with bargaining leverage, and oil-financed industrialization increases the attractiveness of Mexico as an economic partner for the industrial countries.

The politics of oil in Mexico provide an all-important prism through which the economic influences are filtered. The importance of nationalization — indeed, of the history of Mexican oil production — must not be underestimated. Oil policy and PEMEX, the state-owned oil company holding a monopoly on oil and gas production, refining, and primary petrochemical production, have been subject since 1938 to competing pressures from market and economic efficiency calculations, on the one hand, and politically powerful views, on the other. Thus, oil policy and PEMEX must give priority to a social mission of facilitating economic and social development by subsidizing industry and consumers through low domestic oil and gas prices and by generating revenues for the state, while conservationist principles (supply domestic needs, with minimal exports) should govern production levels.[10] Mexico's historical experience (well-chronicled elsewhere), and the tension between these competing pressures in particular, strongly condition the ways in which Mexican policy makers view the strategic importance of oil for Mexican development, a point to which we shall return shortly.

In utilizing oil revenues to promote economic development, the Mexican political system confronts a major challenge to its capacity to adapt to changing economic and political circumstances.

Despite the prevalent conceptualization of the Mexican political system in authoritarian terms, it has in fact become more open in the sense of political competition, while the distribution of power within the Partido Revolucionario Institucional (PRI), the dominant party, has shifted to favor more professional, middle-class, and technocratic elites prone to view oil as an engine of development. The bureaucracy itself is organized along lines that are more horizontal than vertical, with numerous agencies, often displaying quite different policy philosophies, involved in the same policy area. This frustrates planning, and contributes to frequent shifts in policy emphasis, even during the same administration, as the president seeks to hold together his coalition.

Oil policy in Mexico hardly enjoys unanimous political support. The opposition parties on the Left, though still minor factors politically, have vocally attacked current policy for squandering Mexico's oil resources, and have been particularly critical of exports to the United States. More important, the bureaucracy is divided over oil policy, especially over production plans. The Secretariat of Programming and Budget, the Bank of Mexico, and PEMEX have favored expansion of exports, while the older-line ministries, such as Agriculture and Industrial Development, which are strongholds of conservationist and "social mission" thinking, have advocated a slower approach.

These political divisions over oil policy were apparent in two episodes in 1981. The first involved a PEMEX plan calling for oil production to rise to 2.9 mbd by the end of 1981. The revelation of this plan early in 1981 caused a furor with several other ministries, because PEMEX appeared to be making policy on its own rather than following ministerial directives. As a result, the official ceiling was set at 2.5 mbd only .25 mbd above the target set in 1980 under the revised six-year plan of 1976.

The second occurred in June 1981, when the director general of PEMEX was summarily fired after lowering prices by $4 per barrel in order to retain sales during the oil glut, and the minister of patrimony subsequently sought to restore $2 of this cut. Foreign companies walked away from shipments, and Mexican exports fell by half. Eventually, Mexico reinstated the $4 reduction, and most sales were restored.

These episodes demonstrate several facts of life regarding Mexican oil. First, although PEMEX is an oil company and, as such, is increasingly subject to the discipline of the international market, it is not free from domestic political pressure. PEMEX's perfectly rational response to market forces – to lower its prices – ran against the grain of the position that PEMEX should not behave like just another oil company, but should pay greater heed to domestic political and social influences and needs. (It must also be pointed out that PEMEX's director general, who had his share of political enemies, apparently failed to consult extensively enough before deciding on the price reduction.) Second, as will be discussed later, the tension between international market pressures and domestic political considerations will likely grow in intensity, setting the stage for renewed policy debate. Third, the consequences of growing dependence on oil revenues were made clear by the June episode. The lost sales and lower prices resulting from it, and the subsequent continuation of a depressed world oil market, kept 1981 oil export revenues at approximately $14.5 billion, over $5 billion below the target for 1981. The deficit, consequently, had to be borrowed abroad. The events of June and the following months had the further effect of stimulating internal debate over the stability of an oil-financed economic strategy.

The social backdrop against which oil policy must be made is sobering. Mexico arguably has the worst distribution of income in all of Latin America.[11] The bottom 40 percent of the people receive 10-12 percent of the income, with no real change in this distribution in almost two decades. Under- and unemployment reach 40 percent. The greatest challenge of all to Mexico is to rectify this imbalance amid orderly economic development, political stability, and increasing democratization. Whether this can in fact be accomplished is of fundamental importance, and clearly overshadows questions of how much oil will be available to the United States and the West. Given the scope of this chapter, this question can only be raised here, but for Mexico it is indeed the "bottom line."

Oil Exports

Mexican oil export policy under President Lopez Portillo has come to center on several points: maximizing revenues via high prices rather than by rapid expansion of the volume put into trade; market diversification; and large exports to the United States. Although not a member of OPEC, Mexico has been well placed to follow a free-rider strategy regarding pricing when the international oil market is tight. Mexico did not play the surcharge game, and did not allow its oil to be sold in the spot market. The high prices Mexico was able to charge in 1979 and 1980, and through most of 1981, allowed exports to expand at a more incremental pace. Throughout this period Mexico sought stable, long-term contractual relationships with consumers that would assure steadily expanding markets, and thus revenues, for its oil.

The latest in a series of plans and pronouncements of production ceilings or "platforms" is the National Energy Program, announced in early 1981. The program, while projecting a 78 percent increase in oil output and a 97 percent increase in gas production by 1990 (to 4.1 mbd and 6.9 billion cubic feet per day, respectively), would hold exports at the current target levels — 1.5 mbd of oil and 300 million cubic feet per day of gas — over the same time period. This essentially would pass the issue of raising exports on to the next president. Nonetheless, just before the announcement of the plan, a PEMEX bid to increase production and exports had been rejected, and within a year of issuance of the plan, negotiations with U.S. gas companies to double gas exports were under way, while the Mexican Petroleum Institute (IMP), affiliated with PEMEX, had issued a report calling for abandonment of artificial ceilings and greater sensitivity to market trends and customer preferences.[1,2]

The program also enunciated principles to guide oil policy. No more than 50 percent of oil exports could go to any one country, and Mexico should supply no more than 20 percent of any country's needs. Both principles were intended to alleviate fears that Mexico would sell too much oil to the United States. Several of the program's key premises have already been invalidated. The program proposed that the level of exports be geared to the revenue needs of the 8 percent GDP growth rate (assuming a 5-7 percent per year real increase in oil prices) that Mexico has experienced the past few years, and that was the target for economic policy. Economic growth in 1982 may prove closer to 0 percent, while Mexico has had to shave the price of its oil by nearly $8 per barrel (weighted 50:50 Isthmus to Maya).

Projecting just where Mexican oil production and export policy will go over the next decade is not easy, and rests as much on simple hunches as on calculations. Although some early analyses foresaw production reaching 10 mbd, and exports to the United States alone hitting 3 mbd by the 1990s (the "new Saudi Arabia" thesis), these forecasts rested upon assumptions of reserve levels substantially higher than current levels and an almost unslakable Mexican thirst for foreign exchange and international prestige. Several technical considerations suggest that such levels, if ever reached, would not long be sustained, based on what is now known about Mexico's oil resources.[13] Some factors — such as the current inability of the Mexican gas market to consume all associated gas, thus forcing the Mexican government to flare it, sell it to the United States, or restrain oil production — may be less compelling, since Mexican domestic gas demand is burgeoning, and most flaring is confined to offshore wells for which gas delivery systems to the shore are only now becoming available. The geology of the Chicontepec region would be an important constraint on the high production scenario (8-10 mbd), since the high output levels would require high recovery in Chicontepec, which may be achievable only over very long periods of time and at great expense.

Technical constraints only set some bounds, however. More important are the political and economic factors determining policy choices within these bounds.

The economic factors at play in Mexico — the external sector of the economy, the financial demands of economic growth, and the inflation rate — will be of major, if not overriding, importance. A PEMEX analysis prepared in early 1981 indicated that in a low economic growth scenario of 0-2 percent per year in 1985-2000, with a weakening of nonoil industry, oil exports and production would have to rise substantially to cover foreign borrowing and a worsening current account deficit.[14] Production could reach 8 mbd by 1986 and exports almost 5 mbd, but they would then fall precipitously (based on reserves of 60 billion barrels of crude equivalent), and domestic demand would exceed domestic supply by 2000. With a higher economic growth rate (8 percent per year), nonoil exports presumably would be stronger, with less pressure to raise oil production and exports rapidly but, ironically, domestic demand would rise faster. According to PEMEX's analysis, Mexico would become a "new Saudi Arabia" only where the worst economic circumstances for Mexico compelled it to.

The dramatic shift in the world oil market from tight supply and price leapfrogging to glut and price cutting, coupled with adverse trends in the Mexican economy, may serve to force a revision of the economic framework within which Mexican oil policy is made. Inflation, overvaluation of the peso relative to the dollar, and a flight from pesos into dollars necessitated a 70 percent devaluation of the peso in February 1982, and continued erosion of the peso is likely. Depressed oil export earnings (as well as for other resource exports) precipitated the crisis, because oil exports had been relied upon to prop up the peso. The widening current account deficit and burgeoning external debt further reinforced the urgency of devaluation, which theoretically would help nonoil manufactured exports. The principal cost will be added inflationary pressure resulting from more expensive imports.

Because of infrastructure bottlenecks impeding industrial growth, oil and gas exports offer the only effective near-term means of acquiring large new increments of foreign exchange through trade. However, oil market conditions prevailing in 1982, if they persist, would appear to necessitate a shift in PEMEX strategy toward one based more on volume than on high prices. Since Maya crude is so difficult to refine, retaining the requirement, imposed on customers since mid-1980, that half of the oil imported from Mexico must be Maya would substantially impede sizable expansion of sales. There are already indications that this requirement and export ceilings are being rethought. The IMP report cited previously recommended greater leeway in setting the Isthmus:Maya ratio in the export barrel, and relying more on market forces to determine overall volumes and prices. At May 1982 prices, Mexico would have to sell another 300,000 barrels per day just to recoup the revenue lost through lower prices, and would have to sell more to shrink the size of the current account deficit.

Opting for a more volume-based strategy would have its political costs within Mexico. It would impart greater intensity to the debate on the alleged overdependence of the economy on oil revenues. The Left in Mexico, most notably the Mexican Workers Party, though unable to change the outcome of the 1982 presidential election, sees oil policy as one of the principal electoral issues, and argues for a conservationist policy of minimal exports (perhaps 500,000 barrels per day). Larger overall export volumes could be seen as implying more to the United States. Increasing exports, in general, would run afoul of strong conservationist and nationalist sentiment, and a deliberately rapid expansion could be especially controversial.

How long the Mexican oil era can be sustained is quite another question, in view of the too frequently overlooked factor of domestic demand, currently growing at 10 percent per year. The National Energy Program placed particular emphasis on reducing the growth rate of domestic energy consumption, especially that of oil. That plan had as a goal restraining domestic oil consumption to no more than 2.6 mbd in 1990, with coal picking up much of the rest. The path of least political resistance, however, is to continue subsidizing industry through cheap energy. Even a shift to coal and nuclear energy (Mexico had announced a very ambitious program in this area) to generate electricity still will have only a moderate impact on oil and gas consumption. Burgeoning demand for petrochemical feed stocks, gasoline, and process heat for heavy industry will continue to push up domestic oil demand. Exports could decline in the 1990s in order to free oil for domestic demand unless reserve additions continue at a high pace.

Just what level of exports will be realized is difficult to say, given the uncertainty of the market, the prospect of perhaps no economic growth rather than the 8 percent assumed in Mexico for planning purposes, and the as yet unmeasured political strength of domestic critics of rapid expansion of production and exports. However, it appears increasingly probable that the recent projections found in more tempered analyses of Mexican oil policy – perhaps 2.5 mbd of oil exports in 1985 and 5.5 mbd overall production – will be reached before that date under the weight of economic needs.[15] It remains just as probable, in the opinion of this observer, that the "new Saudi Arabia" thesis will not be validated.

MEXICO AND THE WORLD OIL SYSTEM

There is little if any doubt that Mexico will play a significant role in the world oil market. Exxon foresees Mexico as accounting for much of the increase in production outside OPEC, and a number of studies now see OPEC output as holding fairly steady in the 23-25 mbd range.[16] It is not likely, however, that Mexican production will have the OPEC-busting impact envisioned by the proponents of the "new Saudi Arabia" thesis. What Mexico will provide is a new and presumably secure source of incremental oil that will help cushion the world market. In the process, an important but by no means preponderant portion of U.S. needs will be met.

As exports expand, PEMEX's behavior will likely become increasingly sensitive to international market conditions, especially under a technocratic presidential administration, creating tension between the need to be responsive to these conditions and domestic political forces. The selection of Miguel de la Madrid Huerta, the head of the Planning and Budget Secretariat and just such a technocrat, as the PRI's presidential candidate, and thus as the next president, suggests that, within limits, PEMEX will operate on the basis of economic efficiency calculations. Under de la Madrid's direction, the Planning Secretariat has stressed the importance of securing a steady stream of oil export revenues and the operation of state and private enterprises along more technocratic/economic efficiency lines. Thus, international market conditions may provide an increasingly important external factor, joining internally generated economic and political ones, in influencing Mexican oil policy.

The constraining effect of world oil market conditions on Mexico is quite apparent. Many of the factors depressing demand for OPEC oil — depressed consumer demand, buyer resistance to high prices, and oil company stock drawdowns — also adversely affect Mexico's ability to sell its oil. Mexico's treasury secretary observed, while introducing an especially gloomy economic forecast in May 1982, that even additional price cuts would likely not result in increased oil exports.

Mexico is not the marginal source of supply, and thus is not in a position to manipulate world price levels. Mexican exports are only 7 percent of OPEC exports. It is conceivable that total Mexican output could reach 15-20 percent of OPEC production by the end of the 1980s, but, after correction for domestic demand in both cases, Mexican exports may still be only a little over 10 percent of total OPEC exports. While Mexican production is by no means trivial in global terms, its impact on the world market is still limited.

One other frequently overlooked area in which Mexico and other suppliers of heavy oil, especially Venezuela, will affect the world oil system is the economic viability of synfuels. A steadily rising output of heavy oil priced significantly less than higher-quality oil could encourage investment in extensive refining facilities to upgrade this oil into premium distillate products, thereby creating a potentially less expensive alternative to oil shale, tar sands, and coal liquefaction as sources of fluid hydrocarbons. A number of potential synfuel developers in the United States are known to be worried about this prospect.

Mexico alone will not be a determining factor in the functioning of the world oil market. The expansion of the non-OPEC oil stream will be such a determining factor, and Mexico will be a primary contributor to that stream. The expansion of this stream is clearly in the West's interest. It will not, however, eliminate the importance of the Persian Gulf region, nor will it allow the United States and its allies to neglect the political and strategic dynamics of that region. In a fundamentally important sense, the politico-strategic contours of the energy supply and security issues are not identical with the structure of the world oil supply system. Thus, Mexico is not, and cannot be, the deus ex machina that suddenly relieves the United States of an important aspect of its responsibilities as a global power. This is not to say that substituting Mexican for potentially insecure Persian Gulf oil is not beneficial to U.S. interests, but it is to warn against false perceptions of the strategic significance of such a substitution.

MEXICO, WESTERN OIL REQUIREMENTS, AND CONSUMER COMPETITION

Even granting that Mexican oil exports will likely not, by themselves, significantly redefine the parameters of the world oil system, Mexico's role in the efforts by individual Western oil consumers to diversify their supply sources is of potentially considerable importance. In considering this, particularly of interest are the underlying constellations of interest for both parties that are served by oil transactions, and the forms of consumer-state behavior that are evident in regard to oil relations with Mexico.

The United States has been, and undoubtedly will remain, the single largest market for Mexican oil exports. By conscious Mexican decision, the proportion of Mexican oil exports destined for the United States has fallen from 87 percent in 1977 to about 60 percent. At the same time the volume of exports to the United States expanded through 1981. The Mexican share of the U.S. oil import market (approximately 12 percent in March 1982) has also risen, although that was due largely to the drop in overall U.S. oil imports.

The subject of oil exports to the United States is politically controversial within Mexico, and is capable of eliciting strong nationalist feelings, expecially at the left end of the Mexican political spectrum, where fear of dependence on the U.S. market (and of U.S. dependence on Mexico) is strong. This factor, in the end, has not blocked the Mexican government from negotiating oil and gas export deals with the United States. It has affected how quickly, and visibly, exports to the United States can expand, and this nationalist factor has encouraged Mexican authorities to stress steps to avoid overdependence on the U.S. market

Mexican oil nationalism, it must be pointed out, is more complex than simple "gringo-baiting." It manifests itself in different ways along the Mexican political spectrum, and in the end it may not prevent an expansion of bilateral energy relations, if U.S. policy is correspondingly sensitive to this sentiment and aims at mutually satisfactory resolution of other bilateral issues, notably trade and immigration, which Mexican authorities regard as being more important than oil.

U.S. oil diplomacy vis-à-vis Mexico has become more adroit, as demonstrated by the signing of an agreement whereby PEMEX would supply a total of 110 million barrels of oil to the U.S. strategic petroleum reserve (SPR), at an average rate of 200,000 barrels per day from September 1 to December 31, 1981, and at 50,000 barrels per day from January 1982 to the end of August 1986. At a fill rate of 205,000 barrels per day (January-April 1982), Mexico was supplying 25 percent of the daily addition to the SPR.

This deal neatly serves a number of U.S. and Mexican interests. Mexico, which proposed it after having rebuffed a similar U.S. Department of Energy (DOE) proposal in 1980, clearly needed a market to take up volumes lost due the June 1981 hiatus (the actual volumes destined for the SPR had been earmarked for U.S. oil companies). The agreement, furthermore, fit with Mexico's strategy of seeking long-term contracts with governments and large oil companies as a means of stabilizing its export market. The DOE at the time was supplying SPR from the spot market, and its earlier purchases during tighter market conditions had been criticized for propping up prices. The Mexican price was below the weighted average OPEC price at the time. Although there was criticism within the United States of the government-to-government nature of the agreement, the signing of the agreement was an important step in overcoming the legacy of somewhat strained U.S.-Mexican relations during the Carter administration.

The importance of this deal should not be exaggerated. By itself it does not signal the establishment of a United States-Mexico special oil relationship; indeed, there have been previous purchases of Mexican oil for the SPR. The deal does, however, indicate the extent to which market calculations are now driving Mexican policy and what can be accomplished through quiet diplomacy, without the glare of a search for a North American accord.

Through the early 1990s Mexico could be an important incremental source of U.S. oil import needs and, perhaps more important, a steady and major source of strategic stockpile crude. Mexico could supply 15 percent or so of total U.S. import needs (assuming total exports of at least 2.2-2.4 mbd, with half going to the United States, and U.S. imports in the range of 6-8 mbd). By comparison, Saudi Arabia in mid-1981 supplied 20 percent of U.S. imports and Nigeria 15 percent (before the spring 1981 drop in Nigerian export totals). Mexico thus could conceivably rank among the top foreign suppliers of the U.S. market. In the short run, constraints on U.S. refinery flexibility might limit how much additional Mexican crude can be taken because of the refining problems encountered with Maya crude. This is an essentially generic problem, however, and substantial investments in upgrading U.S. refining capacity are required in any event to accommodate an increasingly heavy barrel of international oil.[17] In the long run, the growth in Mexican reserves and the rate at which Mexican domestic oil demand increases will determine how long Mexico can remain a major exporter.

Mexico would be a vital component in any U.S. strategy of supply diversification, but it would be that strategy, not just oil from Mexico, that would materially affect U.S. vulnerability through the early 1990s. Moreover, to the extent that even a reduction of direct U.S. import vulnerability would be offset by continued European and Japanese vulnerability, it would be incorrect to think that growing U.S. imports from Mexico would change the overall structure of U.S. foreign policy choices and problems deriving from international oil.

Mexico's role in supplying the oil needs of other Western countries is of particular interest, especially if one accepts the argument that U.S. interests are better served by more Mexican oil going onto world markets than by trying to maximize exports to the United States. (Mexico's oil sale agreements through December 31, 1980, which marked the end of the principal period of Mexican contracting activity, are listed in Table 7.1.) For most of the countries in question, Mexican oil has provided a means of supply source diversification, a cushion against loss of access elsewhere. However, given the volumes in question, the resulting market shares in the customer countries, and the vestigial resiliency of the international oil market, the availability of oil from Mexico has not materially transformed the nature of these countries' energy security problems.

TABLE 7.1
Mexican Oil Exports, by Destination, as of December 31, 1980

Contract Volumes (barrels per day)		Additional Oil Export Commitments (barrels per day)	
United States	733,000	Sweden	70,000
Spain	220,000	Jamaica	13,000
Japan	100,000	Philippines	10,000
France	100,000	Panama	12,000
Canada	50,000	Guatemala	7,500
Israel	45,000	El Salvador	7,000
Brazil	40,000	Honduras	6,000
India	30,000	Haiti	3,500
Costa Rica	7,500		
Nicaragua	7,500	Total	129,000
Yugoslavia	3,000		
Total	1,336,000		

Total contracted and committed: 1,465,000 barrels per day.

Source: Petroleum Intelligence Weekly, February 2, 1981

While U.S. perspectives on Mexican oil have tended to emphasize the energy security aspects of substituting Mexican for Persian Gulf oil, the calculations behind oil agreements signed by other Western countries with Mexico have been quite multifaceted, and in many cases have had less to do with energy security concerns and more with broader economic interests vis-à-vis Mexico. Whereas the competition-for-oil argument would suggest that customer states would fall all over themselves to get more oil from a particular supplier, the opposite appears to be the case in several instances regarding Mexico — the competition is over access to the Mexican market for industrial and high-technology goods. Signing oil agreements is a means of building goodwill in support of gaining such access.

Japan, of the other oil-consuming countries, has perhaps placed the greatest emphasis on substituting Mexican oil for insecure supply from elsewhere, most notably Iran since 1979.[18] Nevertheless, with over 75 percent of its oil coming from the Middle East, Japan's overall dependence of the Middle East would not be greatly affected by Mexican oil. As it is, Mexico supplies only around 5 percent of Japan's oil requirement.

The price Japan has paid for Mexican oil has been high. Japanese interests made two loans to Mexico in 1978. A $600 million credit from a consortium of Japanese banks was the largest single credit without strings ever granted to a foreign borrower to that date. Another $460 million loan went to finance construction of a Mexican petrochemical complex and port, rail, road, and pipeline expansion. A $500 million Japanese credit to PEMEX in 1980 was the first credit negotiated by Mexico that was tied to oil sales. Another $750 million "no strings" loan package in 1981 included $150 million at an interest rate of 4.2 percent, with the rest in credits from the Japanese Import Export Bank. Because the interest rates in such packages are frequently below market, the effect is to make the price of Mexican oil higher than it otherwise would be. Moreover, as the Japanese learned, the loans do not guarantee that a higher volume of Mexican oil will be forthcoming, only that requests for more oil will be given favorable consideration. It was not until market conditions in late 1981-early 1982 changed so dramatically in favor of customers that Mexico offered Japan the 300,000 barrels per day that only eight months earlier it had declined to supply.[19] The Japanese case demonstrates that supplier diversification is both expensive and limited in strategic terms, and that market conditions beyond the control of both Mexico and Japan are of crucial importance in affecting what kind of arrangements are possible.

Supplier diversification has figured less prominently in oil agreements with other customer states. The 60,000 barrels per day Canada agreed to take would satisfy approximately 12 percent of Canadian import requirements (at 1981 levels), but the Maya component has presented serious refining problems. Canadian interest in Mexican oil had as much to do with the Trudeau government's desire to establish government-to-government oil supply relationships that would circumvent the middleman role of the international oil companies it distrusted as it did with the volume obtainable from Mexico.

A more prevalent rationale for oil agreements with Mexico is their tactical potential to broaden economic relations with Mexico. Canada made no effort, upon signing its agreement with PEMEX, to conceal its goal of widening the range of bilateral economic cooperation to include a host of industrial and technological goods. Canada offered a $1.58 billion credit to Mexico in 1979 to help finance this extension of economic ties. The Swedish agreement for 70,000 barrels per day was of relatively marginal importance in energy security terms and, indeed, was suspended by Sweden because no Swedish refinery could handle Maya, and because of the much better deals Sweden has had with Great Britain and Norway for far superior quality North Sea oil. The oil agreement with Mexico did have political utility, however, in cementing economic ties with Mexico that would be more valuable to Sweden in the heavy industry and technological areas.

France also has been courting the Mexican market. Mexico has sought to rectify its persistent bilateral trade deficit with France, and in 1980 the two countries negotiated an economic agreement for French investment in the urban and rail transport sectors, telecommunications, autos and auto parts, chemicals, steel, and port facilities, among other areas.[20] A Franco-Mexican mixed commission, at the ministerial level, coordinates bilateral economic relations. Nonetheless, while France receives 100,000 barrels per day of oil from Mexico, this represents only 5 percent of French oil requirements, despite the fact that Mexico, along with Venezuela and Norway, plays an important role in France's effort to diversify its sources of oil.

The competition over nuclear reactor orders is perhaps one of the best examples of how oil consumer state dealings with Mexico are driven by dynamics that only in part, and possibly minor part, have to do with oil. The stakes are very high in Mexico's ambitious 20,000 megawatt nuclear power program announced in 1981. The depression in many industrial countries nuclear markets places correspondingly greater weight on winning export orders as a means of occupying surplus industrial capacity. Reactor orders, moreover, are seen as means of opening up nuclear-related and other industrial markets to companies from the reactor-supplying country. Mexico appears to be one of the few potential "boom" nuclear markets at the present time, thus heightening the more zero-sum nature of the reactor competition there. It is also the one major Latin American nuclear and heavy electrical market not dominated by West Germany. There is thus an industrial "spheres of influence" aspect to the competition. This is a sensitive point for the French in particular, who see reactor sales as overcoming France's lack of reputation for technological leadership in advanced countries. The major competitors — the United States, France, Sweden, and Canada — have made major efforts to win these orders. To the extent that they help favorably dispose Mexican authorities to deal with a particular vendor country, oil agreements have a strategic importance in economic terms much broader than their purely energy-related dimension.

Just as the economic circumstances of mid-1982 have affected the Mexican economy as a whole, so the future of the Mexican nuclear program appears to be questionable. Certainly the 20,000-megawatt target is in all likelihood unrealistic, and, given the magnitude of the effort, probably was unrealistic even before harder times arrived. In the short run the cost of the first two reactors — at least $5 billion — is a daunting figure in the face of rapidly rising foreign borrowing and stagnant export earnings. Just as happened with the ambitious nuclear program announced by Brazil in 1975, high capital-cost projects with substantial import requirements are very vulnerable to changing economic circumstances, and by relying upon steadily rising oil revenues to finance such forms of technological modernization, Mexico opened itself up to fluctuations in a world oil market that has already seen several price cycles since 1973.

Attempts to strike oil for investment deals, such as those between some consumer states and Mexico, raise the issue of whether they ultimately undermine a broader international trade and investment system whose regime still rests on free trade principles. The Mexican case provides further evidence of the extent to which mercantilist trade strategies have eroded these principles, and raises the question of how to integrate Mexico and other industrializing countries into an international economic regime professing to be based on liberal economic principles.

OIL, THE CARIBBEAN BASIN, AND ALLIANCE TENSIONS

Oil and oil-related economic factors have influenced Caribbean Basin affairs, and U.S. perceptions of what is at stake there, in three fundamental ways. First, the existence of sizable oil reserves in Mexico has helped feed the Reagan administration's anxieties over Central America and the inclination in some sectors of the administration to subscribe to a "domino theory" in which the ultimate Soviet and Cuban objective is to extend unrest to Mexico, and specifically to Mexico's oil-producing region, which is very close to the border with Guatemala. Second, the devastating economic impact of inflation and rising oil prices on the terms of trade for many countries in the region has contributed substantially to the economic malaise there, further undermining the prospects for political stability. Third, a large share of U.S. crude and refined product imports enter U.S. ports via the Caribbean, and Caribbean refineries play an important role in the East Coast fuel oil market, imparting an additional security importance to the region.

Other members of the alliance do not share these perceptions in their entirety, and where there is common ground, there are differences over strategies to deal with commonly perceived problems. This divergence over the Caribbean has contributed to tensions within the alliance, and while one clearly cannot ascribe these tensions to energy concerns, the role of these concerns in influencing at least U.S. perceptions needs to be examined.

Reagan administration officials have, on a number of occasions, stated their fear that domestic instability, guerrilla activity, and "revolutionary" movements might eventually spread to Mexico. The end result would be to deny the United States, and everyone else, access to that oil, thus increasing U.S. vulnerability to disruption in the Persian Gulf. The spread of unrest to Mexico would also, presumably, unleash a tidal wave of immigrants on the United

States, creating serious social dislocations in the Southwest and elsewhere. In this view, Cuba and the Soviet Union are not simply engaging in idle mischief in Central America, and perceiving Central American unrest within an East vs. West framework is entirely appropriate.

There is, of course, considerable disagreement over the validity of this administration viewpoint. A discussion of this issue is beyond the scope of this chapter; what is more relevant is how Mexican views of the security issues differ from those held by the Reagan administration.

Just as denial of access to Mexican oil is a serious concern for U.S. policy makers, for many Mexicans that issue raises fears of U.S. intervention to secure that access. The question of U.S. dependence on oil imports, and thus the weight it gives to Mexico as an alternative to the Middle East and North Africa, reinforces these fears. As a result, U.S. domestic energy policy carries a foreign policy significance of considerable interest south of the Rio Grande.

Both countries have expressed their concern about the spread of conflict in Central America, but they diverge substantially in both the relative emphasis given the various sources of that conflict and, importantly, their views on how to deal with it. Intensification of conflict in Central America, especially in Guatemala, could pose serious security and economic problems for Mexico. The southern region of Mexico is poor, populated largely by Indian *campesinos* who are relatively marginal to the larger economy, and vulnerable to an influx of illegal immigrants from countries to the south. Both Mexican security forces and leftist political parties have been strengthened there in the past year. Mexican authorities are also concerned that devoting more resources to the Mexican military might disrupt the military's relatively inactive political status and siphon off revenues that might otherwise go toward economic development.

Mexico places considerably greater emphasis on the economic and political roots of unrest in Central America, relative to outside subversion, than does the United States.[21] Accordingly, Mexico has lent its support to center-Left groups in El Salvador and to the Sandinistas in Nicaragua in the expectation that these forces, even if not necessarily democratic, can end the violence and guide economic reconstruction. This approach places Mexico – which, it should be pointed out, has been governed since 1976, and will be until 1988, by a basically technocratic and not some wildly leftist administration — at loggerheads with the United States, which has backed the Christian Democrats in El Salvador and views Nicaragua as a Cuban outpost. U.S.-Mexican differences extend to disagreements over the utility of elections, which the Mexicans regard as an ineffective measure to resolve domestic conflict. Mexico's experience with co-opting disparate interest groups in a pluralistic, if not strictly democratic, political system leads it to stress the same approach to dealing with regional problems, including Cuba.

The Mexican initiative, launched in February 1982, to act as a communicator in the various disputes afflicting the region, and to encourage separate negotiations dealing with the three "knots" of tension in the region — U.S.-Cuban relations, El Salvador, and Nicaragua — stems from rising concern at the dangers posed to Mexico by spreading conflict and the view that the problems must be dealt with from a regional rather than an East-West perspective. The emergence of Mexico as a potential mediator in these conflicts, and as an established regional leader, indicates the extent to which Mexican economic development, and thus the underlying factor of oil wealth, is changing the structure of power in the Caribbean Basin.

Disagreement with the U.S. approach to Central America does not stop with Mexico. The seeming U.S. preoccupation with Central America has contributed substantially to the current agitated state of U.S.-European relations. Only Great Britain has lent its political support to the United States on the issue. European attention has focused on the potential for U.S. military intervention in the region, the divisive effect of "another Vietnam" on their own publics' support for military alliance with the United States, and the perceived inclination of some sectors of the Reagan administration to go it alone without European support. Moreover, many European governments regard any strategy of supporting authoritarian governments as doomed to failure, and reject the Reagan administration's tendency to view the world in East vs. West terms.

The most dramatic expression of European discontent with the U.S. approach to Central America was the Franco-Mexican communiqué of September 1981, recognizing the democratic elements in the leftist opposition movement in El Salvador as legitimate participants in the political process. Other European governments have not gone quite so far, but there are considerable links between

European Social Democratic parties and their counterparts in El Salvador. These transnational links at a party level offer a means for Europeans to extend political and financial support without formally intervening in El Salvador's internal affairs.

The European-American division over Central America should be seen as one element of a much broader and deeper rift in the Atlantic Alliance that has been building for some time at the economic and strategic policy levels. The dynamics of this broader process are clearly separate from, and much more significant for alliance relations than, such relatively narrow questions as who is getting how much oil from Mexico. The problems of Central America, and the intra-alliance disagreement over how to deal with them, would exist even if there were not a drop of oil. Nonetheless, to the extent that oil gives Mexico a greater diplomatic role, including participating in transatlantic wrangling over Western strategy on Central America, and influences U.S. perceptions of the stakes involved in the region, it clearly complicates the handling of Caribbean Basin affairs.

A second major area where oil, and oil-related economic factors, affect the region is economic growth. In view of the importance of economic growth as a precondition for rectifying social and political problems, this relationship is especially crucial. Although disagreement between the United States and some of its allies over appropriate strategies for dealing with the problems are less significant than in the preceding area, they nonetheless exist.

The rise in the price of imported oil and the existence of depressed commodity markets have had a devastating impact on the economies of many of the island and Central American countries. For example, by 1979 most of previously prosperous (in a relative sense) Costa Rica's export earnings had to be spent on imported energy. By 1981 high interest rates undermined Costa Rica's ability to cover its balance-of-payments deficit by borrowing abroad. Domestic inflation, rising unemployment, and a collapse of the Costa Rican currency threatened domestic socioeconomic progress in one of the region's few successful democracies. The situation elsewhere is little different, because the external sector of the economy occupies a very large place in many of the countries.

A number of measures to deal with the economic problems of the region have been implemented or proposed. Several of these measures focus specifically on energy. Venezuela and Mexico announced in 1980 that they would help finance the oil import bills of Caribbean Basin customers with loans whose terms would soften substantially if the proceeds were devoted to the development of indigenous energy resources. In 1980 Venezuela also proposed the establishment of a fund for hemispheric energy development that would provide seed capital for energy development projects in energy-importing countries. The Carter administration did not respond enthusiastically to the Venezuelan proposal, and suggested it be melded into the World Bank energy affiliate concept then being developed. By default or conscious decision, the Mexican-Venezuelan oil financing mechanism is the principal instrument in place to help countries pay their oil bills.

The Reagan administration's opposition to the establishment of an energy affiliate for the World Bank, its skeptical attitude toward multilateral lending in general, and its own proposed Caribbean Basin plan, which relies primarily upon private investment in the region to generate economic growth, have dominated the debate on economic development strategy since mid-1980.[22] The administration's position reflects a number of considerations. It believes that World Bank energy lending disproportionately favors the public sector in recipient countries at the expense of the private, and too frequently funds inefficient or unnecessary programs. Its attitudes toward multilateral lending reflect concern at loss of influence over who receives loans or assistance and on what terms. The Caribbean Basin initiative is consistent with these views, in that it relies heavily upon one-way free trade, tax incentives to encourage U.S. private investment in the region, and direct bilateral financial assistance.

While debate rages over how to promote the region's economic development, there is little question that the potential for an important degree of energy self-sufficiency exists. A number of the Caribbean Basin countries possess undeveloped or underdeveloped natural resources and hydroelectric potential.[23] Oil resources may exist in several areas, but exploration has been minimal because of the heretofore much more attractive production possibilities outside the region. The biomass and solar energy potential is considerable, and of potential importance to rural areas. What are lacking are capital, industrial infrastructure, and (in many cases) a competent energy bureaucracy capable of enabling the government to bargain effectively with multinationals.

Finally, the Caribbean region plays a crucial role in the U.S. oil supply system. Much of the nearly 5 million barrels per day refinery capacity in the Caribbean region (the island states plus Venezuela) is oriented toward serving the U.S. product market and particularly the East Coast residual fuel oil market. In 1980 over 60 percent of U.S. imports came from the Caribbean region; 58 percent of this was the residual fuel oil used in electric utility and industrial boilers. Although total U.S. product imports in 1980 satisfied only 9 percent of U.S. product demand, Caribbean refineries satisfied 37 percent of U.S. residual fuel oil demand and 70 percent of residual fuel oil demand on the East Coast. Venezuela remains an important U.S. supplier (it was the leading U.S. supplier until 1976) and, over the long run, could increase in importance as the Orinoco heavy oil belt, with an estimated resource of anywhere from 1 to 6 trillion barrels (only 10-15 percent may actually be recoverable) is developed.

Thus, strictly from an energy security standpoint, the United States possesses a particular set of interests in the domestic stability of the islands and open sea-lanes that is not shared by the allies. That the Reagan administration is attaching greater weight to these interests, especially the sea-lanes issue, contributes to the conflict of perceptions between the United States and it allies over regional affairs. While one may argue that defining U.S. interests in this particular way leads to an overemphasis on physical security considerations, the differences between the stakes involved for the United States, and for its allies contribute to the disagreement over strategies to deal with regional problems.

CONCLUSIONS

One has to regard the "competition for oil" thesis, as applied to Mexico, with some caution. Mexican oil does not offer a true alternative to Persian Gulf oil, and even couching a discussion of Mexican oil in such terms is misleading. Industrial state approaches toward Mexico see oil agreements as a means as much as, if not more than, an end, with the Mexican market for capital goods the most lucrative target. To the extent that there is consumer-state competition over Mexico, it is driven more by dynamics that go far beyond access-to-oil considerations, and might operate regardless of how much oil could be acquired in the process. The nuclear reactor competition, which is driven by underutilized domestic reactor manufacturing capacities, is clearly one case where oil export agreements, rather than being a goal, are more a means to build economic ties with Mexico.

Moreover, were there really a competition for access to Mexican oil, one could not objectively regard it as immensely successful. The Mexican share of many Western markets is marginal, and there are crude quality problems to boot. The oil-for-investment deals actually offer somewhat less than that, since, as the Japanese learned in early 1981, more investment does not guarantee additional oil exports. In the end, changing market conditions have had more influence on Mexican willingness to increase export volumes than have new steel mills.

The perspective on Mexican oil policy presented here emphasizes the underlying economic and political factors, rather than outside consumer-state influence, as the primary determinants of that policy. These factors point toward a steady rise in production and exports, and to the extent that economic conditions compel it, at a rate faster than Mexican authorities might otherwise select. Ironically, before the 1981-82 oil glut Mexican authorities expressed their fear of economic "indigestion" if exports expanded too rapidly, resulting in an influx of dollars and higher inflation. By mid-1982 inflation had doubled, but oil revenues had fallen. While the question of overdependence on oil revenues may be debated within Mexico, in the near and medium terms oil exports are the easiest sources of foreign exchange.

The growing importance of market conditions as an influence on Mexican oil export policy also tends to support the belief that Mexico does not have a great deal of latitude in setting its oil policy. The period of rapid expansion of output and exports coincided with a relatively tight market, and Mexico was in the driver's seat so far as its own policy was concerned. If predictions of a looser market (at least until the mid-1980s) are borne out, then this will be much less the case, and Mexico may find itself having to be more responsive to market trends and conditions. Efforts to reduce the level of heavy oil exports and to strike deals with refiners able to process Maya oil are examples of how changed market conditions have already affected Mexican policy. Greater emphasis on long-term contractual relationships with major oil companies, and even govern- ments, as a means to ensure access to markets (the reverse of the "access to supply" syndrome feared by Henry Kissinger and others) would be another. Abandonment of production and export platforms or ceilings could be a third. The choice of a technocrat to be the next president suggests that such calculations of a more economic than political character will, with appropriate fence-mending with more nationalist and conservationist forces in Mexico, play a more prominent role in Mexican oil policy.

One area where such fence-mending moves may come is Mexico's position on Central America, where maintaining distance from the United States can have domestic political utility. While it is not evident just how much influence Mexico wields in shaping events in El Salvador and elsewhere, it is not likely to retreat from a more activist diplomatic role there. There may be cooperation of a tactical sort between Mexico and the United States on regional problems, but the underlying basis for a convergence of strategic views does not appear to be present, and may not materialize, given Mexico's different domestic political situation and experience.

Thus, although the "competition for oil" thesis is suspect with regard to Mexico, oil and Mexico are relevant to Western alliance relations and issues in a number of respects. Access to oil may, in fact, be a relatively small part of that connection. Nonetheless, the combination of oil and industrialization, each of which generates its own set of international dynamics, will ensure that the importance of Mexico to the economies and foreign policies of the countries in the Western alliance will increase.

POSTSCRIPT 1982: THE YEAR OF ECONOMIC COLLAPSE

In the second half of 1982, several dramatic and profoundly disturbing events transpired in Mexico that have cast a very dark shadow over that country's economy, and possibly over the world financial system. Mexico's oil-financed economic boom collapsed utterly. Only extraordinary measures by the central banks of the leading industrialized countries, in making available $1.8 billion in currency swaps, prevented the total collapse of the peso. Other emergency measures included a $2.8 billion credit from the United States ($1 billion in advance payments for oil and a $1.8 billion Commodity Credit Corporation credit guarantee for U.S. grain exports), a larger contract for Strategic Petroleum Reserve oil, and decisions by private banks, some of which have loans equal to over 50 percent of their equity outstanding in Mexico, not to immediately call those loans. Mexico teetered at the brink of default, and it is not evident that a $3.8 billion loan arranged with the International Monetary Fund at the end of 1982 will be enough to help Mexico past this period.

The impact of Mexico's financial crisis on its energy programs has been very marked. The nuclear program was indefinitely deferred. Oil exports, which in 1982 provided over 90 percent of all export earnings, are being stepped up toward the 2 mbd mark, and possibly beyond. PEMEX has had in the short run to curtail its expenditures on exploration, development, and refinery construction, as debt service requirements on the country's external public debt (private debt is hardly being touched) siphon off most of PEMEX's revenues. At the same time, $20 billion must be spent over the next six to eight years on exploration, development, and infrastructure to keep the oil industry strong. There are clear economic incentives to continue to boost oil exports to ease the economic crisis, but Mexico will still have to borrow extensively to finance industrial and social development. This time, however, Mexico will have to pay premium interest rates and curb public expenditures to control inflation running at the end of 1982 at around 100 percent on an annual basis.

The Mexican case demonstrates the fragility of economic growth based on the export of a commodity over whose price a country has little control. In a soft world oil market, the more Mexico (and other non-OPEC countries produce), the greater will be the downward pressure on price. A collapse of world oil prices, while gleefully entertained by some economic and political pundits in the United States, would devastate Mexico, resulting in economic and likely political chaos, and could provoke a world financial crisis as some oil-supplier states default on their debts. Where there may once have been competition for markets in Mexico, there may now be a recognition among industrialized states of a common interest in propping up that country's economy.

NOTES

1. See. for example, Bruce Netschert, *Mexico: Potential Petroleum Giant* (Washington, D.C.: National Economic Research Associates, 1978); William D. Metz, "Mexico: The Premier Oil Discovery in the Western Hemisphere," *Science* 202 (December 28, 1978): 1261-65; and Richard B. Mancke, *Mexican Oil and Natural Gas* (New York: Praeger, 1979).

2. Interview with James Reston, *New York Times*, October 13, 1974, p.1. See also Kissinger's address to the Society of Pilgrims, London, December 12, 1973.

3. George W. Grayson, *The Politics of Mexican Oil* ((Pittsburgh: University of Pittsburgh Press, 1980), ch. 3; Laurence Whitehead, *Mexico from Bust to Boom: A Political Evaluation of the 1976-79 Stabilization Program*, Working Paper no. 44 (Washington, D.C.: Latin American Program, Woodrow Wilson International Center for Scholars, 1979).

4. See the articles by Isidra Sepulveda, René Villarreal, and Laura Randall in J. Ladman et al. eds., *U.S.-Mexican Energy Relationships* (Lexington, Mass.: Lexington Books, 1981).

5. Data reported in Banco Nacional de Mexico, *Review of the Economic Situation of Mexico*, March 1982, p. 89.

6. Banco Nacional de Comercio Exterior, S.A., *Comercio Exterio de Mexico*, September 1980.

7. Previously, Mexican authorities had tended to hold up Venezuela, where oil provides over 95 percent of export revenues, as a primary example of a "petrolized" economy, which Mexico would never follow.

8. Laura Randall, "The Political Economy of Mexican Oil, 1976-1979," in Ladman et al., op. cit.

9. See Susan Kaufman Purcell and John F. Purcell, "State and Society in Mexico: Must a Stable Polity be Institutionalized?" *World Politics 32 (De-*cember 1980): 194-227.

10. See Grayson, op. cit., esp. ch. 2; and Isidro Sepulveda, "PEMEX in a Dependent Society," in Ladman et al., op. cit.

11. Joel Bergsman, *Income Distribution and Poverty in Mexico*. World Bank Staff Working Paper no. 395 (Washington, D.C.: World Bank, June 1980).

12. *New York Times*, February 4, 1982 p. 2 Sec. D.

13. David Ronfeldt et al., "Mexico's Petroleum and U.S. Policy: Implications for the 1980s," RAND Corporation, R-2510-DOE (Santa Monica, Calif.: RAND, 1980).

14. Reported in *Oil and Gas Journal*, August 24, 1981, pp. 79-84.

15. See Ronfeldt, op. cit., for such a moderate prognosis. The report by the Mexican Treasury Secretary, Jesus Silva Herzog, which predicts economic growth in the 0-2 percent range for 1982, would, if borne out, suggest an acceleration of exports. *Los Angeles Times*, May 19, 1982, p. 1, Business section.

16. *Wall Street Journal*, February 25, 1982, p. 4.

17. See Sabri A. R. Kadhimd, "Options Open to Producers for the Increased Utilization of Heavy Crudes," in J. Dunkerley, ed., *International Energy*

Studies, (Cambridge: Oegelschlager, Gunn, and Hain, 1980), pp. 299-320; and *Oil and Gas Journal*, May 31, 1982, pp. 117-25 and March 24, 1980, pp. 75-88.

18. See Peter A. Petri, "High-Cost Energy and Japan's International Economic Strategy," in Ronald A. Morse, ed., *The Politics of Japan's Energy Strategy* (Berkeley: Institute of East Asian Studies, University of California, 1981).

19. *Petroleum Intelligence Weekly*, December 14, 1981.

20. *Comercio exterior de Mexico*, June 1980, p. 203.

21. Susan Kaufman Purcell, "Mexico-U.S. Relations: Big Initiatives Can Cause Big Problems," *Foreign Affairs* 60 (Winter 1981/82): 379-92.

22. U.S. Department of the Treasury, Office of the Assistant Secretary for International Affairs, *An Examination of the World Bank Energy Lending Program* (Washington, D.C.: Treasury Department, July 28, 1981).

23. See D. G. Fallen-Bailey et al., *Energy Options and Policy Issues in Developing Countries*, World Bank Staff Working Paper no. 350, (Washington, D.C.: World Bank, August 1979); and World Bank, *Energy in the Developing Countries*, (Washington, D.C.: World Bank, August 1980).

169-192

8

ECONOMIC NATIONALISM AND
THE DISRUPTION OF WORLD TRADE:
THE IMPACT OF THE THIRD OIL SHOCK

Walter Goldstein

The argument advanced in these pages can be succinctly stated: Three waves of change swept through the world oil industry between 1973 and 1982, and their significance can be most effectively gauged in the turmoil that they brought to the flow patterns of world trade. The standoff between the three great trading blocs in the system was upset on each occasion that oil supplies and oil prices were radically altered. The 24 "postindustrial" and oil-importing economies of OECD recorded a long-term fall in real GNP and economic wealth; the oil-exporting countries (both within and outside OPEC) enjoyed a sensational growth in revenue, followed by an acute reduction in their bonanza cash flow; and most of the 100 or more less-developed countries (LDCs) resigned themselves to increasing debt, economic hardship, and trade deficits. The turmoil in world trade has come to match in severity the systemwide dislocation that we conventionally know as the Great Depression of the 1930s. There is no sign that the faltering of world trade flows will be corrected in the 1980s; and there is no nation, rich or poor, that can hope to escape its dread consequences.

The central argument does not suppose that the depression in world trade and economic growth can be attributed to one factor alone — the onset of revolutionary change in the oil industry. It is argued, instead, that the three successive stages of change can best be observed in the trade wars and the economic upheaval that came to disrupt the 20 years of growth (roughly from 1950 to 1970) that had created a *belle époque* in the international economy. But other factors must be considered, too, in studying contemporary disruptions in world trade. The spiraling of inflation was not principally caused by the 1,000 percent increase in world oil prices that began in 1973. Nor can the upswing of global unemployment and economic dislocation be attributed exclusively to the mounting of energy anxieties. It is true that most nations were hard pressed to secure safe oil supplies and to finance their soaring oil bills. But it cannot be argued that their despair in recession was created by the three-stage upheaval in the world oil market.

There is one consistent phenomenon, however, that can be linked to the waves of change that forced apart the supply and demand curves of the oil industry. In many countries the generation and distribution of wealth obviously were fundamentally changed. The richer oil-consuming nations tried, unsuccessfully, to mount a collective defense against the steep rise in oil prices that the oil-producing countries triggered in 1973 and again in 1979. The OPEC bloc gained new confidence and a gigantic cash flow as its market power increased, but its affluence was short-lived. The second wave of oil price rises was followed by a period in which its trade and income surplus melted away.

OPEC's downfall was not prompted by a collective effort of the consumer nations to safeguard their economic strength. It resulted from the sharp falling off of industrial production and international trade among the oil-exporting countries' best customers. The allegation cannot be sustained that a conspiracy of consumers was launched to strike back against the greed of the OPEC cartel. It will be argued instead that the forces of inflation, recession, and unemployment forced a war of all against all in the international order, and that the oil factor played a significant role in reviving the passion for trade wars. Protectionist measures, currency devaluations, and monetarist policies were employed to preserve each nation's job reservoirs, its balance of payments, and its terms of trade. As a consequence, the zero-sum struggles for growth in the 1970s were replaced by a negative-sum conflict in which nearly every nation forfeited economic advantage.

THE THREE WAVES OF CHANGE

The first oil shock began in 1973, when the OPEC cartel asserted its power to hike the world price of exported crude by 300 percent. The 13 members of OPEC were accused of resorting to "outrageous exploitation"; it was alleged that their "greedy profiteering" had wreaked havoc on the global economy. Economic growth turned sharply downward within a year and a full-scale recession set in. Unemployment and budget deficits increased in most of the OECD economies, and an unwelcome boost was given to the inflation of the world money supply. These were to outlive the decade. A few responses were recommended in the early 1970s by Western and Third World conferences that were hastily convened to alleviate the disruptions created by the oil shock. But after years of talk no decisive or collective agreements were reached. Discord in the economic order was pervasive, and anxiety increased as the military security of the Middle East deteriorated.

- UNCTAD and the U.N. General Assembly sponsored a series of conferences to structure a new international economic order (the NIEO), and to revise its monetary system and commodity pricing, as well as the inequities built into North-South trade. Declarations supporting a NIEO were adopted but never implemented. A conference on international economic cooperation struggled for three years to devise a triangular deal among the OPEC, the OECD, and the LDC blocs; but it too failed to shore up the free trade system that was breaking apart under the oil strain. Year after year the United Nations, UNCTAD, the Common Market, and NATO failed to take collective action.[1]

- A multilateral response was launched by 21 industrial nations in OECD to create an emergency sharing scheme, under the auspices of the International Energy Agency, and to establish a disciplinary limitation on imports among the largest oil-consuming nations. Further efforts were made at the annual summit meetings of Western leaders to curb consumption schedules and to create emergency stockpiles; and the special drawing right (SDR) facilities of the IMF were extended to help the developing nations cover their rising oil bills. But these measures did little to correct the imbalance between supply and demand or to restore stability in the world market.[2]

- Collective security arrangements, especially within NATO, were not effectively improved. Western nations disagreed sharply among themselves in voting on Arab-Israeli issues at the United Nations; and they competed hastily to sell armaments and nuclear equipment in the new, lucrative markets of the Middle East. Nothing was done to safeguard the security of Western oil supplies in the Persian Gulf or in the tanker lanes leading from it.

- More important, the giant multinational banks of New York, London, Paris, and Tokyo scrambled to syndicate placements of surplus petrodollars among their impoverished clients in the Third World. This created a huge pool of credit funding in the world money market and helped accelerate the pace of worldwide inflation.

The second oil shock came five years later when the revolution in Iran forced a withdrawal of its production from the oil market. Unfortunately, the reliance of the United States and Europe on imported oil had increased steadily between the 1973 and 1979 crises, and a brief panic set in when oil prices were raised once again. When the Shah of Iran was overthrown in 1979 and an autarkic regime seized power in the second greatest exporter in OPEC, the insecurity of supplies prompted further anxiety. Five million barrels a day (mbd) were withdrawn from global supply; 52 hostages were imprisoned in the U.S. Embassy for over a year; the basic reference price of oil shot up from $14 a barrel to $23, and then to $35 or more. In 1980 a war broken out between two major OPEC exporters, Iran and Iraq, and it was assumed (erroneously, it later appeared) that oil reserves would be reduced to a dangerously low level.[3]

OPEC claimed that its price increases had been justified by the relentless inflation that had undermined its terms of trade with the West. The cartel leaders pointed to the precipitous decline in the value of the dollar, the currency in which oil transactions and cash reserves were denominated. The devaluation of the dollar against the stronger Western currencies had reduced some of the purchasing power that they needed to finance their economic development and the modernization of their armed forces. They angrily claimed that their one, golden opportunity to leap from feudalism to industrialized wealth has been eroded by Western inflation and monetary fluctuations. Accordingly, they had tried to recoup their bargaining strength by seizing the price leadership advantages offered by a sellers' market.[4]

The draining of revenues to the OPEC countries was condemned every summer at the summit conclaves of Western leaders. OPEC was accused of inducing a massive shift in purchasing power from the consuming to the producing nations, yet the buyers failed to organize a multilateral response to the outrage of "price gouging." Instead of forming themselves into an OPEC of importers, the second oil shock prompted many of the OECD countries to resort to unilateral bursts of competitive protection and trade rivalry. Import barriers were raised to turn back the rising tide of unemployment and to repair deficits in their balances of payments. In 1979-80 the United States and the EEC each recorded deficits of $30 billion and an unemployment rate of 8 percent. Notwithstanding the Tokyo round of agreed tariff reductions, import surcharges were raised on an ever wider range of goods and produce; "orderly marketing" limits were imposed in the form of steel trigger prices, multifiber limitations, automobile quotas, and government purchasing contracts; and several European nations began to imitate Japan by providing their export industries with favorable subsidies, tax exemptions, and cheap credit.

Western leaders insisted that they were still committed to free trade and an open money market. In practice, however, they relied on a battery of trade war tactics to protect their export earnings and currency reserves. Multinational firms and banks transferred short-term funds and long-term placements through the burgeoning offshore money markets, and their corporate clients piled up unprecedented debts in Eurodollars. The trading system became awash with excess liquidity; the dollar fell steeply in the late 1970s; and the spiral of inflation wound tighter in developed and developing nations alike. Inflation topped 15 percent in the United States, 20 percent in Italy and Great Britain, and 200 percent in the weakest economies of the Third World.[5]

The third oil shock appeared after the Reagan administration took office. The proximate cause was attributed not to the pricing policy of OPEC but to the monetarist policy of the United States and other Western governments. Interest rates on Wall Street climbed to a new high, and in 1981 the dollar appreciated against many currencies by 25 to 30 percent. Credit funds flowed in large volumes into U.S. Treasury bills and certificates of deposit, and the relative world price of oil (denominated in dollars) increased for the third time in ten years. West Germany and Japan cut their oil imports by nearly one-quarter, but the dollars paid for their oil imports flowed out more and more rapidly. Indeed, both countries suddenly moved from an overall surplus on current account to a surprisingly large deficit.[6]

During 1980 and 1981, in the face of near-zero growth in real GNP, mounting shortfalls on external account, and continuing stagflation, most of the EEC countries retaliated against the U.S. dollar. They raised their own interest rates and intervened in world currency markets. Japan, Belgium, France, and Mexico − among many others − devalued their currencies in order to boost their exports and improve their terms of trade. Unfortunately, this hiked their oil and other factor costs and lowered the value of their central bank reserves. As industrial production began to fall in the industrial and developing countries, severe cuts had to be made in their imports of oil and oil derivatives (such as petrochemicals). In 1981 and 1982 the price of oil on the spot market declined by 25 percent and the production of OPEC oil fell by 44 percent, from 32 to 17 mbd. Sellers outnumbered the buyers, and a glut of oil remained unsold. The impact of U.S. monetarist policy and rising interest rates had pushed prices too high. Business activity and investment fell as the U.S. dollar appreciated; oil reserves were drawn down; and great efforts were made to conserve energy by automobile users, by industrial oil consumers, and by millions of homeowners. Within a year the demand for OPEC oil fell below the level set in 1970, and many of the cartel members moved from an ample surplus to a sizable deficit on their external accounts.[7]

THE CONSEQUENCES OF THE THIRD OIL SHOCK

It is still too early to determine what the consequences of the third (and certainly not the last) of the crises will be. Recession and inflation have depressed the levels of business activity worldwide, and oil demand in the non-Communist world has fallen. The World Bank's *Annual Report* (September 1981) forecast that economic recovery will be sluggish in the 1980s. World trade has become more competitive and less profitable for many national actors; and, worse still, the spiral of inflation has become tightly wound.[8] In 1982 real growth in the industrial world will reach an average of only 1 percent and 4.6 percent among the developing nations. (But the LDCs operate from a smaller and poorer base than do the industrial states.) Great Britain and the United States were likely to record negative growth and less than 70 percent utilization of industrial capacity. Inflation would hover close to 10 percent in most countries, and only Japan could anticipate a real growth exceeding 3 percent.

The most notable aspect of the third shock, however, is its origin. It was not OPEC that engineered the sudden crisis in the energy market. It was the leading consumers of oil – and especially the United States – that radically changed the terms of trade to the buyers' advantage. The escalation in interest rates and in the value of the dollar reversed the balance between the scarce supply and the excessive demand for oil. After the cost of raising capital had doubled, refineries reduced their stocks and production runs. Oil consumption fell steeply, prices on the spot market declined, and OPEC lost its commanding leadership in the marketing of crude oil. More important, the conservation of energy was highly cost-sensitive. It became more profitable to economize in consumption than to promote the expansion of production facilities.

The dimensions of the contemporary crisis can be measured with different sets of indicators. First, the tightening of monetarist policy has brought about the squeezing of industrial credit, a decline in employment and business investment, and a serious shortfall in current accounts. In 1981 the collective deficits of the OECD bloc approached $30 billion, and in the LDCs it reached beyond $70 billion. The bond and stock markets registered record down-swings as business confidence waned and long-term capital dried up. Major investment projects were scaled down or abandoned; stocks of capital goods or raw materials were depleted; and it became less costly to switch to coal or natural gas than to import dollar-denominated oil.

Many examples of retrenchment in trade and investment could be cited, but one stands out dramatically. The former president of the World Bank had recommended in 1980 that $25 billion should be invested in the most promising energy exploration and development projects in Third World countries over the next five years. The investment could help relieve the LDCs of their towering deficits and debt-servicing payments, and it could assist many of them in developing the oil and gas resources that they need to achieve energy independence. The incoming president has chosen to cut the commitment in half because long-term money has become too expensive and because the falling price of oil has turned many of the projects into high-risk and low-profit ventures.[9] Opposition by the Reagan administration also has influenced these decisions.

A second dimension of the crisis can be gauged in the surprising volte-face in the fortunes of OPEC. In 1980 the 13 cartel nations earned $272 billion, an increase of $84 billion over 1979 — even though oil exports had already declined by 14 percent in volume. The cartel was split between the hawks, who wanted to compete for higher prices, and the doves, who wanted to stabilize market prices through a voluntary curtailment of supply volume. The latter then prevailed because of the determination of one member, Saudi Arabia. Able to lift 10 mbd without strain, the Saudis provide 40 percent of OPEC's export and 20 percent of the oil production of the non-Communist world. The Saudis cut back their exports by 30 percent in late 1981 to subdue the rivalries among their cartel colleagues. Their reduction came too late, though, and a surplus of 5 mbd remained unsold, a glut on the market. Spot prices were slashed from $40 a barrel to $30 by some sellers — such as Nigeria, Mexico, and Iran — and OPEC's decision to limit exports to 17 mbd was flouted by several members. The biggest buyers in the market, including the multinational giants, demanded for the first time since 1969 that their suppliers renegotiate the price of long-term contracts or barter agreements (as in the French swap of military and nuclear hardware for Iraqi crude). Indeed, it hurt the companies hardly at all when the United States curtailed all purchasing from a major OPEC hawk, Libya.

In the meantime, the cash surplus of the six leading Arab exporters has tumbled from the $100 billion peak of 1980. Several nations in the Organization of Arab Petroleum Exporting Countries (OAPEC) are now piling up debts, to their surprise, and their petrodollar placements in Arab and multinational banking syndicates have been stringently curtailed. This has hurt many actors in the system as well as the OPEC paymasters themselves.[10] Sharp cuts were made in the petrodollar flows to the international banks and to the debtors who desperately need to borrow (such as Poland, Mexico, and Turkey) in order to relieve their debt-burdened economies. The soft loan agencies of the World Bank have had to retrench, and so have the Islamic countries that (until 1978) had received extensive grants in aid. The curtailment of OPEC funding helped tighten the global supply of capital, thus raising interest rates and adding to instability in the currency markets. At one point in 1981, the rush of industrial funds out of sterling, francs, and deutsche marks threatened to topple the fragile base of the European monetary system (EMS). Unprecedented deficits appeared in the external accounts of several EEC governments, and they were forced into costly devaluations. The countries that had converted most of their reserves out of dollars in the 1970s were badly hit; their oil imports were cut by 15 percent or more, but the relative cost of their energy soared as the dollar appreciated.[11]

There is no good indicator to measure the upturn in economic nationalism that has swept through the world trade system. If an indicator had been devised, it would show a remarkable increase in the political control of economic activity. Free market, *dirigiste*, and centrally planned economies have responded to the international recession with a range of protectionist measures. In many cases their resort to economic nationalism threatens to undermine the open-trading ideals incorporated in the Bretton Woods agreements, GATT, and the Treaty of Rome. Currency values have been manipulated, national debts have been allowed to multiply, and subsidy payments have been lavished on the "national champions" in the export industries that excel overseas. For import-threatened industries, restrictions and tariff barriers have been raised to shelter domestic companies and to safeguard their vulnerable work force. In short, the competitive rules of free trade and open market rivalry have been softened in one industrial sector after another through neomercantile interventions of the nation-state. As the French put it, Japan is free to export as many cars as it can sell – up to 3 percent of the French market – and other nations (especially Italy) are likely to do the same.[12]

A brief sampling of these deflections of market forces can suggest the degree to which economic nationalism has become the accepted, if not the dominant, mode of international commerce.

• The ideology of the Reagan administration emphasizes the sanctity of the free trade and of laissez-faire economics. Nevertheless, import quotas were imposed on Japanese cars, Korean clothing, and European steel; foreign aid was slashed to 0.2 percent of GNP; and imports of raw materials and finished goods from the LDCs were cut back severely as aid and trade diminished.

- Oil imports in the United States were curbed by decontrolling prices, by subsidizing the conversion of oil-burning boilers, and by imposing mandatory conservation standards (for auto gasoline and industrial distillates). Oil imports were cut in 1980-82 from 8.5 mbd to 4.8 mbd, and the critical ratio of oil consumption to GDP dropped by 28 percent between 1973 and 1981. Oil-producing countries chose to intervene in their home markets with different tactics. Canada and Mexico supplied their domestic industry with oil and gas well below the world price order to boost GDP and export earnings; Great Britain and Norway levied royalty taxes on their oil exports to improve their balance of payments; France and Canada turned to the nationalizing of multinational oil companies in order to regulate the industry and its investments.[13]

- The Federal Reserve Bank in the United States maintained a spread of nearly ten points between the prime rate and the consumer price index. The high rate of interest drew so much money from overseas that it helped thwart the recovery of the EEC economies. The dollar came back to the trade-weighted strength it had enjoyed until 1971, though it left the U.S. economy with a $28 billion merchandise deficit and a sluggish recession that could survive for several years to come.[14]

- Recovery from the recession in the EEC was virtually halted after 1980. In Great Britain, France, and Germany, interest rates were hiked to compete with the United States, unemployment increased to new heights, and conflicts waxed over monetary and fiscal policies. Great Britain chose to prolong its course of painful and crippling deflation, while the new French government chose to reflate — partly by imposing exchange controls, by nationalizing the banks, and by spending 25 percent of French reserves in a hasty attempt to prop up the value of the franc. Germany managed to control its inflationary spiral by opting for zero growth and a deficit on current account. But the diverging policies of the three countries, coupled with the weakness of all other EEC currencies against the dollar, might yet destroy the EMS. Basically, the EMS was meant to restrain European exchange fluctuations and to stabilize the EEC's joint recovery plans. If it should disintegrate, trade within Europe and with the United States could be severely impaired.[15]

- The Japanese solution, sustaining export-led growth with a boost in export subsidies and currency supports, might prove to be counterproductive in the late 1980s. If the United States and the EEC should clamp down on its competitive, high value-added exports, Japan will no longer be able to sell 50 percent or more of its production of cars, electronics, and engineering products overseas. Nor will it succeed indefinitely in subsidizing its currency against the dollar, its low interest rates, and its high level of employment. Threats have been made to require 75 (or even 90) percent of its manufactures to be made in the country of final sale, and to force the devaluation of the yen from 250 to 150 to the dollar, in order to scale down its protectionist maneuvers.

- The LDCs will be the "weak link" in trade wars. The collective debt owed to the OECD banks and to their OPEC suppliers now exceeds $500 billion. If they should falter in their debt servicing, the LDCs could grievously impair the cash balances in the hands of their Western bank creditors; they would then have to slash their imports from the West – which account for 35 percent of the export earnings of the United States and the EEC, and 46 percent of Japan's balance of payments.

- Despite this alarming prospect of shrinking trade, Western governments have refused to widen the LDCs' access to IMF credits and soft loans (worth $13 billion a year) and SDRs; they have refused to renegotiate the Lomé and multifiber agreements. Several of the LDCs, and also of the COMECON countries, could conceivably collapse under the burden of their huge debts to OPEC and OECD creditors. If any one of them should default, a chain reaction could rock the world, as it did in 1931 when the Austrian Credit Bank went under.

- Export subsidies for agricultural and industrial products have been raised by the leading OECD nations. The United States has threatened to penalize with high tariffs the subsidized goods and food imported from the EEC and Japan, but it still pays costly farm price supports at home. Japan has awarded valuable sole-source contracts and cheap-interest loans to its prime exporters, and it has balked at removing the nontariff barriers that discourage the entry of foreign exports. Japan has already run up a trade surplus of $18 billion with the United States and another $10 billion with the EEC. The spirit that once moved the Kennedy Round and the Tokyo Round efforts to liberalize world trade now seems to be spent.[16]

ECONOMIC NATIONALISM AND THE CHANGING WORLD ORDER

It is apparent that divisions among the Western allies over foreign and defense policy will widen as the full force of their economic nationalism gathers strength. Most of the NATO allies have refused to match the increased defense spending or to join the embargo on Soviet trade sought by the Reagan administration. Objections were raised regarding the cost and the political consequences of deploying expensive new weapons systems, despite U.S. insistence that the Soviet military buildup will threaten the NATO security zone and Japan. No ally has offered to share the expense or the risks of deploying a rapid intervention force to defend the Persian Gulf, or to police its vital tanker lanes and facilities.[17]

The greatest outstanding trade dispute in the West has focused on the European proposal to finance a $10 billion pipeline, 3,500 miles long, to tap the natural gas fields of Siberia. The U.S. Defense Department argued that the gas line would furnish invaluable hard-currency income to the Soviet economy, and would make the Federal Republic of Germany vulnerable due to its dependence on Soviet sources for 30 percent of its gas supplies. Chancellor Schmidt disagreed. He felt that the deal would help reduce unemployment and Germany's current account deficit, and that it would bring much-needed relief to the German steel industry. Schmidt's enthusiasm was shared by most of EEC partners; they preferred to expand trade contacts with the East than to follow the U.S. embargo.[18]

Their advocacy was well-timed. The costly surplus and the underutilized capacity of the EEC steel industries have stimulated various proposals (including the d'Avignon plan) to create an "orderly marketing agreement" among Europe's bankrupt steel foundries. The Europeans foresee less danger in extending their reliance on Soviet gas supplies than in maintaining current levels of unemployment and underutilized industrial plant. They steadfastly refuse to consider alternative U.S. proposals – to extend North Sea gas wells or nuclear reactor programs – because of long lead-times and because the return on these investments is too uncertain when the price of money is so high.

No one dares forecast how long-lived or disturbing the present crisis will be. If inflation, unemployment, and zero growth should extend throughout the 1980s, severe damage will be done to the multilateral principles of the world trading system that evolved in the postwar years. The consequences could be startling and destructive. It is possible that the OPEC cartel will split apart if its members continue to compete aggressively against each other to dispose of their oil surplus at discounted prices. It is possible, too, that the trade war maneuvers of the OECD nations will acquire greater sophistication. Democratic governments need to foster the illusion, especially before a general election, that they can act vigorously – either to insulate the national economy from the turmoil surging through the world market or to seize zero-sum advantages in a declining world economy. It is an illusion, of course, that the autonomy of a nation's growth can be maintained in an interdependent and closely integrated market. But it is logical, if not practicable, for governments to pretend that economic autarky can still be attained. Mass electorates rarely vote for governments that confess their inability to boost GNP growth or to defend domestic industry – and jobs – against the dumping of cheap imports by foreign rivals.[19]

It is not public opinion, however, that drives nation-states to compete in grueling trade wars in order to claim a larger slice of world markets. It is in the logic of the international economy that nation must strive against nation, no holds barred, when the trade flow is shrinking. No comparison can be made with the era of expanding trade in the 1950s and 1960s. Then the volume of interstate commerce multiplied at a faster rate than the GNP growth recorded by most national economies. Only the newly industrialized countries (NICs) – such as Taiwan, South Korea, and Singapore – can hope today to score significant growth by raising their world trade income and doubling their exports within a decade. They have done so by rejecting the stratagems advocated by theorists of free trade, and they have achieved a phenomenal economic take-off by ignoring domestic demands and subsidizing their export sales. They have harnessed their resources to establish a position in the fastest-growing and the most profitable marketing area, the world trade system.[20]

The older industrial countries were not blind to the benefits that could be recaptured through offshore trading. They recognized that a high standard of living and industrial prosperity must depend to a large extent on their prowess in competing against the NICs and other protectionist rivals.[21] Especially in the EEC, governments encouraged home-based multinational firms to invest heavily in overseas subsidiaries in the most affluent economies. Most OECD members gave the greatest encouragement to their export industries, and in several cases scored notable victories. France pushed its exports to a new high, and its export earnings rose to 18 percent of GDP. West Germany achieved a ratio of 23 percent, the Netherlands 46 percent, and Belgium at one point topped 50 percent. The export portion of GDP in the United States almost doubled in the 1970s, going from 4.3 to 8.2 percent. The growth came partly because U.S. multinational firms had implanted profitable subsidiary operations overseas, and partly because the 1971 devaluation of the dollar made American exports cheap and competitive. By 1980 one-third of U.S. farmland and one-fifth of the manufacturing work force were employed in some form of foreign trade. After 1980 the U.S. could afford a tight money policy and an expensive dollar.[22]

The reliance on export prowess and foreign trade was even more striking in Japan. Government, industry, and the banks combined into a joint "Japan Inc." strategy to fulfill the most cherished goal of economic nationalism, export-led growth. When the recession hit in Japan in 1981 and domestic demand began to falter, export earnings were boosted by 18 percent and a trade surplus of $30 billion was run up with its strongest clients, the United States and Europe. The benefits were formidable. Domestic inflation and bank rates were kept low, business activity levels were raised, and the yen was subsidized at an artifically low rate – to promote export competitiveness. As a consequence, Japan cornered a valuable share of the world market for automobiles, electronics, semiconductors, and integrated chips. It also paid for its rising oil bills, as the dollar strengthened in value, by redoubling its export efforts.[23]

The example set by Japan was condemned and also envied by all of its trading rivals, but few of them succeeded in imitating its mercantilist thrust. Japan mounted an array of tariff and import barriers to protect its industrial base. It held down its imports to one-third of the per capita purchases of any country in Europe, even though it depended on foreign supplies for practically all of its raw materials, grain, and oil. Complaints were raised against its contravention of GATT rules and the Tokyo Round agreements to lower trade defenses, but the Tokyo government refused to budge. It rallied the leading firms in its most promising and high value-added industries to create giant combines and to push their expansion of exports. Japan also was accused of dumping goods overseas at artificially low prices and of subsidizing its export "champions" in order to enlarge their worldwide position. Within a few years it captured 70 percent of the market for integrated circuits, nearly one-quarter of the automobile sales in the U.S. and several EEC countries, and a major share of the sales of electronic, machine tool, and engineering products.[24]

The labor displacement effect of these low-cost sales was enormous. The most evident effect appeared in the U.S. automobile industry, where sectoral employment fell by 350,000 and, in 1981, unprecedented deficits were recorded by Ford, GM, and Chrysler. The recession hit Detroit badly, but the Japanese undercutting was even more painful. Japanese cars sold for $1,800 less per unit than their American competitors. Their engineering and gas efficiency were of superior quality, and their sales appeal was formidable. But their successful marketing was attributed to the cheap capital and the cheap yen that Japan had furnished to its leading manufacturers. By contrast, it was alleged that a markup of nearly 100 percent had been added to the price of American and European cars entering Japanese salesrooms.

By 1980 there had been a fundamental shift in the production and distribution of the world's wealth. The nations with falling real GNP had borne a marked decline in comparative cost advantages and in the international division of labor.[25] They had forfeited both dynamic growth and economies of scale in their leading industries. Many of them turned to industrial and monetary protection to repair their damaged standing, but few of them gained the benefits won by Japan. Their industries and infrastucture had been too long neglected, or their capital formation was not adequate to the massive task of modernizing their economic and social bases. Many had failed to curb the inflationary surge that bloated their money supply, impaired their currency, and restricted the employment of their work force and the deployment of their industrial capital. Worse yet, they had made no provision to pay the "wealth transfer tax" that OPEC had imposed on the consuming countries when it transformed their surplus on current and capital accounts into a set of massive deficits.[2][6]

The wealth transfer tax paid by the OECD economies (in lost GNP) came to $1 trillion in 1979-81, and the loss in personal income was $1,300 per capita. The rise in energy prices accounted for 12 percent of their inflationary burden, and each $4 rise in the price of a barrel of oil added another 1 percent to the inflation rates in 1980. The Reagan administration mastered the inflationary spiral by cutting back on investment funding, employment, social services, and real wage rates; as a consequence, GNP remained stationary and the growth of the money supply began to flatten. The use of monetary policy to curb the supply of credit was successful in halving the inflationary burden, but it prolonged the recession in the U.S., in Europe, and in the OPEC countries. The raising of interest rates led to the suppressing of capital investment and industrial modernization, to a downturn of nonoil imports by trading nations, and to a further decline in the world demand for oil.

By 1982 OPEC had collectively agreed to cut back production to 17 mbd, but it was obvious that many of its members had ignored the agreement. As the cash surplus of many OPEC members drained away, they became major borrowers in an already tight money market and began to unload their oil at discount prices. The revolutionary regimes in Iran, Iraq, and Libya ignored the marker price, $34 a barrel for Arabian light crude in mid 1982, and sold more than their agreed share of OPEC offtake. Nigeria and other states ignored the self-imposed quota and pricing system, too, and thus undermined the expectation that OPEC not only would survive the century but also would tighten its market grip.[2][7]

The abrupt fall in the price and volume of oil supplies after 1980 must not be seen as a permanent or unmitigated benefit to world trade. The third oil shock did not just pit one OPEC country against another as a remarkable shake-out began to work its way through the oil industry. The pound sterling fell in 1982 when BP was forced to close several refineries, sell its loss-making petrochemical plant, pull out of a few countries, and slash the price of North Sea oil. The currencies of Norway, Canada, Mexico, and the EEC nations suffered a comparable decline. Many of the giant U.S. multinational companies encountered a grave problem with cash flow in a falling market beset by high interest rates and low profit margins. New drilling and exploration ventures were aborted, investments in synfuel projects were canceled, and diversified business holdings (in real estate or manufacturing subsidiaries) were shed at considerable loss. Clearly, their pricing and capital forecasts had been fraught with error.[2 8]

It was the movement of money that prompted the third wave of oil changes. Though the U.S. trade deficit remained at $30 billion, $41 billion in transfer payments flowed into dollar holdings as U.S. interest rates rose. In 1981 the record surplus on the U.S. current account was paid, in effect, as another wealth transfer tax by OECD and OPEC trading partners. It reversed the "benign neglect" of the dollar in the 1970s — though it is not likely that the surplus will survive for many years to come. If the U.S. dollar stays strong but the U.S. trade balance goes to $35 billion in the red, as the forecasts for 1982 envisage, there will be another realignment of trade and currency positions, and the oil market might be subjected to a fourth major jolt.

PROJECTED OUTCOMES FOR THE 1980s

Three or four outcomes have been projected for the near future. All of them, unfortunately, are likely to lead to intensified trade warfare. It is assumed today that the scramble for comparative advantage will force nations to protect more of their key industrial sectors, to subsidize their export and deter their import trade, and to realign their currencies' worth. These changes in trading practice cannot be easily anticipated, but a set of projections can be made with regard to the parameters of development in the oil industry in the 1980s:

- If interest rates remain high and capital stays tight and expensive, the recession in the oil-producing and oil-consuming economies will levy yet another wealth transfer tax. This time the $1 trillion tax will not be paid to anyone; it will be forcibly extracted from purchasing power as industrial and employment resources are increasingly idled.[2 9]

- If a realignment of currencies takes place, possibly with turbulence, the lira, pound, and French franc will probably decline appreciably against the deutsche mark. If Germany brings its economy under control, while its neighbors remain trapped in stagflation, the EMS and even the IMF could falter. Were the United States to relax its tight money policy, the simultaneous weakening of the dollar and oil prices could threaten the stability of the money market. The EMS mechanism is supposed to assure a joint European float against the dollar, but it would be overwhelmed it the dollar went down while the deutsche mark rose against all other currencies (except the subsidized yen).

- If OPEC were to cut oil flows from 17 mbd to 14 or 15 mbd in the next year, it might regain its cartel grip and hold a benchmark price of $34 a barrel. This will be difficult to secure because consumption world wide has fallen by nearly 20 percent since 1979. In the peak years of its power, OPEC contributed 64 percent of the non-Communist supply of oil; its production has since fallen by 32 percent and its cash surplus has turned to an overall deficit. Given the mounting efforts to economize and conserve energy in the consuming states, and the relative increase of oil drilling in non-OPEC countries, it is not likely that OPEC will regain its dominant position or its price leadership.[30]

- If the international division of labor should shift considerably before the current recession is finally played out, the NICs and other protectionists will enjoy a faster recovery potential. The NICs and the modernizing economies will achieve comparative advantages that are vital for success in the cutthroat competition in tight export markets. The laggards, by contrast, will suffer a labor displacement in their domestic industries, a continuing weakness in their internal and external accounts, and a low growth in economic productivity. They will be strongly tempted to compensate for their deficiencies by resorting to trade wars and the mercantilist interventions of economic nationalism. A new tactic will be used in forcing extraterritorial restraints on multinational subsidiaries located overseas. A first move appeared in 1982 when the U.S. government ordered U.S. subsidiaries and licensees in Europe to cancel their gas pipeline contracts with the Soviet Union — even though their host governments in the EEC chose to ignore the U.S. embargo.

- If the fall in real income continues in the 1980s, yet another crisis will hit the world markets for oil, money, and export earnings. It will also lead to greater layoffs of labor and plant in those industrial sectors that cannot be "saved" by public subsidy or protectionist devices. Roughly 5 million workers in each of the obsolescing industries — steel, shipbuilding, automobiles, textiles, and intermediate manufacturing — will be permanently displaced if free market forces sweep the OECD economies. Added to 30 million already without work, and a plant utilization capacity running at 70 percent, the forecasts suggest that there will indeed be a "rough ride ahead" in the 1980s.

- If a Middle East war were to break out among the revolutionary shiekhdoms and the radical military regimes, the third oil shock would be quickly superseded by a fourth crisis. The oil glut caused by the current recession and inflation would immediately terminate. If 5 mbd were taken offstream, the benchmark price would soar and the spot market would be besieged by anxious buyers. Failing the onset of war or revolutionary upheaval, however, the shift from a buyers' to a sellers' market must wait until the world trading system moves into a strong recovery. And that, conceivably, may not occur during the 1980s.

The conclusion to be drawn from the analysis of the three oil shocks and the scenarios for future development is strongly pessimistic. Political intervention in the free flow of trade and money has become a dire necessity. As the rivalry for economic development becomes more aggressive, the imperative for intervention will mount and the rewards intensify. Mercantilist maneuvers may harm the commercial system as a whole, but they have become politically expedient to the cause of economic nationalism. Separatist maneuvers may harm the commercial system as a whole, but they have become politically expedient to the cause of economic nationalism. Separatist maneuvers may hinder the collective determination of the Western bloc to improve its economic recovery and its energy self-sufficiency; but they will also have a stronger appeal to the nationalist electorates of the industrial world. In doing so, the force of mercantilist pressure will turn attention increasingly from a concern with energy issues toward the struggle for national trade advantage and trade warfare.

The problem that is vital but still unresolved (in mid-1982) is that of improving long-range energy forecasts. They have been wrong too often in the past, but they are urgently needed. For example, will the 44 percent decline of OPEC production since 1979, from 32 to 17 mbd, continue in the 1980s, and will OPEC succeed in hanging on to the 35 percent share that is left of its position in the world market? Will non-OPEC sources of oil continue to expand – in Mexico, Canada, the North Sea, the United States – thus crowding the Middle East exporters from their depressed Western markets? More important, will the long awaited economic recovery of the OECD countries raise oil demand in the non-Communist world? If so, will this make the West once again dependent on the price maneuvers and the boycott threats of the Middle East, or will the recovery be fueled by a determined thrust of conservation (and conversion from oil), so that Western societies can achieve an even greater rate of energy efficiency and independence?

It is difficult and hazardous for forecasters to handle these issues. A report in the London *Observer* (July 4, 1982) contrasted the forecasts recently issued by the International Energy Agency (IEA) in Paris with a range of conflicting projections that were advanced at a technical conference held at Cambridge by the International Association of Energy Economists. Underpinning each forecast were contradictory assumptions about the price elasticity of oil – both on the demand and on the supply side – and about the capacity of the world trade system to change course from permanent stagflation to a new burst of economic growth and trade expansion.

Optimistic forecasters, such as Prof. Morris Adelman of MIT, estimated that oil dependency will shrink overall as the energy input needed to expand GNP growth continues to fall; hence, demand will not be restored to its previous peaks even if an economic recovery should be sustained. Pessimists assume, as in the OPEC Downstream Project in Hawaii, that the Persian Gulf States will have 9 mbd in refining capacity in place by 1986 (as against 6 mbd today), and that they will recover price advantage and market leadership by forcing consumer nations to buy refined as well as crude products – even if they are saddled with costly surplus refinery capacities at home. Prof. P. R. Odell from the Netherlands disagreed. He had not prepared an obituary for OPEC, but he saw the Middle East producers becoming more vulnerable to competition as consumer nations finance new drilling in the Western Hemisphere,

Africa, China, or the Soviet Union. Of course, no one dared forecast whether a violent war would erupt in the Persian Gulf, thus blocking the 12 mbd that now flow from Saudi Arabia, Kuwait, the United Arab Emirates, Iraq, and Iran. If the Saudis or any combination of their neighbors were forced to close their pipelines, the panic and market alarms of 1979 could quickly return. Anxieties over future supplies and pricing strategies, whether they were well founded or not, could then bring a leap in prices on the spot market of from $30 to "a few hundred dollars a barrel" — as one forecaster in the U.S. government was prepared to envisage.[31]

The mid-1982 forecast of the IEA envisaged a 6 percent fall in the year's consumption of oil by its 21 member states; they now take 70 percent of all non-Communist production, and their actual consumption has fallen by 13 percent since 1979 — a slump equal in volume to more than twice the annual British production in the North Sea. The forecasting record of the IEA was criticized by *The Economist* (June 5, 1982) for promoting a false sense of well-being; it urged instead that stern measures should be taken by OECD governments (through raising oil taxes, new drilling efforts, and synfuel production projects) in order to fend off a return to dependence on the OPEC cartel. It was assumed that a steep price for Western economic recovery would have to be paid in any case, since the oil exporters outside OPEC could not lift sufficient supplies to support a fast rate of growth in world trade. The assumption is widely shared, but debate rages over the degree of dependency that will materialize. Will the non-Communist countries require 20, 30, or 40 mbd from OPEC by 1990, and will this represent 40, 50, or 60 percent of the oil supplies available on the world market?

These are the critical questions that forecasters cannot answer with confidence, largely because their predictions have been wrong so many times since 1973. If a coordinated form of contingency planning for the 1980s is ever to be adopted by the West, however, an agreed-upon and accurate methodology of forecasting must first be devised. It must determine what consequences of the third wave of oil changes are likely to occur within the trade flow patterns of the international economy. More important, it must determine what impact on energy supply and demand curves will be wrought by the changing flow of world trade. There is little beyond intuitive judgment to guide the forecasters at the present time, and thus energy planning remains at a precarious level of accuracy or political accord.[32]

NOTES

1. For a survey of the trade impacts of the succession of oil shocks during the 1970s, see Walter Goldstein, "Redistributing the World's Wealth: Cancun Summit Discord," *Resources Policy* 8, no. 1 (March 1982).

2. A useful array of trade data appears in Ian M. Torrens, *Changing Structures in the World Oil Market* (Paris: Atlantic Institute, 1980).

3. In 1979 and 1980 the spot market price of $13 a barrel nearly trebled. The consequences are analyzed in Hollis B. Chenery, "Restructuring the World Economy: Round II," *Foreign Affairs* 60, no. 2 (Summer 1981).

4. The strategy and timing of OPEC's price policy were noted by one of its most acute critics: Walter J. Levy, "Oil: An Agenda for the 1980s," *Foreign Affairs* 60, no. 2 (Summer 1981).

5. The economic anxieties of the time are recaptured in the rich data sources given by Lawrence A. Veit, *Economic Adjustment to an Energy-Short World* (Paris: Atlantic Institute, 1979).

6. A lucid account of change in money flows appears in John C. Ruggie, "The Politics of Money," *Foreign Policy* no. 43 (Summer 1981).

7. The downturn surprised even the sharpest forecasters. Melvin A. Conant, *Access to Energy: 2000 and After* (Lexington: University of Kentucky Press, 1979), provided a set of projections for the 1980s and the 1990s that were widely praised. But by 1981 they had been overtaken by a sudden, unexpected decline in OPEC's fortunes.

8. The World Bank, *World Development Report, 1981* (Washington, D.C.: World Bank, 1981).

9. Andrew MacKillop wrote a thoughtful piece, "Global Economic Change and New Energy: A Proposal for Enhanced Economic Growth in Low Income Countries," *Energy Policy* 9, no. 4 (December 1981). His suggestions to develop the energy resources of the LDCs became obsolete as the cost of credit rose and the price of oil fell.

10. Another author failed to anticipate current changes in OAPEC's standing in the oil and investment world: Mary Ann Tétreault, *The Organization of Arab Petroleum Exporting Countries* (Westport, Conn.: Greenwood Press, 1981).

11. P. R. Odell and K. E. Rossig, *The Future of Oil* (London: Kogan and Page, 1980), prepared a set of pricing projections for the next decade with considerable subtlety. Their baseline assumptions were already in error in 1981 because their extrapolations hinged on consumer demand schedules that were relatively inelastic in price and volume.

12. *The Economist* (February 6, 1982), provided a detailed analysis of the trade war tactics utilized by Japan to secure its highly prized and widely envied goal: export-led growth. Japan has been more ingenious, if not unscrupulous, in practicing "free trade when it suits its interests." Hence, its example is likely to be imitated by its rivals in future years.

13. An extensive survey by the present author of the "nationalizing" of oil policy in Canada and Mexico can be found in *Energy Policy* 9, no. 1 (March 1981); and 9, no. 4 (December 1981).

14. See Robert Solomon, "The Elephant in the Boat?: The United States and the World Economy," *Foreign Affairs* 60, no. 3 (Fall 1981), for a stern analysis of U.S. economic and monetary policies overseas.

15. Flora Lewis, "Alarm Bells in the West," *Foreign Affairs* 60, no. 3 (Fall 1981), investigates each of these developments in detail.

16. The questions involved in the survival of a liberal world order are raised by G. K. Helleiner, Lawrence G. Franko, Helen B. Junz, and Peter Dreyer, *Protectionism or Industrial Adjustment?* (Paris: Atlantic Institute, 1980).

17. The growing disunity of the Western alliance over energy issues and geopolitical strategy is noted in Robert J. Lieber, "Europe and America in the World Energy Crisis," *International Affairs* 55, no. 4 (October 1979); and David Deese, "Energy: Economics, Politics, and Security," *International Security* 4, no. 3 (Winter 1979-80).

18. An excellent monograph on western European energy supplies and détente politics is Hanns W. Maull, *Natural Gas and Economic Security* (Paris: Atlantic Institute, 1981).

19. Numerous efforts have been made to establish the linkage between domestic electoral expectations and the conduct of foreign economic policy. Among the best of the analyses are Robert O. Keohane and Joseph S. Nye, *Power and Interdependence* (Boston: Little, Brown, 1977); and Peter Katzenstein, ed., *Between Power and Plenty* (Madison: University of Wisconsin Press, 1978).

20. The rapid growth and change in world trade forms the analysis of an outstanding book on competition in commerce and currency: Joan E. Spero, *The Politics of International Economic Relations* (New York: St. Martin's, 1981).

21. A theory of industrial rivalry and the struggle for comparative advantage is articulated in Klaus Knorr, *The Power of Nations: The Political Economy of International Relations* (New York: Basic Books, 1975).

22. A set of conservative, free market essays has been collected in Michael J. Boskin, ed., *The Economy in the 1980s* (New Brunswick, N.J.: Transaction Books, 1979). They stress the need for the United States to raise productivity and lower factor costs in order to compete more effectively with an expensive currency.

23. A popularized and sociological explanation of Japan's success has been widely quoted. See Ezra F. Vogel, *Japan as No. 1: Lessons for America* (Cambridge, Mass.: Harvard University Press, 1979).

24. Several contributors examine the impact of state intervention on the free market flow of goods and money in a timely collection of essays: R. Dornbusch and J. A. Frenkel, eds., *International Economic Policy: Theory and Evidence* (Baltimore: Johns Hopkins University Press, 1979).

25. Each of these factors is examined, both in theory and in historical context, in Richard N. Gardner, *Sterling-Dollar Diplomacy in Current Perspective* (New York: Columbia University Press, 1980).

26. The tax and welfare consequences of the oil price rise are given considerable attention in W. M. Corden, *Inflation, Exchange Rates and the World Economy* (Chicago: University of Chicago Press, 1981). Useful data are also provided on the relation between inflation and currency exchange rates.

27. A conventional, Establishment forecast of the problems anticipated in the 1980s appears in Atlantic Council, *U.S. Energy Policy and U.S. Foreign Policy in the 1980s* (Washington, D.C.: Atlantic Council, 1981).

28. See Geoffrey Bartlett and the Economist Intelligence Unit, *Rising Oil Prices and World Economic Output*, Special Report no. 94 (London: *The Economist*, 1981). The analysis focuses on the potential growth of GDP in the industrial countries and their dependency on future conditions of oil supply and demand.

29. The taxing effects of inflation and tight money policies are examined in a set of essays that are still pertinent today: Fred Hirsch and John H. Goldthorpe, eds., *The Political Economy of Inflation* (Cambridge, Mass.: Harvard University Press, 1978).

30. The price of investment capital and the price of oil are the concerns that move Christopher Johnson, "Alternatives to OPEC Oil: Investment Costs and Financing Prospects," *Energy Policy* 9, no. 2 (June 1981).

31. A report on war games and crisis forecasting by IEA and U.S. government officials appears in the *New York Times*, July 19, 1982. The U.S. team wanted to "test" the emergency oil sharing and contingency plans of the IEA, as well as the likely U.S. response to an emergency situation, now that it is committed to a free market form of energy policy planning. Another report on team forecasting, at the U.S. Foreign Service Institute, appears in the *Observer* of July 4, 1982.

32. Three meetings of the OPEC Council were held in 1982 to reach a basic agreement – to limit production to 18 mbd and to hold to a fixed reference price of $34 a barrel. All three meetings failed. The radical and the cash-hungry members of OPEC refused to limit their oil exports to an agreed and stringent quota; and they refused to stop selling oil at price discounts ranging up to 30 percent in the case of Iran, Mexico, and other debt-burdened exporters. As the last of the meetings adjourned in confusion, there appeared to be no way in which OPEC could bring on-stream its unutilized capacity of 10 mbd, at least in the early to mid-1980s; and speculation increased as to whether the cartel could possibly survive the decade. See the editorial by the present writer, "Discounting World Oil," *Energy Policy* 11, no. 1, March 1983.

9

DOMESTIC POLITICAL CONSTRAINTS ON AN ATLANTIC ENERGY POLICY

Ronald Inglehart

INTRODUCTION

Securing an adequate energy supply at bearable cost may be the most important problem facing industrialized societies during the next few decades. Though a major technological effort will be needed for its solution, an intractable aspect of the problem is not technological but attitudinal. Heated controversy among various segments of the public threatens to block the vigorous pursuit of any of the conceivable policy alternatives, whether they emphasize nuclear power, coal, hydroelectric, or solar power, or reducing the demand for energy. As a result, despite significant gains in some areas, and a short-term petroleum glut linked with the recent recession, Western nations have on the whole made little progress toward any long-term solution of the energy crisis since it became manifest in 1973.

The critical factor today depends on value conflicts, deeply rooted in different segments of Western publics. The authors of the Resources for the Future National Energy Strategies study conclude:

> Energy has become the testing ground for conflict over broader social choices. . . . In public discourse, they are often posed as questions

of the morality of using nuclear power, the legitimacy of economic growth, the proper distribution of income, and to what extent human wants should be satisfied when they conflict with the preservation of environmental amenities, to mention only a few. In essence, value systems are in conflict. (Schuur et al., 1979, p. 432).

Politically, the acceptance or rejection of nuclear power constitutes the most sensitive aspect of the energy problem. It reflects societal cleavages in a particularly acute way, tapping a whole cluster of related values ranging from whether one is for or against economic growth to attitudes toward large bureaucratic organizations, and attitudes toward the costs/benefits of high technology. Quite often, attitudes toward nuclear power reflect differing visions of the kind of society in which one wants to live (Nelkin and Pollak 1981; Otway et al. 1978).

Public acceptance of nuclear power is crucial in another sense, for it constitutes the most controversial aspect of the problem, on which the solution may hinge. Energy conservation, on the other hand, is relatively noncontroversial: conservation means more efficient use of energy, and at today's energy prices virtually no one is against it. Accepted as an important part of the solution by virtually all parties to the energy debate, there is disagreement only over the degree of emphasis – and funding – to be accorded to conservation. Clearly, any policy worth discussing is a combination of conservation plus something else. Among the energy policies receiving serious discussion, one school of thought would rely on conservation very heavily, until presumably safe and limitless supplies of energy such as solar power and nuclear fusion can carry the burden.

The position advocated by the Harvard Business School Energy Project (Stobaugh and Yergin 1979) comes relatively close to this pole, placing heavy emphasis on conservation and solar energy, though conceding the need for increased use of natural gas and – where absolutely necessary – coal as interim measures.

But direct solar power and nuclear fusion will not become major sources of energy until well into the twenty-first century. By 1981 – more than seven years after the first major OPEC price increase – only one out of 800 homes in the United States was obtaining some part of its heating from direct solar energy. Moreover, solar energy's contribution to electrical power was still insignificant and likely to remain so, barring a major technological breakthrough that has often been predicted but keeps receding into the future. And though conservation can play an important part in reducing growth of world energy demand, it cannot be expected to offset it entirely — much less to replace petroleum as a major energy source. Accordingly, the U. S. National Academy of Sciences (1980) report concludes that only coal and nuclear energy offer a reasonably assured ability to support significant electrical generating capacity over the next few decades. In keeping with these findings, at summit meetings in both 1980 and 1981 the leaders of the seven leading non-Communist industrial powers endorsed the policy of placing major emphasis on increased development of nuclear power and coal during the 1980s — on the ground that these countries would otherwise encounter huge economic difficulties by 1990. Despite significant changes in national leadership between 1980 and 1981, the conclusions remained basically the same.

Though a strong case can be made for the argument that reliance on coal would be even more dangerous than using nuclear energy, coal remains relatively noncontroversial: it is a familiar energy source that was the mainstay of the industrial world until the 1950s. Coal retains a fairly benign image, and for the present, domestic opposition tends to focus on nuclear power. As coal comes under increasingly close scrutiny, its economic, environmental, and safety drawbacks are likely to limit the role it can play; but we will probably need to develop both coal and nuclear energy. Will domestic political constraints allow nuclear fission to play a significant role in meeting energy demand in the Atlantic region?

In their overview of the energy future, Stobaugh and Yergin (1979) dismiss this option as "the nuclear stalemate" — accepting the current American stalemate more or less as a fact of nature, almost on a par with the fact that petroleum is being consumed more rapidly then new fields are being discovered. But is it? I would argue that it is not; far from being a constant, the "nuclear stalemate" reflects the political pressures and political institutions of given nations at given times.

Thus, after a period of rapid growth, the development of nuclear power in the United States and West Germany has been paralyzed in recent years. But in other settings it has been growing rapidly. France provides a particularly striking contrast: in the mid-1970s nuclear power provided only about 5 percent of its electrical power;

by 1979 this figure had risen to 16 percent; in 1980 it was 24 percent; and during the first seven months of 1981 it was 37 percent. By 1985 nuclear power will provide 50 to 60 percent of France's total electrical power supply, and by 1990 it is expected to provide 75 to 80 percent. Belgium will also be getting over half of its electrical power from nuclear sources by 1985. Sweden constitutes an almost equally striking case; by 1985 nuclear power is expected to furnish 35 to 40 percent of the total electrical power supply. After a relatively late start Japan is now moving ahead rapidly in developing nuclear power. And in a quite different institutional setting, the Soviet Union has undertaken to quintuple its production of nuclear power between 1980 and 1985.

The "nuclear stalemate" does not reflect insurmountable technological or economic problems so much as domestic political constraints. What is the basis of these constraints? Public opposition to nuclear power has been one of the major factors, playing a decisive role not only in Sweden, Denmark, Austria, and Switzerland, where national referenda have been held on nuclear power, but also in West Germany and the United States, where well-organized opposition had virtually halted the development of nuclear power by the end of the 1970s. The effectiveness of such opposition depends partly on the institutional structure of a given nation: public opposition is no more widespread in Germany than in France, but the relatively centralized structure of their country's political institutions has given French political leaders somewhat more insulation from the impact of antinuclear pressure groups. But the intensity and distribution of public support or opposition has clearly been a major limiting factor. The balance of this chapter will examine support for and opposition to nuclear power at both mass and elite levels, using cross-national survey data that enable us to analyze the social bases of political constraints on nuclear power in western Europe and the United States.

DIFFERING VIEWS OF DOMESTIC CONSTRAINTS
ON NUCLEAR POWER

Domestic constraints on the nuclear option exist on at least three levels. They reflect support or opposition to nuclear power among the general public, among key elite groups, and in the institutional arrangements of a given country.

One of the leading analysts of nuclear politics, I. C. Bupp, emphasizes the rigidity of both pronuclear and antinuclear groups in refusing to accept any possible compromise — a rigidity that tends to be exacerbated in certain institutional settings:

On the whole, the evidence of the 1970s strongly suggests that in the developed countries nuclear power is vulnerable to criticism where political authority is fragmented by federalism and/or where judicial authorities exercise broad mandates to challenge administrative agencies. Conversely, nuclear development benefits from centralization of government and narrow limits on rights of judicial review. Only in France and the USSR have nuclear advocates been able, for the time being at least, to prevent their opponents from tying reactor licensing and other aspects of nuclear decision making in a tangle of procedural knots that will take time and political power to undo. (Bupp 1981, p. 70)

The central fact about the political environment in which the Three Mile meltdown occurred is that the nuclear advocates and the nuclear critics both in and outside the federal government can in large measure block each other's goals, frustrate each other's policies, and hence prevent the development of any coherent strategy in reactor licensing. This breakdown raises very serious questions about the future of the approximately seventy nuclear plants that were operating at the time the meltdown at Three Mile Island occurred. It also represents a clear and present danger to the operation of the ninety plants that were being built and the forty that were on order. (Bupp 1981, p. 73)

Bupp concludes that we seem headed toward the worst of all possible outcomes, in which nuclear power may make only a marginal contribution to energy supply, while at the same time effective barriers to the proliferation of nuclear weapons disappear.

In their insightful analysis of antinuclear movements in France and West Germany, Nelkin and Pollak (1981) also emphasize institutional factors. They attribute the failure of the antinuclear movement in France to a centralized decision structure that insulated political decision makers from political pressures. But is an implicitly undemocratic "insulation" the only factor, or is a relative weakness of antinuclear sentiment also involved? France undeniably has a far more centralized political structure than West Germany or the United States. But this does not automatically confer immunity from political pressures on its leaders — witness the total paralysis of France that the 1968 protest movement was able to bring about. I suggest that the difference lies in the fact that the May 1968 movement had a much broader popular base than the antinuclear movement has. We must consider the strength and social location of domestic opposition to nuclear power, in addition to institutional factors: the attitudes of the public and of key elite groups can be crucial.

Up to the present the debate has taken place with remarkably little reference to empirical evidence of representative public attitudes. Those who take a strongly pronuclear position tend to view the antinuclear opposition as a small group of fanatics who are sometimes able to block the needs of society, imposing their will on the vast majority. This viewpoint is sometimes presented in advertisements sponsored by large energy companies. The strongly antinuclear position tends to replicate this image in reverse — viewing pronuclear policies as something that can only be foisted on the hapless public by a conspiracy of industrial, bureaucratic, and scientific elites.

Among the leading authorities on nuclear power, Amory Lovins probably comes closest to embodying this viewpoint. He argues that, throughout the Western world, domestic support for nuclear power is weak — so weak that the pronuclear policies of other Western governments would collapse if they were not propped up by American support:

> In almost all countries the domestic political base to support nuclear power is not solid but shaky. However great their nuclear ambitions, other nations must still borrow that political support from the United States. Few are succeeding . . . . My own [judgment], based on the past ten years' residence in the midst of the European nuclear debate, is that nuclear power could not flourish there if the United States did not want it to. (Lovins 1977, pp 52-53)

Lovins retains a remarkable faith in the omnipotence of American influence — a faith that most others have gradually abandoned. He goes on to argue that is unlikely that France will actually proceed with the ambitious program of nuclear power plant construction that was adopted in 1974 (Lovins 1977, pp 203-04), and to argue that if the United States were to abandon the export market for nuclear power plants, France would be unable to step in: "Those who believe such a move would be seized upon gleefully by, say, French exporters are seriously misjudging French nuclear politics" (Lovins 1977, p. 54).

Another analyst of French nuclear politics, Robert Lieber, comes to diametrically opposite conclusions:

> Even the area of nuclear reactor exports is unlikely to experience major policy shifts. A Socialist-dominated government of France, no less than a Gaullist-conservative one, would have had compelling reasons to maintain nuclear export sales, despite the risks of proliferation. The presumed benefits of expertise in nuclear energy technology, export competitiveness, and the substantial balance-of-payments effects would probably have been too compelling to abandon.
>
> In the realm of domestic nuclear power, any French government would have strong incentives to continue policies for expanded use of nuclear-generated electricity, including the breeder reactor program. Despite demands from ecologists and from some within the Left, and problems of mounting costs and technological uncertainty, the enoromus balance-of-payments dependency resulting from imported oil and gas would create pressures for a leftist government to continue this nuclear program. (Lieber 1980, p. 199)

Which of the two interpretations are we to believe? I would bet on Lieber. For, as we will see below, domestic support for French nuclear policy is not nearly as weak as Lovins seems to believe. Since Lieber wrote the above lines, a Socialist-dominated government actually has come to power in France, an event that Lovins thought likely to curb that country's development of nuclear power. Nevertheless, there already are indications that the new French government will continue the previous regime's program of nuclear power plant construction, and will vigorously pursue nuclear power plant orders in the international market, regardless of what the United States does. Already the French have taken a number of orders away from American suppliers; the question is becoming less and less "Can they survive without us?" than "Can we keep up with them?"

SUPPORT AND OPPOSITION TO NUCLEAR POWER IN ATLANTIC SOCIETIES

People with antinuclear convictions tend to agree with Lovins that domestic support for nuclear power is weak almost everywhere.

Pronuclear activists tend to perceive public opinion as overwhelmingly favorable. What is the reality?

Our initial remark is banal but necessary: it's not that simple. First, we must bear in mind the fact that the level of support one finds depends, in part, on how one measures it: the answer necessarily reflects the question to some degree, because different questions have different connotations and imply different cutting points between "pro" and "con." It follows that any given set of responses must be interpreted in context with the question that evoked them — and ideally, the question should be as simple, clear, and neutral as possible.

But even assuming that we use a simple and neutral question, reality itself is complicated. We cannot provide a simple description of it: it turns out that domestic political support for nuclear power is strong in some countries and weak in others. Similarly, the parties of the Left are pronuclear in some cases and antinuclear in others. Moreover, the levels of support in given countries change over time.

Finally, we have to specify what we mean when we speak of "domestic political support": do we mean the general public, regardless of how well informed or strongly motivated they are, or do we mean political elites? The evidence indicates that Lovins is partly right and partly wrong, and exactly how right or wrong we consider him depends, in part, on which of the above definitions we consider most relevant.

Despite these reservations, some findings seem reasonably clear. No matter how we slice the data, it is virtually impossible to reject the conclusion that Lovins is right about Denmark. And no matter how we slice the data, it is difficult to avoid the conclusion that he is wrong about France. Let us examine the evidence.

The spring 1979 European Community survey (*Euro-Barometer* 11) included a battery of 13 items, introduced as follows:

> We'd like to hear your views on some important political issues. Could you tell me whether you agree or disagree with each of the following proposals? . . . How strongly do you feel?

The second item in the series was "Nuclear energy should be developed to meet future energy needs." Table 9.1 shows the percentage agreeing or disagreeing with this proposition among the publics of the nine European Community nations in April-May 1979. The question measures support or opposition to nuclear power at a given point in time, and this particular time happened to be immediately after the March 1979 nuclear accident at Three Mile Island, which received an immense amount of coverage in the mass media of these countries. On the whole, public attitudes toward nuclear power have been relatively stable over time, but in this case there is reason to suspect that public support for nuclear power was at a low ebb at the time of the surveys. This clearly was the case in the United States, where public support for the nuclear option dropped by ten points or more in the aftermath of Three Mile Island, but recovered by early 1980.

TABLE 9.1
Support for Developing Nuclear Energy
Among European Community Publics: April-May 1979
(percent)

	Agree Strongly	Agree	Disagree	Disagree Strongly	N
United Kingdom	28	47	14	11	(1,126)
France	26	35	20	19	(891)
Germany	24	37	19	19	(896)
Belgium	23	30	24	23	(815)
Italy	19	32	21	28	(1,004)
Ireland	15	32	26	28	(845)
Denmark	16	22	27	35	(901)
Netherlands	14	24	22	40	(954)
European Community	23	36	20	21	(7,432)

"Nuclear energy should be developed to meet future energy needs."

Source: European Community public opinion survey (*Euro-Barometer* 11, June 1979).

The results from spring 1979 may underestimate current mass support for nuclear power, but let us take it as a conservative base line. At that time, developing nuclear energy was supported by 59 percent of the European Community public as a whole (weighted according to population) and opposed by 41 percent.

But perhaps the most striking finding from Table 9.1 is the fact that public support varied dramatically from one country to another. There is little justification for generalizing about support for nuclear power "in almost all countries" because the situation varies greatly from one country to another: in the United Kingdom support overwhelmed opposition to nuclear power by a 75:25 ratio; in the Netherlands, at the opposite end of the continuum, 62 percent of the public opposed nuclear power and only 38 percent supported it. Pronuclear sentiment heavily outweighed antinuclear sentiment among the publics of France and Germany in 1979, and the pronuclear position prevailed narrowly in Belgium, Luxembourg, and Italy. Opposition narrowly outweighed support in Ireland, and was strongly predominant in Denmark.

Undoubtedly the absolute level of support or opposition will fluctuate somewhat, but we suspect that the rank ordering shown in Table 9.1 – with Britain, France, and Germany at the top and Denmark and the Netherlands at the bottom – will remain relatively stable. It seems to reflect long-term factors that have helped shape the outlook of the respective nationalities. In particular, support tends to be strongest among the publics of those countries that have long established, relatively large-scale nuclear power programs; it is weakest in those countries that have new or nonexistent programs. Table 9.2 demonstrates this point.

The first nuclear power plant in the world went into operation in Great Britain in 1954. In 1979 the United Kingdom still led the European Community in the number of nuclear power plants, with 33 in operation. It is probably no coincidence that public support for nuclear power was stronger in that country than anywhere else in the Community. France ranks second in both tables, operating 16 plants in 1979 (though by now it has surpassed Great Britain in the production of nuclear power). Conversely, the three nations in which the public is predominately antinuclear were operating a combined total of only two nuclear power plants.

This could be interpreted as evidence of the decisive influence of public opinion: in those countries where nuclear power is unpopular, nuclear power plants don't get built. And there unquestionably is a good deal of truth in this interpretation: public opinion can prevent the utilization of nuclear power, as is illustrated by the fact that not long after these surveys, in a 1981 national referendum, the Danish public voted against nuclear power — effectively killing the nuclear option in that country.

But it seems very likely that the causal process works both ways. The 33 nuclear power plants operating in Britain might not be there if the British public were overwhelmingly opposed — but in all probability, one reason why the British public is favorable is the fact that nuclear power has been operating there for over 25 years on a relatively large scale, producing electrical power but not producing the soot or the deaths that would be linked with coal-burning plants. For the British public, nuclear power is not particularly new or frightening; it has been around for a long time.

TABLE 9.2
Number of Nuclear Power Reactors Operating in European Community Nations, 1979

Nation	*Number*
United Kingdom	33
France	16
Germany	13
Belgium	3
Luxembourg	0
Italy	4
Ireland	0
Denmark	0
Netherlands	2

Source: Kidder, Peabody, and Company, "Electric Utility Generating Equipment: Status Report on Worldwide Nuclear Reactors" (October 1979).

Historically the United States was the second nation to develop nuclear power plants. If the foregoing interpretation is correct, the American public should also be relatively favorable to nuclear power. How does it compare with the other nine publics? It is not possible to make a cross-national comparison based on data gathered at the same time. But an item similar to the question shown in Table 9.1 was included in the September 1980 survey of consumer attitudes carried out by the University of Michigan Survey Research Center.

The precise wording, and results, were as follows:

Please tell me if you agree or disagree with the following statement: "Nuclear power should be developed to meet future energy needs. . . ." Do you strongly agree, somewhat agree, somewhat disagree or strongly disagree?

Strongly agree	33%
Somewhat agree	38
Somewhat disagree	13
Strongly disagree	15
	99% (682)

As of September 1980, 71 percent of the American public supported the development of nuclear power, and 28 percent opposed it. We must bear in mind that the wording varied slightly (since only one item was used here, instead of a battery of 13 items) and that the American survey took place a year and a half after the accident at Three Mile Island, rather than immediately afterward. Bearing these caveats in mind, it is interesting to note that the American public ranked second in support for nuclear power, immediately after the British — which is precisely where one might expect the Americans to be, on the basis of the length of their experience with nuclear power.

The validity of this interpretation remains to be tested against further evidence, but we will draw the provisional conclusion that long-term experience with the use of nuclear electric power tends to increase its public acceptance in a given nation.

But, needless to say, time is not the only factor. Nuclear power has become a hotly contested, highly ideological topic in recent years. In this struggle the antinuclear forces tend to identify themselves with the Left. But the antinuclear Left is a New Left that does not fit easily into traditional categories, for the leaders of both the ruling Communist parties of eastern Europe and Asia, and the major nonruling Communist parties of western Europe, are strongly pronuclear. Nevertheless, the antinuclear segments of Western electorates tend to support the parties of the Left, as Table 9.3 illustrates. In this table the numerous political parties of nine nations are grouped together according to the six major party groupings of the European Parliament. The first four groupings are truly transnational, with significant representation in all or almost all of the European Community nations. The last two groups are more narrowly based: the Progressive Democrats are primarily a French grouping, consisting of Gaullists, plus the Irish Fianna Fail and the Danish Progress Party; the Conservatives (officially known as the European Democrats in the European Parliament) are primarily the British Conservatives, together with smaller Danish groups.

The fact that the last two groups in table 9.3 are largely French and British distorts the picture slightly, for these are the most pronuclear nationalities. Nevertheless, it is readily apparent, even

TABLE 9.3
Support for Developing Nuclear Energy,
by European Political Party
(percentage favoring development)

Party	Percent	Number
Communists	48	(414)
Socialists	54	(2,131)
Liberals	71	(761)
Christian Democrats	63	(1,554)
Progressive Democrats	82	(512)
Conservatives	80	(490)

Source: European Community Surveys, April-May 1979.

from the simplified overview provided by Table 9.3, that the Socialist and Communist electorates are significantly less favorable to nuclear power than those of the other parties. It is by no means a case of black-and-white polarization: on the contrary, the Communist and Socialist electorates are very evenly split on this issue, and even the electorates of the Right fall far short of unanimity. But there is a definite tendency for an antinuclear stance to be more congenial to the Left than the Right. Why? We will return to this question later.

First, however, let us examine support for and opposition to nuclear power among political elites of western Europe. Our evidence is based on a survey of candidates for the European Parliament carried out immediately before this body was elected by popular vote for the first time, in June 1979. Fieldwork for this survey was supported by the Volkswagen Foundation, the Commission of the European Communities, and the European Parliament (for details of fieldwork, see Inglehart, Rabier, Gordon, and Sorensen 1980). Our sample of 672 candidates includes 62 percent of those who were actually elected to the European Parliament, covers all nationalities and all political parties that won seats, and is weighted in proportion to the number of seats won by a given party from a given nation. The members of the European Parliament are relatively young but are roughly equivalent in social background to members of the lower houses of the respective national parliaments – in which many of them also hold seats. Hence, this sample should provide a reasonably good, and cross-nationally comparable, indication of the views of west European political elites.

In these interviews we used the same battery of questions concerning 13 key issues that had been employed in surveys of the publics of the same countries at about the same time. The elite responses were coded into five categories rather than four, however: a neutral "neither agree nor disagree" category was included, in addition to the four agree-disagree categories. Table 9.4 shows the results from political elites in each of the nine nations.

As in Table 9.1, the nations are ranked according to their relative levels of support for nuclear power. Table 9.4 replicates the rank ordering of Table 9.1 with almost incredible fidelity. At both mass and elite levels the three most pronuclear nations are Britain, France, and Germany. At both mass and elite levels the three least pronuclear nations are Denmark, Ireland, and the Netherlands. And at both mass and elite levels Denmark, Ireland, and the Netherlands are the only countries in which opposition to nuclear power equals or outweighs support for it. Virtually the only notable difference between elite and mass patterns is found in France, which ranked second in Table 9.1 but rises to first place in Table 9.4. Closer inspection of the results reveals that the British elites are no less favorable to nuclear power than is the British public (the respective figures are 73 percent and 75 percent), but the French elites are appreciably more pronuclear than the French public.

TABLE 9.4
Support for Developing Nuclear Energy Among Candidates
for European Parliament, April-May 1979

"We'd like to hear your views on some important political issues. Could you tell me whether you agree or disagree with each of the following proposals? How strongly do you feel?" [Third item in series of thirteen items]: "Nuclear energy should be developed to meet future energy needs."

(percent)

Nation	Agree Strongly	Agree	Neither Agree nor Disagree	Disagree	Disagree Strongly	N
France	46	33	6	11	4	(100)
United Kingdom	24	49	19	6	2	(108)
Germany	17	50	14	13	6	(144)
Italy	24	30	16	21	10	(156)
Belgium	14	30	26	22	9	(34)
Luxembourg	0	46	13	36	6	(10)
Denmark	26	13	23	16	23	(35)
Ireland	13	20	27	23	18	(19)
Netherlands	5	25	24	20	26	(42)
European Parliament	25	37	16	14	8	(648)

Source: Survey of candidates for the European Parliament, Spring 1979.

The striking similarity between the national patterns of support at both mass and elite levels tends to confirm the interpretation that we are dealing with a relatively stable aspect of the given political cultures, linked with the historical experiences of the respective nations.

When we examine attitudes toward nuclear power by political party, we find an interesting contrast between the electorates and the elites of the Left. Table 9.5 shows support for an opposition to nuclear power among the candidates of the major groups in the European Parliament.

Among the general public the Communist electorate is least favorable to nuclear power: only 48 percent support developing it. At the elite level, however, the Communist group is overwhelmingly pronuclear: 67 percent "agree" or "agree strongly" that it should be developed. When we subject our elite data to a more refined breakdown by party and nationality, as in Table 9.6, we observe

TABLE 9.5

Support for Developing Nuclear Energy, by Political Party

(agreement or disagreement that "Nuclear energy should be developed to meet future energy needs"; percent)

	Agree Strongly	*Agree*	*Neither Agree nor Disagree*	*Disagree*	*Disagree Strongly*	*N*
Communist	30	37	15	17	2	(52)
Socialist	6	28	17	31	18	(237)
Christian Democrat	24	48	18	9	2	(154)
Liberal	39	41	11	8	1	(66)
Conservative	33	53	14	0	0	(45)
European Progressive Democrat	74	15	12	0	0	(42)
Other	12	9	22	18	39	(52)

Source: Survey of candidates for the European Parliament, Spring 1979.

TABLE 6
Support for Developing Nuclear Energy, by Party and by Nation

"We'd like to hear your views on some important political issues. Could you tell me whether you agree or disagree with each of the following proposals? How strongly do you feel?" [THIRD ITEM IN SERIES OF THIRTEEN ITEMS:] "Nuclear energy should be developed to meet future energy needs."

(Percent "agreeing strongly" or "agreeing")

Nation	Communist	Socialist	Christian Democrat	Liberal	Conservative	Progressive Democrat	Other	N
Belgium	*	27	65	60	*	*	0	(34)
Denmark	0	7	*	60	100	100	0	(35)
Germany	*	39	92	50	*	*	*	(144)
France	83	43	100	95	*	97	*	(100)
Ireland	*	0	25	*	*	73	0	(19)
Italy	55	35	60	80	*	*	32	(156)
Luxembourg	*	0	25	100	*	*	*	(10)
Netherlands	*	6	43	67	*	*	0	(42)
United Kingdom	*	43	*	*	85	100	20	(108)
European Parliament	67	34	72	81	86	92	18	(648)

*Not applicable.
Source: Survey of candidates for the European Parliament, Spring 1979.

209

that this pronuclear majority masks a sharp contrast between the French and Italian Communist parties — which are overwhelmingly pronuclear — and the Danish group, which is solidly antinuclear. The Communist party group as a whole is strongly pronuclear simply because the French and Italian delegations are much larger than the Danish.

The Socialists are in the converse situation: while their electorate tends to favor nuclear power, the Socialist candidates are predominately opposed. Thus, while the Socialist and Communist electorates are rather similar in their attitudes, the two parties differ starkly at the elite level: 67 percent of the Communists favor developing nuclear power — as compared with only 34 percent of the Socialist candidates. The Socialists are cross-nationally divided on this issue. While support is about as widespread as opposition within the British, French, and German parties, it is virtually nonexistent among the Danish, Dutch, and Irish groups.

No party group is as severely divided over nuclear power as the Socialists. The transnational Socialist party federation splits on this issue along national lines; within given countries there is a disparity between relatively pronuclear electorates and relatively antinuclear elites; and in the larger countries with substantial nuclear power capacities, the elites are divided into pronuclear and antinuclear factions. This was particularly true in Germany, where Helmut Schmidt was performing a difficult balancing act, trying to hold together a coalition of pronuclear politicians and labor union leaders with a sizable young Socialist wing that is militantly antinuclear. In the West German institutional setting, the result has been a paralysis of nuclear power plant construction.

The remarkable pace at which nuclear power has developed in France in recent years seems to reflect a situation in which a predominantly pronuclear public was led by overwhelmingly pronuclear political elites, operating within a judicial and regulatory structure in which antinuclear groups could not readily block nuclear power plant construction, or make it prohibitively expensive through protracted and repeated delays.

The coming to power of a Socialist-led government makes the future of nuclear power uncertain in France. At the elite level the Socialists are least favorable to nuclear power of all the major French parties. On the other hand, President Mitterrand's electorate tends to be pronuclear, and his governing coalition is partly dependent on the support of Communist labor unions and party activists who are overwhelmingly pronuclear. Moreover, the development of nuclear power may give French industry significant cost advantages over its competitors in neighboring countries. According to Electricité de France, oil-generated electricity in France is now more than twice as expensive as nuclear power and 75 percent more expensive than coal-generated power. The French government forecasts that by 1990, the average price per nuclear-produced kilowatt-hour will be $.03, compared with $.05 for coal and $.10 for oil (*Business Week*, June 1, 1981, p. 45). Italian electricity is generated primarily by oil and coal, with only a small nuclear component; Italian economists estimate that the cost to Italian industry of having more expensive energy than France will be on the order of $10 billion in the 1980s (*The Economist*, May 23, 1981, p. 34). Furthermore, nuclear power may make an enormous difference in France's balance-of-payments problems. The cost of imported oil to Germany alone is currently in the neighborhood of $50 billion per year.

By a greater reliance on nuclear power, the French will be able to spend much less on imported oil, and to offset part of the remaining costs through the sale of nuclear power plants in an export market in which French technology is now extremely well placed. Finally, nuclear power offers the French economy a degree of security if the supply of petroleum from OPEC countries should be interrupted. To be sure, it will still need to import uranium — but the volume and cost involved are trivial by comparison with those of an equivalent amount of energy in the form of oil or coal. With a nuclear power plant the main cost is the hardware; fuel is a relatively minor item. Subsequent increases in the cost of fuel, therefore, have relatively little impact on the price of electricity — a partial hedge against inflation and, even more important, a safeguard against the recessions that have followed each of the major OPEC price increases.

All of these factors suggest that the impact of the change in government on French nuclear energy policy will be only marginal.

THE ROOTS OF PRONUCLEAR AND ANTINUCLEAR ATTITUDES

Up to this point we have examined support for and opposition to nuclear power among Western elites and publics, and proposed a possible explanation of why attitudes are relatively pronuclear in certain countries but antinuclear in others.

But we have not attempted to explain why, within given nations, some groups and individuals hold pronuclear convictions while others are antinuclear. In seeking such an explanation, two types of factors play a central role: one's information and one's values. The two seem to interact, with cognitive factors sometimes influencing one's values, and one's values screening the information one receives and assimilates. Let us start with the cognitive aspect.

Paradoxically, both pronuclear and antinuclear groups tend to offer rather similar explanations of why their opponents disagree with them: they are inadequately informed. From a pronuclear viewpoint, opposition results from an inadequate understanding of the economic and environmental advantages of nuclear power, and a failure to understand the actual safety of nuclear power plants. From an antinuclear viewpoint, the problem is inadequate public awareness of the long-term costs and hazards of nuclear power; far from leading to increased acceptance of nuclear power, it is argued that more information simply mobilizes latent fears about nuclear hazards (Kasperson 1980).

If the information springs from a controversy over whether a specific nuclear power plant should be allowed to operate, debate is likely to be limited to the question "Will this nuclear power plant result in 50,000 deaths or none?" Under such circumstances the resulting information almost certainly will simply mobilize latent fears. On the other hand, when the risks and costs of not using nuclear power are weighed, as well as the risks and costs of using it, the result may be quite different. But this approach involves considering a nation's energy policy as a whole, rather than just the risks connected with one aspect that lends itself to sensational treatment. Sweden and the United States provide illustrations of the two contrasting approaches to public information.

Sweden's referendum on nuclear power in 1980 was preceded by what was probably the most thorough information campaign that has ever taken place on the subject in any country. Since 1976 nuclear power had been the central issue in Swedish politics. During the months preceding the referendum, the issue was debated at great length, not only in the mass media but also through extensive campaigns organized by the major political parties, labor unions, business and environmental organizations, and other interest groups. The Swedish public was actively involved in the debate, to an unprecedented extent. Approximately 80,000 Swedes participated in discussion groups dealing with the nuclear power question.

In the ensuing referendum the Swedish public voted in favor of an option that gave lip service to the goal of phasing out nuclear power a generation later, but will enable the production of nuclear power to be doubled by 1985. To argue that more information simply results in more opposition to nuclear power seems to be an oversimplification. It depends on the quality and balance of the information, as well as its quantity.

In terms of sheer volume, nothing can compare with the deluge of information concerning nuclear power that poured out in the aftermath of the 1979 accident at Three Mile Island. But one can question its quality and balance. It has been estimated that 40 percent of the prime-time news coverage on the major American television networks was devoted to Three Mile Island during the weeks immediately after the accident. During the following months nuclear power was on front pages and television newscasts almost daily, and was the subject of cover stories in news magazines throughout the Western world. But though millions of words were spoken and printed about nuclear power, the news media failed to convey some of the most basic facts the public would need to know in order to make an informed judgment about what was involved.

To take one crucial example: in 1980 only 9 percent of the American public was aware that it would by physically impossible for a Hiroshima-type explosion to take place in the nuclear power plants now operating in the United States; fully 87 percent believed it could happen. In September 1980 a national sample was asked the following question:

> People have been talking about the possibility of accidents taking place in nuclear power plants. What about a nuclear explosion like that of the bomb used in Japan in World War II — would you say that an explosion of this type in one of the nuclear power plants now operating in this country is very likely, somewhat likely, not very likely, or physically impossible?

The vast majority of the American public indicated that they thought these plants could explode like atomic bombs, and assigned this prospect various degrees of probability, as indicated in Table 9.7. Only 9 percent were aware that such an explosion was physically impossible (the remaining 4 percent said they didn't know).

Similar results were obtained from a 1982 survey of the publics of the European Community nations. In the European Community as a whole, 76 percent of those interviewed thought that a Hiroshima-like explosion could take place; 15 percent said they didn't know; and only 10 percent said that it was physically impossible.

Western publics have been poorly informed on this subject – for such an explosion is, of course, physically impossible. The light-water nuclear reactors operating in the United States and most European countries utilize uranium-235 enriched to a concentration of about 3 percent. An explosive chain reaction requires a much higher concentration. And this concentration could not be reached by any conceivable accident: enriching uranium is an extremely difficult process, requiring sophisticated technology and complex equipment.

As one might expect, whether or not one was correctly informed was related to education: in the American public, for example, among those whose education did not go beyond high school, only 5 percent were aware that such an explosion was physically impossible; among college graduates the figure was 17 percent. But perhaps the more striking fact is how poorly informed even the college-educated were. During the weeks after the accident at Three Mile Island, even people as highly educated as Ralph Nader were making comments to the effect that "If Three Mile Island blows up, it'll take eastern Pennsylvania with it." The greater the possible danger appeared, the greater the news value of the Three Mile Island story. Perhaps for this reason, the mass media did not go out of their way to reassure the public that their worst fears might be unfounded. Contrary to what most of the public believes, the worst conceivable accident that could take place is not a Hiroshima-type explosion, but a meltdown or steam blast that could allow radioactive waste products to escape into the groundwater or atmosphere.

This misconception may have played a major role in public reactions to mass media reports of a potential disaster at Three Mile Island. After a lengthy investigation the Kemeny Commission, appointed by the president to investigate the accident, concluded that – in the most serious accident ever to befall the nuclear industry

TABLE 9.7
Public Perceptions of the Danger that a Nuclear Power Plant Could Explode Like an Atomic Bomb

"People have been talking about the possibility of accidents taking place in nuclear power plants. What about a nuclear explosion like that of the bomb used in Japan in World War II – would you say that an explosion of this type in one of the nuclear power plants now operating in this country is very likely, somewhat likely, not very likely, or physically impossible?"

(answers in percent)

	U.S.A.	Germany	France	Neth.	United Kingdom	Denmark	Italy	Belgium	Ireland	Greece
Very likely	12	8	6	11	11	13	10	12	19	24
Somewhat likely	32	21	26	30	31	22	31	35	37	41
Not very likely	43	40	47	43	40	43	31	27	20	19
Don't know	4	19	12	7	9	14	20	21	21	12
Physically impossible	9	12	10	10	9	9	9	6	4	4

Note: U.S. data based on 682 telephone interviews with a representative probability sample of the American public. The numbers of interviews in the European countries (in the order above) were 1,063; 999; 1,028; 1,259; 1,003; 1,084; 1,006; 983; 999.

Sources: United States – Survey of Consumer Attitudes, Survey Research Center, University of Michigan, September 1980; Europe – Commission of the European Communities, *Euro-Barometer* Survey no. 17, April 1982, June 1982.

215

in the Western world – no one had been physically harmed, even slightly; no lives had been endangered; the amount of radiation to which people living in the vicinity of Three Mile Island were exposed was about one-tenth that from a routine chest X-ray (or from the normal amount of sunshine in Denver); and the most serious harm done was damage to the mental health of the people in the vicinity – who suffered severe psychological stress from worrying about what they thought might happen. Part of this psychological stress came from living with a danger that was wholly imaginary: if the residents of the Harrisburg area were like the rest of the American public, the great majority of them believed that the Three Mile Island plant might explode like a huge atomic bomb.

This does not mean that opposition to nuclear power plants is simply based on ignorance. Many very well informed people oppose them because of concerns about such problems as waste disposal and proliferation. But uncertainty about the difference between a nuclear power plant and an atomic bomb does seem to be a crucial factor in support for the nuclear option. Among those Americans who believed that an atomic bomblike explosion in a nuclear power plant was "very likely," a clear majority – 60 percent – opposed the development of nuclear power plants. Among those who realized that it is physically impossible, only 12 percent opposed developing nuclear power and 88 percent supported it. Misapprehension on this subject could cost many lives and increase Western dependence on imported petroleum.

During the decade preceding 1978, the contribution that nuclear power made to American energy resources grew more than twelve-fold. At the start of this period it generated less than 1 percent of total American electrical output; by 1978 it furnished more than 12 percent. After Three Mile Island this development stopped. In 1979 and 1980 nuclear power furnished only about 11 percent of American electricity, and just 3 percent of primary energy supply. In the present atmosphere of delays and uncertainty, no new nuclear power plants are being ordered, and at least a dozen of those already ordered have been canceled. There is a serious possibility that the American nuclear power industry, which led the world until quite recently, may shut down completely.

No law of nature or economics determines that this must be so. Many other nations have decided to pursue the nuclear option vigorously, and a number of them (including Belgium, Sweden, Switzerland, France, and Great Britain) already surpass the United States in the percentage of electricity they produce from nuclear sources. The United States is capable of achieving similar goals; doing so would reduce its dependence on imported oil, strengthen the dollar, and reduce pollution. Quite probably it would also save lives.

If one is genuinely concerned with the safety of the American people, one needs to weigh the risks of not using nuclear power along with the risks of using it. If we do not use nuclear power, we will probably use something else, and at present the chief alternatives are coal and oil. Nuclear power is not totally risk-free — but neither are the alternatives. Approximately 100,000 Americans have died in coal mine accidents in the twentieth century. From the start, nuclear power has been viewed with an almost superstitious awe, and the safety standards imposed on nuclear power plants have been incomparably more demanding than those imposed on coal- or oil-powered plants. These standards have grown steadily more stringent, with the reaction to Three Mile Island bringing an additional wave of tighter safety requirements. In this respect the antinuclear movement has played a constructive role. The danger is that by going to extremes, it could inadvertently cost lives. The escape of radioactive material from a power plant could cause casualties, though in 25 years of operation it has never done so, either in the United States or anywhere else in the Western world. But each year hundreds of miners die in coal mining accidents, and in the United States alone about 3,000 coal miners die from black lung disease each year. No one knows exactly how many additional deaths among the general public can be traced to pollution from coal — but a study estimates that 53,000 Americans die each year from industrial pollution caused by burning coal and oil (Wilson et al. 1981). It seems reasonably clear that any switch from nuclear power to coal, however well intentioned, would in the long run wind up costing many lives.

Continuing to rely on oil might be even more reckless. Like any form of energy, it has unavoidable occupational hazards: a North Sea oil platform collapsed in 1980, killing 123 people in a single accident (which was forgotten within a few weeks). But an even more serious danger in relying on imported oil is that it threatens to involve the West in war in the Middle East. The Rapid Deployment Force that the United States is developing is designed to protect Middle Eastern sources of petroleum from Soviet inter-vention. If it were used, and the Russians responded in kind, it is difficult to say where escalation would stop.

Nothing is perfectly risk-free. Despite their impressive safety record, nuclear power plants cannot be guaranteed to be totally free from accidents. On the contrary, if they continue to operate, we must assume that people eventually will be killed or injured; but the human impact of such an incident, if it does take place, will probably be on the scale of a coal mine accident or an oil drilling accident, and not on the scale of Hiroshima.

A Hiroshima-type explosion is impossible. Nevertheless, if one is asked to think up the worst conceivable accident involving a nuclear power plant, regardless of how improbable it is, one can readily reach a figure that borders on Hiroshima. If everything went wrong simultaneously, and if the back-up systems failed, and the back-up systems to the back-up systems failed, and if on top of this the containment structure were breached, and the plant were situated near a large city and if there were an atmospheric inversion, and if a sufficiently strong wind were blowing in just the right direction, then enough radioactive waste might get blown over the city to kill 50,000 people. This is, of course, conceivable – but highly unlikely.

Western publics are highly sensitive on this topic. In the barrage of publicity about Three Mile Island, the attitudes of the American public shifted from being predominantly pronuclear to being un-favorable toward the development of nuclear power. More recently there are indications that this mood may be shifting. Despite the persistence of some major misconceptions about the risks of nuclear power plants, the American public again seems relatively favorable to constructing them, although the results depend partly on how the questions are phrased. For example, in November 1980 the American public was asked the following question:

> Some people say that the nation needs to develop new power sources from nuclear energy in order to meet our needs for the future. Other people say that the danger to the environment and the possibility of accidents are too great. What do you think? Are you in favor of build-ing more nuclear energy power plants, would you favor operating only those that are already built, or would you prefer to see all nuclear power plants closed down?

This question contains the phrases "danger to the environment" and "the possibility of accidents." As we have seen, for most people the word "accidents," in connection with nuclear power, implies the possibility of Hiroshima-type explosion. In response to this question, 33 percent of the public favored building more plants, 42 percent favored operating only those already built, and 16 percent wanted to see all nuclear plants closed down (8 percent had no opinion or were undecided) (Miller 1981). When the dangers of nuclear accidents are explicitly evoked in a question, much of the public shrinks from the idea of building more nuclear plants but does not, for the most part, favor closing down the existing plants; it opts for a compromise course, if it is available.

These results could be interpreted in various ways. One could report that only 16 percent of the American public favors abandoning the nuclear option. Or one could report that only a third of the American public favors building more nuclear power plants. Both findings are accurate — in the context of this particular trichotomous question. But both reports could be misleading in what they imply about the remaining 42 percent. The fact that only one-third chose the option "building more nuclear energy power plants" does not necessarily indicate that the other two-thirds oppose the plants. Another question, in which the Harris Poll simply asked whether one was for or against building more nuclear power plants in the United States, indicates that a majority of the American public favors building more plants: when nuclear accidents are not evoked, and a compromise option is offered, the bulk of the public shifts to the pronuclear side.

Each of these questions uses a reasonable formulation and each set of responses reveals something about public attitudes toward nuclear power. But the responses can be misleading if interpreted out of context with the question that evoked them, for this is a highly charged topic — on the one hand, nuclear power offers possible help in solving the current energy crisis and urgent economic difficulties; on the other hand, it can evoke terrifying, apocalyptic images.

Western publics' first awareness of nuclear power came with the stunning and terrible news from Hiroshima. That a single atomic bomb had suddenly destroyed 100,000 people was shocking, terrifying, almost supernatural. This apocalyptic first impression has remained linked with anything bearing the name "nuclear" ever since. One of the crucial points shaping Western attitudes toward nuclear power is the fact that the majority of the public does not have a clear idea of the distinction between nuclear power plants and atomic bombs – and tends to view nuclear accidents as potential Hiroshima-like explosions. As long as this perception persists, it will constitute a key constraint on Western energy policy.

It wold be false to assert that there is no connection between the two. Historically, the development of nuclear power plants was based on the research that had given rise to atomic bombs. And there is a genuine possibility that the spread of nuclear power plants might facilitate the spread of nuclear weapons, though the relationship is highly problematic. But to simply lump the two together as "nukes" is misleading even when done with the best intentions, and could conceivably cost lives rather than save them.

An awareness of these facts, together with a diminishing impact of the publicity about Three Mile Island, may have led to a gradual shift in the direction of more favorable attitudes toward nuclear power among most Western European publics from 1979 to 1981. Table 9.8 shows support for developing nuclear energy among ten Western publics. In the European Community as a whole, the support level rose from 60 percent to 65 percent during this period. On the whole, the changes are modest; only in Italy was there a dramatic rise in support. Overall, the rank order of the respective countries is remarkably stable, which is consistent with our earlier suggestion that the cross-national differences reflect the respective nations' historical experience with nuclear power. But insofar as change has occurred, there has been a moderate tendency toward increased public support for nuclear power.

CHANGING VALUES AND ATTITUDES TOWARD NUCLEAR POWER

Information may play a key role in shaping attitudes toward nuclear power. But to a very large extent these attitudes also seem to reflect one's underlying value priorities – which may selectively screen the information one assimilates.

There is considerable evidence that during the past few decades, the prevailing value priorities of Western publics have undergone a shift from overwhelming emphasis on "materialist" values (giving top priority to economic and physical security) toward greater stress on "postmaterialist" values that emphasize belonging, self-expression, and the nonmaterial quality of life (Inglehart 1977; 1981).

This process of value change has taken place gradually, as one generation replaces another in the adult population. In large part it seems to reflect the far greater economic and physical security, compared with older generations, that the postwar generation

TABLE 9.8
Support for Developing Nuclear Energy Among West European Publics: Spring 1979 and Fall 1981

"Nuclear energy should be developed to meet future energy needs."
(percentage "agree" among those expressing an opinion)

	April 1979	*October 1981*
United Kingdom	75	72
United States	(n.a.)	71
Germany	62	69
France	60	67
Italy	51	65
Greece	(n.a.)	56
Belgium	53	49
Ireland	46	43
Netherlands	38	43
Denmark	38	36
European Community	60	65

Sources: Europe — *Euro-Barometer* surveys no. 11 (June 1979) and no. 16 (December 1981); United States — Consumer Outlook Survey, Survey Research Center, ISR, University of Michigan, September 1980, listed under the 1981 column.

experienced during its formative years. But its effects have now penetrated deeply into the ranks of young professional, managerial, and technocratic elites, with a pervasive political impact (Inglehart 1981).

Until quite recently it was taken as self-evident that economic growth was inherently good; though there were sharp disagreements on how its benefits should be allocated, the pro-growth consensus embraced both labor and management, capitalist and Communist. Only recently has this assumption been called into question, with the environmentalist movement holding that economic growth does not always justify its impact on the environment, and with some segments of the movement arguing that economic growth is now becoming either undesirable or even impossible, because of the scarcity of natural resources. When environmentalism raises questions of environmental quality versus economic growth (as is often the case), it pits postmaterialist priorities squarely against materialist ones.

It is significant that the environmentalist movement has not collapsed in the post-1973 setting of severe strains on Western economies that are due to skyrocketing energy costs that exacerbate inflation, and that drain away immense sums of capital that might otherwise be invested to produce fuller employment. Despite this economic crisis, and a subsequent backlash against environmentalism, postmaterialist support for environmentalism remains firm and the movement continues to win some victories.

One of the most dramatic and emotionally charged confrontations between materialist and postmaterialist priorities was the struggle over nuclear power. One can conceive of a world in which postmaterialists favored the development of nuclear power on the grounds that it disturbs the natural environment less than coal mines, petroleum wells, or hydroelectric dams, and that it produces less pollution and has a better safety record than conventional energy sources. This is conceivable – but the reality is quite different.

Nuclear power has come to symbolize everything the post-materialists oppose. It carries connotations of Hiroshima, reinforced by fears that nuclear power plants might facilitate the spread of nuclear weapons. Based on complex technology, nuclear power was developed by large corporations and the federal government, in the name of economic growth. Postmaterialists were disproportionately active in the antiwar movement, tend to be suspicious of big business and big government – and give low priority to economic growth. They form the core of the opposition to nuclear power. And, despite the current energy crisis, opposition to nuclear power plants has not died away – on the contrary, it has brought the development of nuclear power almost to a halt in the United States, West Germany, and several other countries. In the face of protracted and unpredictable delays, no new nuclear power plants are being ordered, and many of those already ordered have been canceled. In South Korea, where environmentalist and antinuclear groups have virtually no impact, a nuclear power plant can be built in five years. In the United States the time now averages about 12 years. It seems possible that the American nuclear power plant industry, which led the world until recently, may shut down completely.

Like the environmentalist movement, the struggle over nuclear power reflects a clash of world views. For materialists the use of nuclear energy is desirable insofar as it seems linked with economic growth and full employment. For them highly developed science and industry symbolize progress and prosperity. Among postmaterialists nuclear power tends to be rejected not only because of its potential dangers but also because it is linked with big business, big science, and big government – bureaucratic organizations that are evaluated negatively because they are inherently impersonal and hierarchial, minimizing individual self-expression and human contact. The ideologues of the antinuclear movement argue for a return to a simpler, more human society in which energy is used sparingly and what is needed comes directly from nature – symbolized by solar power (Nelkin and Pollak 1981).

Tables 9.9 and 9.10 show the relationship between value type and support for developing nuclear energy among European Community publics and among candidates for the European Parliament (the measures of value priorities are described in Inglehart 1977; 1981). In every country materialists are far more favorable to developing nuclear energy than are the postmaterialists. At the mass level a majority of the materialists support the development of nuclear power and a majority of the postmaterialists oppose it in eight out of nine nations. The differences are even more pronounced at the elite level; a majority of materialists support nuclear power and a majority of postmaterialists oppose it among candidates from every one of the nine countries. And the percentage spread between materialists and postmaterialists is at least 46 points

TABLE 9.9
Support for Development of Nuclear Power Among West European Publics, by Value Type

Question: "Could you tell me whether you agree or disagree with each of the following proposals?" . . . "Nuclear Energy should be developed to meet future energy needs."
(percentage "agree" or "agree strongly")

	Britain	France	Germany	Belgium	Italy	Luxem-bourg	Ireland	Nether-lands	Denmark
Materialist	79	77	69	56	57	53	52	59	41
Mixed	75	64	58	57	47	59	45	36	40
Post-materialistic	52	44	46	46	45	36	35	27	20

Source: European Community survey (*Euro-Barometer*, June 11, 1979), April-May 1979.

TABLE 9.10
Support for Developing Nuclear Power Among Candidates for European Parliament, by Value Type

(percentage "agree" or "agree strongly")

	France	Germany	Britain	Italy	Belgium	Ireland	Luxem-bourg	Denmark	Nether-lands
Materialist	95	98	77	55	100	54	71	86	64
Mixed	85	65	54	54	40	29	25	14	35
Post-materialist	49	40	24	44	24	0	0	9	5

Source: European Elections Study survey of candidates for European Parliament.

in every country but Italy, where nuclear power has not become a major political issue.

This emerging axis of polarization cuts squarely across traditional Left-Right lines. On the antinuclear side are intellectuals, some Socialists — and much of the upper middle class. On the pronuclear side are big business — and the AFL-CIO — Gaullists — and the French Communist party. It is not a traditional class struggle, but a polarization based on materialist versus postmaterialist values.

One of the most striking features of the nuclear power controversy is the extent to which well-informed members of the public and even competent experts, when exposed to the same body of information, draw totally different conclusions. We believe this reflects a process of cognitive screening in which given facts are retained and weighted in accord with the individual's basic values. Though support for or opposition to nuclear power is usually justified in terms of objective costs, benefits, and risks, an underlying factor is a clash of world views.

Materialists take it for granted that economic growth is crucial, and weigh the costs and risks of nuclear energy against the costs and risks of alternative energy sources. Postmaterialists take economic security for granted and weigh the costs and risks of nuclear power against various no-cost alternatives — among which reduced material consumption seems not only acceptable but, to some, actually desirable; insofar as it might lead to a more decentralized, less impersonal society that allows freer play for individual self-expression, it has a very positive image (see Schumacher 1973; Lovins 1977; Sale 1980). Thus, the debate over nuclear power is based on contrasting visions of the good society, with pronuclear and antinuclear advocates talking past each other because their arguments are implicitly based on different value priorities. To a considerable degree each side is insensitive to the basic premises of the other.

Domestic constraints are a major limiting factor on any energy policy. Despite reports to the contrary, a stronger information effort probably could lead to greater flexibility in these constraints — for public information is manifestly inadequate. But this flexibility is limited. Deep-rooted values are engaged in the nuclear power controversy, and it does not seem likely that they can be readily modified.

REFERENCES

Bupp, Irvin C. 1981. "The Actual Growth and Probable Future of the World-wide Nuclear Industry." *International Organization* 35, no. 1: 59-76.

Commission of the European Communities (biannual). *Euro-Barometer. Public Opinion in the European Community*. Brussels: Commission of the European Communities.

Inglehart, Ronald. 1981. "Post-materialism in an Environment of Insecurity." *American Political Science Review* (December) 75, no. 4: 880-900.

————— . 1977. *The Silent Revolution: Changing Values and Political Styles Among Western Publics*. Princeton: Princeton University Press.

Inglehart, Ronald, Jacques-René Rabier, Ian Gordon, and Carsten Sorensen. 1980. "Broader Powers for the European Parliament? The Attitudes of Candidates." *European Journal of Political Research* 8: 113-32.

Kasperson, Roger E. 1980. "Institutional and Social Uncertainties in the Timely Management of Radioactive Wastes." Testimony prepared for the California Energy Commission.

Kemeny, John G., et al. 1979. *Report of the President's Commission on the Accident at Three Mile Island*. Washington, D.C.: U.S. Government Printing Office.

Lieber, Robert J. 1980. "Energy, Political Economy and the Western European Left: Problems of Constraint." In Leon Hurwitz, ed., *Contemporary Perspectives on European Integration*. Westport, Conn.: Greenwood Press.

Lovins, Amory. 1977. *Soft Energy Paths: Toward a Durable Peace*. New York: Harper.

Miller, Warren E. 1981. "Policy Directions and Presidential Leadership: Alternative Interpretations of the 1980 Presidential Election." Paper presented at the 1981 Annual Meeting of the American Political Science Association.

National Academy of Sciences. 1980. *Energy in Transition, 1985-2010*. San Francisco: Freeman.

Nelkin, Dorothy, and Michael Pollak. 1981. *The Atom Besieged: Extraparliamentary Dissent in France and Germany*. Cambridge, Mass.: MIT Press.

Otway, Harry J., et al. 1978. "Nuclear Power: The Question of Public Acceptance." *Futures* (April): 109-18.

Sale, Kirkpatrick. 1980. *Human Scale*. New York: Coward, McCann and Geoghegan.

Schumacher, E. F. 1973. *Small Is Beautiful*. New York: Harper.

Schuur, Sam, et al. 1979. *Energy in America's Future*. Baltimore: Johns Hopkins University Press.

Stobaugh, Robert, and Daniel Yergin. 1979. *Energy Future*. New York: Random House.

Wilson, Richard, et al. 1981. *Health Effects of Fossil Fuel Burning*. Cambridge, Mass.: Ballinger.

ABOUT THE EDITOR
AND CONTRIBUTORS

ROBERT J. LIEBER is professor of Government at Georgetown University, specializing in U.S.-European relations, energy security, and American foreign policy. Among his books are *British Politics and European Unity*, *Theory and World Politics*, and *Oil and the Middle East War: Europe in the Energy Crisis.* He was also co-editor of *Eagle Entangled: U.S. Foreign Policy in a Complex World.* His most recent book is *Eagle Defiant: U.S. Foreign Policy in the 1980s*, of which he is co-editor and contributing author. In addition, he has held fellowships from the Woodrow Wilson International Center for Scholars, Council on Foreign Relations, and Guggenheim, Rockefeller and Ford foundations.

*   *   *

NILS ANDRÉN has been Professor of Political Science at the Universities of Stockholm and Copenhagen. He is head of the division of international studies at the Swedish Defence Research Institute in Stockholm.

GUY DE CARMOY is Professor Emeritus at the European Institute of Business Administration in Fontainebleau, France. His publications include *The Foreign Policies of France, 1944-1968* and *Energy for Europe, Economic and Political Implications.*

WALTER GOLDSTEIN is Professor of Political Science, Graduate School of Public Affairs, State University of New York at Albany. His recent publications have dealt with world trade wars, economic nationalism, and the oil industries in Canada, the United States, and Mexico. He is the author of monographs on direct foreign investment and the offshore holdings of multinational firms.

FREDERICK W. GORBET was director of Long-Term Cooperation and Policy Analysis for the International Energy Agency (1979-82). He is now Assistant Deputy Minister for Fiscal Policy and Economic Analysis in the Canadian Department of Finance.

RONALD INGLEHART is a Professor in the Department of Political Science, and the Institute for Social Research at the University of Michigan. The author of numerous publications on mass and elite attitudes, values, and political behavior, he is currently working on a study of ideological change among the publics of advanced industrial societies.

BRUCE W. JENTLESON is Assistant Professor in the Department of Political Science in the University of California, Davis. He did his graduate studies at Cornell University and previously has worked on East-West trade policy as a consultant to the President's Commission for a National Agenda for the Eighties and as a legislative assistant in the United States Senate.

REIMUND SEIDELMANN is Professor of International Politics at Geissen University in the Federal Republic of Germany. His special fields include German security and détente policy, European integration, and transnational party cooperation.

EDWARD F. WONDER is a Senior Consultant with International Energy Associates Limited, Washington, D.C. He has written widely on oil and gas policy in Mexico and Canada, as well as on nuclear export and non-proliferation policies. He holds a Ph.D. in Foreign Affairs from the University of Virginia.